Migration, Domestic Work and Affect

Routledge Research in Gender and Society

Migration, Domestic Work and Affect

A Decolonial Approach on Value and the
Feminization of Labor

Encarnación Gutiérrez-Rodríguez

Routledge
Taylor & Francis Group
New York   London

First published 2010
by Routledge
270 Madison Avenue, New York, NY 10016

Simultaneously published in the UK
by Routledge
2 Park Square, Milton Park, Abingdon, Oxon OX14 4RN

Routledge is an imprint of the Taylor & Francis Group, an informa business

Typeset in Sabon by IBT Global.
Printed and bound in the United States of America on acid-free paper by IBT Global.

Library of Congress Cataloging-in-Publication Data

Gutiérrez Rodríguez, Encarnación.
    Migration, domestic work and affect : a decolonial approach on value and the feminization of labor / by Encarnación Gutiérrez-Rodríguez.
        p. cm. — (Routledge research in gender and society ; 26)
    Includes bibliographical references and index.
    1. Women household employees—Europe.   2. Women foreign workers
—Europe.   3. Women immigrants—Employment—Europe.   4. Sexual division of labor.   5. Latin America—Emigration and immigration.   6. Europe—Emigration and immigration.   I. Title.
    HD6072.2.E85G88 2010
    331.4'8164086912094—dc22
                                                        2009052926

ISBN13: 978-0-415-99473-6 (hbk)
ISBN13: 978-0-203-84866-1 (ebk)

To my mother, Pepa

Josefa Rodríguez Santana, October 1964.

Contents

Acknowledgments

This book has traveled with me from Germany to the UK, changing shape and content. When I started my research on "undocumented migrant" domestic workers in European households at the University of Hamburg, the aim of the project was driven by my interest in the interpersonal relationship between the domestic workers and their employers. My move from the Sociology department to the Spanish, Portuguese and Latin American Studies department at the University of Manchester, opened up debates and perspectives that had been forgotten in the rather monolingual and Eurocentric discipline that Sociology tends to be. Connecting back to Latin American and Caribbean epistemology, this project developed new contours as it engaged with the decolonial perspective. But, I would never have reached this point without the insights and the analytical sharpness of the women that agreed to tell me their stories, to share with me their moments of despair, frustration and anger in regard to the devaluation of domestic work, but also their fears and worries because of the threat of deportation and detention. Despite the sadness encountered in some of the accounts of my research participants from Latin America, facing the dehumanizing effects of European migration regimes, their narratives also filled me with energy, hope and strength in our fight for social justice. Their voices also trace for me the transcultural spaces of a creolized Europe, a Europe that cannot be thought of without its colonial and imperial past, a Europe that is intrinsically linked to the misery its conquering endeavors and expansionist capitalist ambitions have brought about. From their perspective I have embarked on this work, which would not have been possible without their contributions. I am deeply indebted to these women. It is to them that this work is dedicated and to whom my full gratitude goes.

Also without the collaborative EU project on "Housework in Europe" conducted with colleagues in Austria, Spain, Germany and the UK, this book would have never seen the light of day. In particular, the support of the Berlin domestic workers and supporters' network *RESPECT* enabled this work as well as my research team at the University of Hamburg, where this research started. My thanks go to all my colleagues in this project, in particular to Susanne Schultz, Patty Caro, Isabel Gomez, Macarena

González Ulloa, Efthimia Panagiotidis, Nina Schultz, Cristina Vega Solís, Silvina Monteros, Mar García, Luzenir Caixeta, Barbara Haas, Bettina Haidinger, Sonja Rappold, Daniela Rechling, and Pamela Ripota. I am also very grateful to Marianne Pieper at the University of Hamburg, who gave immense support to this project and my work. This spirit accompanied my project long after leaving Hamburg and finding a new home in Manchester. In this environment my project flourished in new ways, a process that was made possible due to the generous support of my head of department, Christopher Perriam, who made me feel instantly at home. I would also like to thank Isabel Santaolalla for her insightful feedback and numerous reading suggestions and Jo Labanyi for encouraging me in the establishment of the Migration and Diaspora Cultural Studies Network at Manchester (MDCSN), a project that could only be realized through sharing forces with Margaret Littler. I would also like to thank Günther Dietz for his constant support at a distance and my colleagues Hilary Own and Lúcia Sà for their feedback.

My collaborations with the Austrian project European Institute for Progressive Cultural Policies enriched my perspective on the politics of translation that I have included in this work. In this regard, I would like to particularly thank Therese Kaufmann, Hito Steyerl, Boris Buden, Stefan Nowotny and Gerald Raunig. I would also like to thank my PhD student Lorraine Margaret Pannett for exciting discussions in this regard. Without the generous invitation from Manuela Boatcă to participate in the groundbreaking workshop on "Critical Thought—Transformative Practice" at the Instituto Universitario de Pesquisa (IUPERJ) in Rio de Janeiro, my decolonial perspective would not have undergone its critical transformation. This encounter led to an intellectually enriching collaboration with Manuela Boatcă and Sérgio Costa, documented in our book *Decolonizing European Sociology*, a project that enriched this work. I would also like to thank my colleague Sandra Gil for her invitations to the events of the Latin-American Researchers Network in Madrid (*Grupo Interdisciplinario de Investigaodor@s*), which contributed enormously to a vibrant exchange on Latin American migration to Europe.

Thanks to the generosity of the Humboldt Foundation, I was able to discuss early stages of this research with Scott Lash at the Centre for Cultural Studies, Goldsmiths College, University of London. Also the generous stipend offered by the Five College Women's Studies Centre, Mount Holyoke, and the Ford Foundation enabled me to concentrate on the completion of this book. In this regard, I would like to thank my colleagues at the Five College Women's Studies Research Centre and at Smith College for their generosity and engagement with my work. My thanks go in particular to the research fellows of FCWSC 2007–2008, Janice Irvine and Elizabeth Lehmann. Without the support received from Christine Shelton and Kathleen Gauger I would not have had the chance to enjoy the beauty of Smith campus. My thanks go also to my colleagues Michelle Joffroy, Ginetta

Candelario, Karen Remmler and Marguerite Itamar Harrison. In particular, I would like to thank Sara Lennox, Anna Schrade and my students of SWG214. Without the accurate eye of Tom Norton and the technical support of Max Novick this book would never have emerged.

This book would also never have been completed without the warm support of my friends in Manchester, in particular Adrià Castells Ferrando, Christian Klesse, Nicole Vitellone, Necla Acik-Toprak and Iris Bachmann. And, of course, without Christoph Pilgrim's and Selçuk Yurtsever-Kneer's constant gestures of friendship this project would not have grown. I would also like to thank my sisters, Gracia and Angela. I particularly want to thank my sister Gracia, who has provided me with considerable support by taking care of my parents in Germany, while I have been engaged with my work and this project in the UK. Also my parents' experience and strength has accompanied this project and the smiles and playful spirits of my niece, Alba, my nephew, Dariush, and Shirley's grandson, Tev'ian. I would also like to thank Shirley Anne Tate for her love and support throughout this project.

Introduction
Sensing Domestic Work

To feel within it totally invisible and also completely worthless
because there . . . is no thank you, no, ah, there you are again, you
feel like a ghost. (Verónica, domestic worker, Hamburg)

Verónica's words touch me deeply. I met Verónica, a 25-year-old economist
in Hamburg, Germany, in 2005, four years after she arrived from Ecuador
to continue with postgraduate study. Her family and friends, while sad to
see her leave and uncertain about what she might encounter in Germany,
fully supported her decision to emigrate. For Verónica, arriving in Hamburg "was the most beautiful thing." Though, "it was a gray day," she was
overwhelmed by the images she saw, "the snow, the trees without leaves,"
an unfamiliar image for her, used to Ecuador where "the leaves are always
on the trees." Germany "looked exactly like the photographs" she had
seen, she told me. Verónica's memories about her first months in Germany
resonate with other visitors' stories. Like them she came with her suitcases
full of images and fantasies about Germany. After unfruitful negotiations
regarding the recognition of her Ecuadorian degree with the University in
Hamburg her three-month tourist visa expired. Suddenly, she found herself
among the approximately 1.5 million "undocumented migrants" living in
Germany, a status that forced her to look at her desires, dreams and projects within the crude effects of abjection and exclusion caused by migration policies.[1] Still determined to be accepted as a student by the university,
she remained in Hamburg. Back in Ecuador, Verónica used to employ a
domestic worker, now in Hamburg she is cleaning, washing, ironing and
sweeping for others.

"WAGES FOR HOUSEWORK" RELOADED

Very little has changed since the feminist movement's campaign for "wages
for housework" in the 1970s. Despite the assumed *flexibilization* of gender roles and the option of paternity leave and part-time work in urban
middle-class households, a perpetuation of the classical gendered division
of work is kept alive.[2] Women are still largely opting for maternity leave
and part-time jobs as they principally bear the major responsibilities in
regard to children and housework. This was, in fact, the situation that
we encountered in the women in middle-class urban households that we

interviewed in Spain, Germany, Austria and the UK.[3] While in the majority of the households we encountered a self-reflexive and critical approach to gender roles (for example, some households had rotas for housework), women were largely responsible for domestic work. It is no wonder that when we approached the households for an interview those coming forward were mostly women.

In order to avoid gender tensions and to lessen the immense gap between the philosophy and practice of gender equality, the households interviewed opted to employ another woman to do this work. Numerous studies have delved into the dynamics produced in the employment relationship between two women in regard to domestic work, characterized as "a bond of exploitation."[4] However, as I will show here, this relationship of exploitation is complicated when we regard domestic work as affective labor. What we see then is that while one woman is employed to serve another woman and the household, both are affected by this labor in similar but also different ways, at the same time that this labor is textured by their affects. The vital character of this labor as *living labor* is sustained by the affects produced and absorbed within it. Nonetheless, domestic work as affective labor is an expression and impression of global inequalities. As Pierrette Hondagneu-Sotelo observes, globalization has created new regimes of inequality, in which the intersections of "race," gender and class have been reshuffled.[5] These new regimes of inequalities are reflected in private households. Migrant women from Eastern Europe and the "global South" are taking over the household work that is still left in women's hands.

MIGRATION, COLONIALITY AND THE FEMINIZATION OF LABOR

Paradoxically, while the demand for domestic and care workers in the EU is increasing, due to the growing incorporation of women into the labor market, an aging population and the privatization of social care,[6] the possibility of entry and settlement for non-EU citizens in recent years has been restricted. Meanwhile, State programs that seek societal answers to domestic and care work are rare, as we will see in Chapter 2 of this volume. Offers such as "cash payment for care" have individualized care by giving the responsibility of organizing it back to the individual households. The need for nursery places, after-school centers and cooperative cleaning agencies or community-based projects for child and household support are not on the State agenda. Hence, the provision of childcare and care for the elderly is increasingly reliant on individual arrangements in private households, and new conflicts regarding the gendered division of work arise between the households' members. Refusing to assume sole responsibility for the household, professional women opt together with their household members to employ another woman to do this work. This need is met by female "undocumented migrant" workers trying to make a living in Europe. Left in a working rights gray zone, ranging from partial regulatory measures to complete deregulation, the labor-power of these workers is socially devalued through its cultural predication as feminized and racialized labor. Juxtaposing the private households with the dynamics of global interdependencies, the local face of the gendered and racialized division of work of the modern/colonial world system becomes a tangible and immediate reality in private households in Western Europe. It is in this regard that the legacies of a colonial order, reactivated through racial and gendered segregation in the labor market and dehumanizing migration policies, are felt on an individual level and mobilized in our everyday encounters.

The decline of the "housewife" model in Fordist Western European societies, due to the incorporation of women into the labor market, has not led to a more egalitarian approach to household work, as I will argue in Chapter 3 of this volume. Instead, domestic and care work have been and continue to be outsourced to migrant women. In Germany, for example, from the 1960s to the 1990s, Spanish, Turkish, Greek, Italian, Yugoslavian, Moroccan and Portuguese migrant women were cleaning offices and people's houses. These women are now retired and a new generation of women from Eastern Europe, Africa and Latin America have replaced them. Due to restrictive asylum and migration policies, their working conditions are not regularized and there is a lack of social protection, safe working conditions and fair wages.[7] Though some EU Member States have introduced immigration policies based on fixed-term contracts for certain labor sectors such as agriculture, the IT industry and health service, it is only in a few EU countries, for example, Spain and Italy, where there are regularization programs for migrant domestic and care workers.

However, as Bridget Anderson observes, "some policy interest in the sector, both as potential generator of jobs and of State income" has been shown.[8] For example, the European Parliament held a public hearing in 2000 on "Regulating Domestic Help in the Informal Sector." European organizations of domestic workers in cooperation with the European Trade Unions are also promoting this process.[9] This is even the case in Spain where the household service sector is regulated by a special social security regime only applicable to "regularized migrant" workers. Here, domestic workers' organizations such as *Servicio Doméstico Activo* (SEDOAC), and feminist networks such as the *Assembly of Women in Biskaia and Madrid*, as well as *Precarias a la Deriva*, are campaigning for domestic workers to have a written contract stipulating a 36-hour week with health care, unemployment benefits and bonuses. In the UK domestic work has only been regularized in specific cases.[10] In Germany and Austria where "housekeeper" is a profession, hourly paid jobs, au pairs and undeclared domestic workers are not covered by this status. Further, whilst in some Western European countries a legal framework might exist to provide fair and dignified working conditions for domestic workers, this legal framework has limited coverage. This is so because households are considered by the State to be a "private sphere," in which employment relations are individually negotiated. The State's reluctance to intervene in the privacy of households leaves domestic workers at the mercy of their employers. Moreover, while in recent years provision addressing personal care seems to have attracted the attention of State programs, for example, Spain, Austria, France and the UK have opted for individual incentives to procure care for the elderly through programs[11] like "cash payment for care,"[12] domestic work is not explicitly targeted by these considerations.

Of course, the division between domestic and care work is more artificial than factual. It is utterly impossible to separate domestic and care work from each other as the skills and tasks deployed in them overlap. Nonetheless, political debates tend to distinguish between personal care and domestic work.[13] As I will argue in Chapter 4 of this volume, however, domestic work is intrinsically linked to sustaining personal well-being even where the task involved is only cleaning the stairs. The value actually inherent in cleaning the stairs does not just remain in the spotlessness of the stairs, but includes the creation of an agreeable environment, a value gained by the users of this space. Domestic work as affective labor, thus, always engages with the production of well-being, livability, amiability and comfort. It does so even in the instances where this is not intended.

AFFECTS AND DOMESTIC WORK

Verónica's words not only filled me with ambivalent feelings of (*com*)*passion* and (*im*)*potence* regarding the effects of policies interpellating human beings as "invaders," "cultural threat[s]" and an "exploited labor-force," they also "touched" me, affecting me, making me feel, but also think, about the affective dimension of migration policies. The impression of feelings of "invisibility" and "worthlessness" are symptomatic of the cultural logic of abjection, evolving within a racializing and feminizing script of power, prescribed by migration policies, the coloniality of power[14] and feminization of labor. These feelings form part of a "structure of feeling,"[15] not readily inscribed into a semantic structure or cognitive script. Rather, they represent what Raymond Williams calls the "delicate" and "less tangible parts" of our human existence.[16]

Affecting Verónica and affecting me, these feelings become affects, circulating in our spaces of encounters, in the contact zones of our lives, and mutually recreating our relational bonds and (dis)attachments. They are, as Kathleen Stewart suggests, "ordinary affects," moments of intuition, sensations, bodily reactions emerging through the impulses of life, moving us to act, driving us to think, developing relationality in our daily practices and encounters.[17] Verónica's words affect me and are at the same time affected by her sense of being, by her attempt to capture the corporeal experience of her life. Transmitting the "violent emotional materiality"[18] of her experiences as a domestic worker, Verónica's words capture the ontology of the present, the moment in which words are "made flesh and dwell"[19] in our bodies, but also the moment in which meaning attempts to capture experiences. Already expressing feelings, this pushes us away from affects. Affects are characterized by their evasive force, by the attempt to escape a script of meaning production. Nonetheless, affects unfold context, as Brian Massumi suggests.[20] They become significant through the intensities they produce, through the thoughts and feelings they create.

But, as I will argue here, affects are more than just movements of deterritorialization, flows and circuits, not rooted in material conditions. Rather, affects evolve within the dynamics and in the ambivalent movements emerging out of material social conditions. Affects not only unfold context, but they emerge within a concrete historical and geopolitical context. While they emanate from the dynamics of our energies, impulses, sensations and encounters,[21] affects also carry residues of meaning. They are haunted by past intensities, not always spelled out and conceived in the present. Immediate expressions and transmissions of affects may indeed revive repressed sensations, experiences of pain or joy. Although not explicitly expressed as such, they are temporal and spatial constellations of certain times, intricately impressed in legacies of the past and itineraries of the present/future.

Through this angle, this book aims to show how the social fabric of domestic work is shaped by affection, the expression and exchange of affects. Affects are here not just perceived as emotions and feelings, but as intensities, sensations and bodily reactions disturbing, but also stretching and reaffirming, power relations. While feminist theory has highlighted the emotional character of domestic work, the affects expressed in this study of well-being, happiness, servility, disgust, dismissal and disdain are less connected to the tasks of caring for or being attentive to others than to our immediate bodily reactions and sensations with regard to the energies of others and our environment.[22] This relates to Benedictus de Spinoza's "affectus," which has been translated into English as "emotion" and "passion," in other words, body excitations, in contrast to emotions that he describes as cognitive expressions or feelings: sensations or stimuli.[23] Such an interpretation of affects departs from the observation of the mutual dependency between body and mind. The mind moves the body as the body moves the mind; they are, therefore, interdependent. As Michael Hardt, in reference to Spinoza, notes, the "mind's power to think corresponds to its receptivity to external ideas; and the body's power to act corresponds to its sensitivity to other bodies."[24] For Spinoza then, affect drives us to act, it moves us to transform passion into action.[25] As such it is an energy or "drive" that emerges through contact and encounter. It is a relational force permeating our bodies as well as resulting from our bodily ability to feel. Consequently, our energy increases or diminishes in regard to the life forces driven by desire (*cupiditas*), joy (*laetitia*) and sadness (*tristitia*), which motivates our thinking and actions.[26]

As Sianne Ngai discusses in regard to the analysis of cultural representation, the focus on racialized affects enables us to understand the relationship between states of feelings and action, it pushes us to take a closer look at how actions are "blocked," suspended or channeled through our vital forces.[27] These vital forces, while not always explicit, emerge within a social space, driven by the logic of capital accumulation and processes of differentiation, channeled in particular by historical legacies and contemporary dynamics of racialization and gendering. Feelings of "invisibility" and "worthlessness" are then constituted by the transmission of abjection and negation. These feelings are coupled to a dominant symbolic script, subtly operating within the matrix of hegemonic practices, technologies of governance and discourses of Othering. Within the dominant script, domestic work is considered ordinary, simple and banal and this impacts on the bodies of racialized and feminized subjects employed as domestic workers, as Verónica has shown. While this labor emerges out of the affective character of our lives, it is kept socially and epistemologically outside the framework of recognition and value. Domestic work thus becomes the neuralgic node in which the "multilayered texture" of oppression is crystallized;[28] in which old structures of domination, thought overcome by a post-human logic of dynamics and flows, are revived in their most utterly human appearance. Working with and through the affective texture of our lives, domestic work engages with the twofold and ambivalent character of affects as life drives and resources of exploitation in advanced capitalism.

Over and over again, feminists, critical "race" and decolonial scholars have discussed the effects of racialization and feminization as coupled to a process of devaluation or "dehumanization."[29] In the daily life of household work, affects are transmitted and circulated through the energies incorporated, expressed and impressed in a space marked by local and global inequalities. Though affects seem to transcend a material logic of power, they evolve implicitly in this logic. Affects are also ambivalent as they indicate the unruly and dispersed forces of our vital faculties and activities, at the same time as they evolve and are transmitted in concrete spaces, inflected by the logic of domination and its effects. My analysis of domestic work here makes this evident. In the encounter between domestic workers and their employers, more than an exchange of reproductive tasks or emotional labor occurs. In fact, what shapes these encounters is the transmission of affects, that is, affection, as affects evolve in the extension to other bodies.[30] As Teresa Brennan observes, the energetic dimension of being moved by what drives us emotionally becomes relevant through affection. Thus, affects can "enhance when they are projected outward, when one is relieved of them."[31] For example, in the case of joy and love, one can become energized. However, affects can be depleted "when one carries the affective burden of another, either by a straightforward transfer or because the other's anger becomes your depression."[32] Within the power dynamics present within the employment of Latin American women in European private households, the transmission of affects carries more than what Massumi interprets as the "prepersonal" dimension of affects. That is, an expression of intensity that is not mediated through language.[33] Rather, the transmission of affects in domestic work is expressed by and oriented towards concrete, historicized bodies as affects are affected by external factors and internal dynamics.

Set within the context of migration regimes and the feminization of labor, expressed in the organization of domestic work in private households, the employment of an "undocumented migrant" worker connects the households immediately to the production of what Jasbir Puar defines as "body-as-information."[34] Conveyed within "information and surveillance technologies of control," the body of the interpellated "undocumented migrant" woman expresses the structural violence inherent in the interface of scientific knowledge, migration policies and the capitalist logic of exploitation. The transmission of affects between the domestic workers and their employers evolves in this ambivalence between State codification and the dynamics of affection in private households. In fact, although not explicitly stated by the private households, employing a domestic worker carries the promise of infusing the household with the positive vital forces of animation. This expectation collides with the effects of "de-animatedness" conveyed in the logic and technologies of surveillance and control of migration regimes. Within this logic, the "undocumented migrant" worker experiences what Ngai observes in regard to the cultural representation of racialized affects. The racialization of affects "turns the neutral and even potentially positive affect of animatedness 'ugly,' pointing to the more self-evidently problematic feelings."[35] While the domestic workers are supposed to infuse the private households with positive affective energies, they themselves are constantly perceived by the household members through a projected racialized form of animatedness. As Ngai comments, in "its racialized form animatedness loses its generally positive association with human spiritedness or vitality and comes to resemble a kind of mechanization."[36] It is in this "kind of mechanization" that they are frequently portrayed by their employers (and also in some research) in one-dimensional ways as "pre-modern" subjects lacking any kind of social complexity and individual agency. They are perceived merely as "automatons." While it is true that institutionalized and daily attacks against their personal integrity and dignity drive these women to situations of despair and hopelessness, their accounts also bear witness to incredible strength, faith and hope in individual and social change.

The accounts of the Latin American women that participated in this study demonstrate their capacity to evolve and act beyond the technologies of control and governance imposed on their bodies and movements through their capacity to be affective. Ironically, it is this affective force that becomes significant for the productive character of their labor-power.

Within the framework of migration regimes, domestic work as affective labor becomes a source of exploitation, at the same time that it represents a vital foundation for the sustainability of our lives. Thus, while this labor is constitutive for the production of value, this value is largely not recognized in society because the cultural predication of this labor connotes it as "non-productive" and its labor force is devalued through its prescription as feminized and racialized labor, as I will argue in Chapters 4 and 6 of this volume. These observations will lead to the discussion in Chapter 6 of *affective value* in relation to the cultural predication of domestic work. Dealing with domestic work as an expression of affective labor, this chapter traces the affects of well-being, happiness, servility, disgust, dismissal and contempt expressed, transmitted and exchanged in the encounters between domestic workers and their employers, demonstrating that the extraction of value cannot be analyzed in purely economic terms. Rather, the analysis of value demands a perspective that takes into account the cultural dynamics through which value is symbolically predetermined, revealing the epistemological foundations constituting the ontological character of domestic work and its racialized and feminized labor force. Considering the interconnections between domestic work, biopolitics and value, Chapter 4 of this volume explores the value character of domestic work. Drawing on feminist debates from the 1970s and 1980s on reproductive labor, this chapter discusses how it is that an enormous intensity of life is invested in and produced through domestic work. This chapter gives an insight into the vital and relational character of domestic work by discussing Antonio Negri's notion of biopolitics, Italian post-operaist feminist understandings of the *feminization of labor*, the Madrid feminist group *Precarias a la Deriva's* concept of *trabajo de cuidados* (care work) and feminist debates on emotional labor.

Contextualizing the transmission and circulation of affects in domestic work within the chain of value coding, this study reveals that affects are contextualized. Their context is delimited by the coloniality of labor and migration regimes, Latin American diaspora in Europe and the feminization of labor, the biopolitical character of domestic work and its logic of racialization. It is along these lines that this book proposes a cultural analysis of domestic work as affective labor, delving into its value character. It does so by situating the encounter between Latin American "undocumented migrant" domestic workers and their European employers in private households in Austria, Germany, Spain and the UK within Fernando Ortiz's ethical framework of conviviality, that is, transculturation.

TRANSCULTURALIZING AFFECTS

Set within a decolonial framework, this book sees private households employing Latin American domestic workers without legal residency permits [37] as transcultural contact zones.[38] Mary Louise Pratt defines contact zones as "social spaces where disparate cultures meet, clash and grapple with each other, often in highly asymmetrical relations of domination and subordination—like colonialism, slavery, or their aftermaths as they are lived across the globe today."[39] Pratt develops her notion of contact zones in regard to Fernando Ortiz's concept of transculturation. In his groundbreaking work *Cuban Counterpoint: Tobacco and Sugar*,[40] Ortiz develops the concept of transculturation through a historical, sociological and cultural analysis of the tobacco and sugar industries. He does this in order to understand Cuba's cultural and social heterogeneity. As he notes, Cuba's "history, more than that of any other country of America, is an intense, complex, unbroken process of transculturation of human groups, all in a state of transition."[41] Transcultural conviviality, hence, defines processes deriving from survival strategies, emanating out of the contact zone and configured by different modes of production through which various social groups were forced to live together, but through which also the human ability and creativity to connect and forge common lives was triggered. Through this perspective, Ortiz emphasizes the historical and social dynamics in which transcultural sociabilities are forged, acknowledging the power relations that condition them.[42] Conceiving private households as transcultural contact zones brings us to consider Anibal Quijano's framework of the coloniality of power in regard to contemporary forms of racial segregation, exclusion and devaluation tacitly or explicitly conditioning access to the labor market for Latin American women without a regularized residency status in Western Europe.[43]

Private households employing "undocumented migrant" women represent sites of transcultural conviviality. As I will discuss in Chapter 3 of this volume, the lack of State programs covering the care needs of private households and considering domestic work as a societal issue leave private households to cope with the organization of care and domestic work. State programs like "cash for care" relegate the responsibility for this labor back to the privacy of the households, thus governing the household at a distance through its own "self-governing" mechanisms. At the same time, these programs silence the fact that the majority of these households can only pursue this goal by employing a low-paid and precarious domestic worker, largely a migrant woman, in some cases even without a residency permit. Through the outsourcing of domestic work to another woman, two social groups that usually live in segregated spaces meet in the private household. We could say that due to the need for a cleaner or a carer, the private middle-class professional households become open to a social group to which they do not have any form of attachment. In this space the employers and the domestic workers meet as two women living in divided spaces ruled by different timescales and professional demands. In their encounter, these two women articulate and negotiate their desires, needs and moments of identification and dis-identification. They share some aspects related to the social construction and assignation of "femininity" in the households. However, this common point of departure is interrupted by the social hierarchies structuring their encounter.

As Julie Graham and Katherine Gibson (aka J.K. Gibson-Graham) argue, the private household represents a "social site in which a wide variety of class, gender, racial, sexual and other practices intersect."[44] This study stresses the *effects* of family and migration policies on private households as will be discussed in Chapters 2 and 3 of this volume. In private households we encounter the immediate effects of migration and border regimes, for example, when "undocumented migrant" workers are employed. Their work conditions and access to rights are very often overshadowed by their illegal residency status. In the case of "undocumented migrant" workers, their lack of residency permits often makes this group the target of physical and psychological abuses. Whilst the private household is perceived by its members as a safe haven, for the domestic workers it represents employment in which they need to struggle for respect and for their rights. Two realities intersect here that inform and shape the transcultural encounter between domestic workers and their employers: safe intimate haven and the anonymous site of worker exploitation.

Under these conditions, these two women experience a "living together" entrenched in structural divisions, in which a "living apart" is expressed by the geographical distances embedded in their encounter. Their neighborhoods are divided by "color" and "class" lines. Their children usually do not frequent the same schools and their friendship circles do not overlap. But in the privacy of the households, these two women meet and share moments of unprecedented intimacy. Moments of worries, anxieties, fears and joys are exposed, expressed and exchanged, instating the affective encounters between these two women, leaving sensations of sadness or despair, but also of dislike and disgust, in particular in the domestic workers. The encounter between these two women is textured by what Ortiz defines as "counterpoint," oppositional social positions in which "cognitive categories as well as structures of sentiments"[45] are forged and experienced. It is concretely in the counterpoint of the "mop" and the "smile" in which the encounter between Latin American "undocumented migrant" domestic workers and their European employers evolve.

EUROPEAN COUNTERPOINT: MOP AND SMILE

The "mop" and the "smile" both serve as metaphors for understanding the two poles of domestic work as physical (material) labor, on the one side, and affective (immaterial) labor, on the other. Both the "mop" and the "smile" represent the productive character of this labor, both signal its residual affective force and its social devaluation. Verónica points to this ambivalent character of domestic work in her aforementioned observation. The affective productivity generated in this labor, while indispensable for social (re)production, also shapes the social character of our lives. Through affects, social meaning is infused into bodies. The feeling of "being treated as a ghost," the feeling of being ignored, infuses Verónica's body with a social meaning of valuelessness. As I pointed out earlier in regard to what Ngai describes as "ugly feelings," being treated as "a ghost" carries the effect of "de-animatedness." The symbolic attribution of "inferiority" conveyed in this treatment becomes corporeal, sensed by the subject injured by this behavior as pain. Through the transmission of affects, a symbolic order is transmitted onto the very surface of the skin. Assignations of class, "race" and gender "inferiority" are thus both sensed and inscribed in/on the body, as I will discuss in Chapter 5 of this volume.

For Latin American women, the expression and circulation of affects in the private households are clearly by-products of migration regimes. However, affects also bear the traces of a colonial imaginary with its cultural ascriptions and prescriptions of the "Other" of Europe, constructed in opposition to a "modern" and sovereign European Self.[46] Public discourses on "undocumented migrants" weave their narratives and information streams, drawing on this colonial imaginary by portraying migrants as a threat to "social and cultural cohesion," as will be discussed in Chapter 2 of this volume. Latin American women living without residency permits in Europe are particularly exposed to racializing and sexualizing discourses. As "undocumented" female workers only a few labor sectors are accessible to them. These sectors are characterized by a high degree of precarious, unsafe and violent working conditions. In this context the subjugation and devaluation of these women is reflected in their exploitation as racialized and feminized labor.

In Verónica's case the effects of coloniality are expressed in her racialization as a "Latina" in Germany. Being racialized as a Latina is a new experience that she first encountered in Europe. Back in Ecuador she was part of the White middle class. In Germany she is confronted with stereotypes of Latin American women as exotic and sexually available. As she told me, "here the Germans think that Latin American women are destined for the bed, they think so many bad things about us." The correlation of Latin American women with sex work is a constant assumption that my research participants spoke about in all four countries. Verónica's brief story epitomizes the experiences of subjugation and racialization that "undocumented migrant" women working as domestic workers in private households encounter in Western Europe as they are "Latina-ized."[47]

Latinizing Europe

Structural adjustment programs, economic and political crises as well as international trade agreements have had devastating consequences for the economies of Asia, Africa and Latin America. Thus, a significant number of their inhabitants have moved to the economic centers of the "global North." A "reverse" movement from the peripheries to the centers of global economic and political power is taking place, reminding us of the slogan of the Black antiracist movement in Britain "we are here, because you are(were) there." Latin American immigration, predominantly from the Cono Sur (Chile, Argentina and Uruguay) in the 1970s to Europe was motivated by political exile and mostly sustained by a human rights discourse in France, Germany and the UK, which were seen as safe havens for political refugees. Today these countries and other EU states are concerned with measures to stop the immigration and settlement of non-EU citizens. Caribbean and Latin American migrants increasingly suffer the consequences of these policies. As non-EU migrants they are confronted with visa requirements and restrictive measures in regard to obtaining residency, working and study permits. Thus, the number of Caribbean and Latin American migrants becoming irregular is increasing. Only a few countries, like Spain, introduced programs in the 1990s to regularize "undocumented" migration. Spain is also where we find the highest number of registered Spanish-speaking Caribbean and Latin American migrants.

In Spain, Latin American and Caribbean migration became relevant for researchers in the late 1980s. In contrast, in Germany, Austria and the UK it was not until the mid-1990s that scholars noticed this immigration. Consequently, research on Latin American immigration in Germany, Austria and the UK is scarce, while the research on Spanish-speaking Caribbean and Latin American immigration in Spain is abundant and differentiated by nationalities, demonstrating the organization of this research from the perspective of "methodological nationalism."[48] In the other countries the research on this type of immigration rarely focused on one single national group, although in the British context research on Colombian refugees and migrants is emerging as a particular focus, accompanied by an emerging interest in Brazilian immigration. This reflects the noticeable appearance of these communities, in particular in the London area.[49] The growing Brazilian communities are also attracting research interest in Austria[50] and Germany,[51] although in these countries research on Latin American immigration is more thematically than nationally organized.

The official national figures available on Spanish-speaking Caribbean and Latin American immigration to Europe only include persons with a regular residency status. That is, those with student visas, work contracts and/or those married to a European. The number of "undocumented migrant" workers is not represented in these figures. Thus, as I will discuss in Chapter 2 of this volume, this study engages less with national communities than with the effects of EU immigration policies, resulting in precarious legal, living and working conditions for the persons subjected to them. Consequently, this book distances itself from a methodological nationalism and engages instead with the effects of migration regimes and their impact on the level of the private household. Through this angle it engages with domestic work as a terrain of affective labor, in which affective value is produced within dynamics engaging with colonial legacies of racialization and feminization in the present.

ONTOLOGIES OF THE PRESENT

As feminist theorists in the 1970s have argued, women's labor is reproductive labor. It not only contributes to the regeneration of the labor force but society as a whole.[52] Marxist feminists like Heidi Hartmann, Christine Delphy, Silvia Kontos and Claudia von Werlhof have seen domestic work as the primary source of capital accumulation, from which "surplus-value" originates.[53] From the perspective of global inequalities, Hondagneu-Sotelo has further argued, in regard to the employment of Mexican, Central American and Caribbean migrant women as domestic workers in the United States, that this represents a bargain for the families and societies receiving these personal services. This is so not only because the countries exploiting this labor do not cover the reproductive costs for these women, but also because their social reproduction has taken place in their countries of origin.[54] Consequently, the "surplus-value" extracted from domestic work does not only rely on the fact that this labor is not properly remunerated, but also on the labor force doing this work, as will be stressed in Chapter 6 of this volume. The "surplus-value" accumulated in this labor is not only extracted from its reproductive character, feminists have argued, but in particular through its emotional engagement transferred from the "global South" to the "global North," discussed as "global care chains."[55] In this transaction, it is not only that the "importing society of domestic workers" saves the costs necessary for the reproduction of the labor force, but it also absorbs the emotional labor of domestic workers. Some feminist economists have interpreted this as an articulation of "emotional imperialism."[56]

The analysis of "emotional labor" in domestic work has uncovered the role of personal care and the investment of subjective faculties by stressing the significance of love in women's labor.[57] Frequently, the assumption is made that when we speak of emotions we mean affects. But, as I argue here, the perspective on affects, while it might embrace an analysis of the dynamics of emotions, goes beyond the cognitive framework of emotions. Affects in regard to emotions, as Massumi notes, do not require a subject as their addressee, they are unstructured and dispersed, they fluctuate in space, connecting different elements together, the human and the nonhuman or the post-human.[58] Affects, for Massumi, cannot be captured in "meaningful sequencing" or "narration,"[59] in contrast to emotions, which have a subjective content and can be sociolinguistically fixed as a quality of experience. Emotions, thus, require a subject as they are composed by meaning and transferred value.[60] Situating my approach to affects in the in-between of these two poles, I understand affects here as embedded in a system of meaning and value production. Although I do not consider them as oriented towards a subject, they still fluctuate within an ontologically produced script, not only referring to the post-human but in particular to the human. Thus, while I consider that emotional labor addresses the activities intentionally oriented towards caring for others, like combing their hair, bathing or listening to them, affective labor goes beyond this. Affects are not oriented to a person, nor are they intentionally interwoven into a matrix of meaning. Although they do carry meaning as they work through emotions and feelings, they are diffuse and unstructured (re-) actions, immediate bodily reactions to energies, sensations and intensities that are not always clearly located in a person, but dispersed in space. Affects are energies that derive from encounters, not always conceivable in language, but sensed bodily. While emotions address the cognitive level of personal feelings, affects engage with often "unspecified" energies, linked to our relational and social character as human beings. The role of affects in racialized feminized labor, urges us to understand the relational character of domestic work.

Affective labor engages with the immediate pulses of life and as such it has a biopolitical quality. It is labor that cannot be measured quantitatively.[61] What affective labor produces is thus not tangible and not always material, as its products are attached to feelings, emotions and energies. The perspective on affective labor, hence, focuses on the "uncensored," intuitive expression of our vital impulses in relation to others and our environment. Immersed in the energies of private households, domestic work is not only a receptor of affects, but also its mediator and organizer. Not solely resulting from the energies of the household members, but from their relationship to their household and of the household to society, the affects produced have internal and external origins. Due to their contextual and situational embeddedness, affects are circumscribed by their social context of emergence. While they are not directly conceived in language, they transmit the symbolic power embedded in their matrix of enunciation. For example, the expression of disgust for the "undocumented migrant" domestic workers represents more than just revulsion, it refers to what Ngai defines as an "agonistic emotion (the social relation of inequality) (. . .) constituted by the vehement rejection or exclusion of its object."[62] Confronted with "disgust" inscribed in the space of the household, the relationships between domestic workers and their employers are affected and affect through this feeling, as I will discuss in Chapter 6 of this volume. In other words, while the sensation of disgust is an expression of a diffused bodily reaction, it is embedded in a web of symbolic power, culturally predicated and manifested in the societal devalorization of domestic work.

Thus, affective labor raises the question of the ontophenomenological dimension of value.[63] As this study demonstrates, the correlation between the societal recognition of domestic work and its labor force, commonly racialized and feminized, reveals how labor is not only constituted by its quality, but by its quantifiable character in terms of who does the work. Domestic work is not only badly paid because it is signified as non-productive, but because those doing this work are feminized and racialized subjects considered as "inferior" to the hegemonic normative subject. Again, the devaluation of domestic work is culturally predicated and reflects a hegemonic perception. Accordingly, the value attributed to domestic work cannot be measured in Marxist terms of use-value or exchange-value because these categorizations does not conceive the specific biopolitical quality of this labor as reproductive, emotional and affective labor. In order to decipher the intrinsic value produced and extracted in this labor we need to depart from affective value, as I will discuss in Chapter 6 of this volume. Affective value in regard to use-value and exchange-value as such represents a "third category," one that denotes the relational and societal character of human interactions. It focuses on the value produced through the energies, sensations and intensities of human encounters within a hierarchical system of colonial classification, entrenched in the logic and dynamics of the modern/colonial world system. Affective value, thus, foregrounds the cultural predication of and corporeal dimension in the production of value. In regard to domestic work within the context of "undocumented" migration in Europe, the corporeality of affective value is signified by the racialized and feminized labor force of postcolonial migrants.

Considering this argument, this book ends with Chapter 7's consideration of rights within the framework of a decolonial ethics of affects. In this chapter I conclude that the dehumanizing logic of migration regimes becomes corporeal and affective. This creates the need to revise migrant workers' and domestic workers' rights from a decolonial perspective on the ethics of affects. Exploring claims made by the domestic workers' movements in Europe and considering debates on transnationalizing workers' rights and emancipatory approaches to human rights, this chapter tries to situate the struggle for workers's right within a decolonial framework, connecting it to what Gibson-Graham defines as "new ethical practices of thinking economy and becoming different kinds of economic beings."[64] Arriving at such a perspective has entailed a methodology that departs from translation as a form of transversal understanding, as I outline in Chapter 1 of this volume. Starting from the economic, political, social and cultural differences in the encounter between researcher and research participants, I discuss the necessity of translation in social research, engaging with what Gayatri Chakravorty Spivak has called working "with a language that belongs to many others."[65] It is in this context that the question of translation focuses on two levels of representation, on the epistemological and on the ontophenomenological, an aim pursued throughout the book and demonstrated in the insistence on understanding domestic work as affective labor and its productivity in terms of affective value. Both are an expression of the coloniality and feminization of labor, intricately interwoven and produced through the corporeal and affective quantity and quality of this labor and its labor force.

1   Decolonizing Migration Studies
On Transcultural Translation

When I think of domestic work, different pictures appear: my mother cleaning the kitchen, my mother sewing our dresses, but also my mother cleaning German households. Conducting this research with women from Ecuador, Chile and Peru has meant speaking in my "mother('s) tongue," Andalusian-Spanish, which has also brought to mind my own mother's experiences cleaning houses in Germany in the 1970s and 1980s. My "mother('s) tongue" has experienced transformation, combining its words with German and English. As a Spanish speaker I began fieldwork with a presupposition about the linguistic commonality between the Latin American research participants and myself. However, this was soon challenged. In attempting to explain my interest in the topic of new migration to Germany, I started the conversation by telling the focus group I had organized in Berlin about my own background. I told them that my parents migrated from Andalusia to Germany in 1962 and that I grew up in Germany, where in my childhood I experienced discrimination based on my working-class, migrant background. This experience was situated in the Fordist Europe of the 1960s and 1970s at a distance from the Europe of the twenty-first century, where Spain has become one of the leading European countries in imposing new anti-migration laws. After listening to my story, Carla, one of the members of the Berlin domestic workers' group *RESPECT*, responded,

> Excuse me, that can also happen in your own country, when we are from different cultures, because that also happened to me. I am from a different culture and I used to speak a different language. My mother spoke a different language and I used to speak her language. I began school when I still spoke my mother's language and then learned Spanish in school. When I was six I still couldn't speak Spanish. It does not just happen to you if you are from a different country, it can also happen in the same country.

Carla was a migrant from Otavalo, a city in the north of Ecuador with long-standing tourism and trading connections to various parts of the

world. While I attempted to establish a bridge with the participants by presupposing that migration was a common point of departure, Carla's observation made me aware of the fragility of an assumed commonality. Her
intervention reminded me of a different space and time when the Caribbean
and Latin America were colonized. Carla's inability to speak Quechua is
reminiscent of colonialism. Though after independence from Spain some
Latin American countries attempted to preserve indigenous languages, in
general these languages were not perceived as a national heritage. As she
tells us, when she was a child Quechua was forbidden at school, where she
was forced to speak Spanish and her mother tongue was relegated to the
domestic sphere. Carla indirectly recalls the fact that for three centuries,
from 1500 to 1800, Amerindians were forced to learn Spanish. During the
1800s some Latin American nation-states introduced bilingualism, which
was solely addressed to the indigenous population who needed to learn
Spanish, while the Creole elites were exempt from learning an indigenous
language. It is this background that informs Carla's Spanish, while mine is
shaped by the Spanish State's attempt to impose the Castilian language on
the whole of Spain, as I insisted in the continuation of our conversation.
As we discussed racism, Dani (from Chile and now lives in Berlin, also a
member of *RESPECT*) remarked,

> *Dani:* In Latin America, in general, it happens. There is strong racism
> against the indigenous and black population.
> *Encarnación:* Yes, and in Spain as well if you are Basque or Catalan,
> you couldn't speak the languages and you had to learn Spanish.
> *Carla:* And what did they say in our country: They are White. If you
> are an *Indio*, then you are an *India* that stinks, all of that, and
> if you are a girl, then it sticks to you and it still does to this very
> day.

Carla's words show that Whiteness is always a position of privilege that
exerts its power through naming the Other and normalizing racialization
so that it becomes everyday common sense. My conversation with Carla
demonstrates that my listening is partial. In my attempt to create a commonality between her situation and my own experiences of discrimination,
I relay the fact that during Francoism in Spain, Basque and Catalan were
forbidden. Interestingly, in this juxtaposition of two different geopolitical
contexts linked to two different historical moments of the imperial project of
Hispanidad, what is revealed are similarities in the process of standardiza-
tion of Castilian in the colonies from the sixteenth century and the Peninsula
from the eighteenth century.[1] Nonetheless, these similarities are affected by
the relationship between former colonizer and colonized. Insurmountable
differences become apparent in our encounter that cannot be neutralized by
my evocation of a commonality as "female migrants." As Dani comments
in an attempt to clarify the difference, "the racism against the indigenous

and Black population is strong in Latin America." Thus, the comparison between my experiences of discrimination as a "guest worker's" child in Germany does not resonate with Carla's experiences of racism as an indigenous woman in Ecuador. Carla's intervention delineates our moment of encounter, informed by colonial legacies and the economic and political (inter-)dependencies between peripheries and centres of the modern/colonial world system. It is within this context that the question of the politics of translation in ethnographic research and its representation arises.

In the conversation between Carla and I, what becomes obvious is not that we need a literal translation. Rather what is necessary is a translation that enables me to listen to difference and resist the appropriation of the Other's speech into a hegemonic script. It is in this regard that this chapter engages with the politics of translation on four levels. First, by exploring the epistemic foundations of the politics of translation, delving into the epistemic power of "colonial difference," double translation and transcultural translation. Through this perspective an immanent logic in migration research will be unsettled by interrogating the construction of migrants as "data bodies,"[2] which is sustained by the enduring epistemic power of "colonial difference." Second, the translation process between the researcher and research participants will be discussed in regard to the transference of the experience of migration and "Becoming Woman." This engages with the ability to listen to alterity and resist homogenization so as to enable a language of conflict and contradiction to emerge. Third, the chapter engages with the possibility of "decolonizing migration studies" by pursuing the feminist, postcolonial and decolonial methodological perspectives of situated knowledge, border epistemology and ontologizing epistemology.[3] Finally, this perspective leads to a discussion of the production of knowledge and its conditions, focusing on the precarious working conditions of researchers.

It is in this complex entanglement between epistemology, ontologies and working conditions that this research defines itself within a framework of "transcultural translation." Transcultural translation makes it clear that ethnographic research needs to be contextualized within a framework of social and geopolitical inequalities[4] and "colonial difference."[5] It is with these understandings that this chapter aims to "decolonize migration studies." Let us now turn to look at translation and colonial difference.

TRANSLATION AND "COLONIAL DIFFERENCE"

Within the sixteenth century, Spanish colonial context translation was a tool of empire. Two strategies were followed here: first, the conversion of the indigenous population to the dominant ideology, and second, the appropriation of their knowledge through assimilation. Translation thus helped build the "colonial difference" between Western European languages (languages of the sciences, knowledge and the locus of enunciation) and the rest of the languages on the planet (languages of culture and religion and the locus of the enunciated). Translation was indeed the process within which the coloniality of power articulated colonial difference.[6] The inscription of "colonial difference" as an articulation of colonial epistemic power became fundamental for the constitution of the binary modern/colonial world imaginary and its representation.[7] Rooted in the entanglement of European modernity and coloniality, Enrique Dussel sets the colonization of the *Américas* in 1492 as the pivotal point of departure for an occidental epistemological tradition, based on the insurmountable difference between the "Self" and the "Other."[8] This is present in Hegel's phenomenology of the Spirit and its logic of subjectivity based on the asymmetrical relationship between subject (*das Selbst*) and object (*das Andere*).[9] As Gayatri Chakravorty Spivak notes, this epistemological perception of the "Other" is circumscribed within the concrete metaphysical context of European colonialism.[10] It is in European colonialism that the construction of the "Other" is simultaneously underpinned by and supports the subjugation and oppression of the colonized population. Within these dynamics, as Dussel notes, the "Other" "is obliged, subsumed, alienated, and incorporated into the dominating totality like a thing or instrument,"[11] by processes of enslavement and colonization. In other words, "thingness," (otherness) emerges from the reduction of the colonized population to an exploited labor force.

In my encounter with Carla, "colonial difference" is expressed as an immanent condition of modernity. Within Quijano's logic of the coloniality of power, differences are produced as an expression of the social classification system based on the colonial category of "race," implied in the division between "insiders" and "outsiders" to the European Union.[12] Today, migration and asylum discourses are defined by this fundamental dichotomy. Thus, to presuppose "colonial difference" as an epistemological and ontological precondition for the encounter between Carla and myself is to recognize that our meeting is haunted by colonial legacies, a past that is still present in the political conjuncture framing the European context of migration and asylum. In this regard, the question of how to communicate within a space structured by fundamental and insurmountable differences emerges as a moment of what Freya Schiwy and Walter Mignolo describe as "double translation."[13]

Double Translation

As Mignolo and Schiwy contend, within the modern/colonial world-system translation is evocative of its character of domination by serving as a tool of "conversion" and "assimilation" of the subaltern into the dominant culture. On the other hand, it is also an instrument of intervention and resistance. Translation is a way of uncovering the sphere of plurilingualism. Intelligibility emerges here not as an outcome of similarity and equivalence, rather "double translation"[14] as a process of transculturation enables the forging of an intelligible text based on the acknowledgment of "impassable differences."[15] This notion of translation evokes Walter Benjamin's idea that a good translation is not necessarily one that repeats the idea of the original by creating a copy of it but one that stems from a failed translation of the original.[16] With his concept of "impassable differences," Benjamin discusses the power relations informing the process of translation. In his view, a translation that attempts to incorporate the language of the Other in its own script, fails in its "task" of creating some kind of understanding between two different systems of speech and perception of the world. The goal of a translation, thus, is not to recreate the language from which it departs, but to understand the process of translation as a moment of encounter with differences. The creativity that emerges in this encounter is what enables communication and encompasses the process of translation. Thus, resisting the incorporation of the Other's voice into a dominant script represents the tasks of translation for Benjamin. In a similar way, Schiwy and Mignolo are attentive to "double translation," the two sides of power relations inscribed in a process of encounter, where two different languages meet, representing different power positions within a global scheme of economic and political relations.

Benjamin's perspective on translation should enable us to spell out the differences and the power relations involved in the process of translation itself. As Paul Ricoeur stresses, following Benjamin, a good translation is one that acknowledges the singularity of the original, its specific context and content.[17] Evoking Benjamin's "impassable difference" and acknowledging a "correspondence without equivalence" in the translation process, Ricoeur's focus lies on the mutual transformation of the foreign and the familiar in this process.[18] Benjamin's angle, however, is less the transformation of the poles of the binary of the Self and the Other than the relation between these two poles. Benjamin is interested in the productive process surfacing from an attempt to communicate difference. This perspective on translation leaves aside the dichotomy of the "foreign" and the "familiar" as well as the parameters of equivalence and fidelity. Each translation engages with a "summary of long textuality where whole contexts are mirrored."[19] The translation of concepts demands the deciphering of a historical and cultural context, but also the tracing of heterogeneity. "It is to this heterogeneity that the foreign text owes its resistance to translation and, in this sense, its intermittent untranslatability."[20] It is this heterogeneity that lies in the attempt to recognize "intermittent untranslatability" that Spivak is attentive to in the process of translation as a moment of breaking monolingualism by "hearing-to-respond."[21]

BREAKING MONOLINGUALISM—HEARING-TO-RESPOND

"No speech is speech," Gayatri Chakravorty Spivak writes, "if it is not heard. It is this act of hearing-to-respond that may be called the imperative to translate [. . .] But the founding translation between people is a listening with care and patience, in the normality of the other, enough to notice that the other has already silently made that effort."[22] As Spivak notes, the imperative of translation arises when we attempt to listen in a space of "bringing to silence." But initially we cannot simply grasp this space of "bringing to silence" by our individual intention to listen. Spivak refers here to a structural moment in the encounter of various geopolitical positions. We are stuck in a dilemma because in an attempt to create commonalities, as the example of my conversation with Carla and Dani demonstrates, we keep hitting upon irresolvable gaps, marked by hierarchical differences.

In my conversation with the Latin American research participants, different languages and accents intertwine, revealing various Spanish idioms related to our geographical, social, historical and cultural positionalities. In my case it is a "hybrid Andalusian" influenced by living in Germany in a diasporic Spanish-speaking community of Latin American and Peninsular accents and dialects. Carla's Spanish is shaped by the influence of the Northern Ecuadorian variety of Quechua, Dani's Chilean by the specific slang of her Santiago de Chile neighborhood. Our accents and dialects more than just reveal language variety; they are also indicative of our geopolitical positions and the social and economic divides that shape our encounter. It is in this situation that a commonly held denominator, our Spanish language, produces more differences than commonalities. The need for translation that considers the cultural and political context of each speaker becomes apparent. Bearing this in mind in the case of my Spanish-speaking research participants and me, attempting to make oneself understood does not require a linguistic or literal translation, but one that acknowledges the cultural and political context of each person's speech.

It is in this regard that Spivak's principle of translation as "hearing-to-respond" as a listening to difference becomes relevant for this project. Listening to difference takes place when we go beyond our own perspective by working "at someone else's title, as one works with a language that belongs to many others."[23] Listening to difference is a way of understanding the affective and material interdependencies embedded in the insurmountable societal antagonisms in which encounters occur. Thus, the question of translation implies working around and through gaps, irritations and irrationalities, because the task of the translator starts where the limits of intelligibility are apparent, as Spivak suggests.[24] For Spivak, translation is a way of getting nearer to the limits of our own identity. This captures the persuasive character of translation as:

> one of the ways to get around the confines of one's identity as one who produces expository prose is to work at someone else's title, as

one works with a language that belongs to many others. This, after all, is one of the seductions of translating. It is a *simple miming* of the responsibility to the trace of the other in the self. (Spivak, "The Politics of Translation," 177)

In the aforementioned conversation with my research participants, commonalities of language, gender and migration are crossed by insurmountable differences between the research participants and myself. Carla subtly focused on the differences between my story and hers, situated at the juncture of the modern/colonial world-system. If we start with the Spanish language as something held in common or our gendered identity as women or even our experience with migration, this implies a reduction in the differences that constitute our positionalities. Thus, the articulation of individual particularities, reflecting social positionalities, appears as a point of departure in an encounter where communication can only be established through listening to the Other and hearing difference. Listening to the Other and hearing difference speaks directly to what Schiwy and Mignolo have discerned as the epistemic power of "colonial difference" in the context of transcultural translation.

Transcultural Translation

From the perspective of coloniality, translation demands that we inquire about the historical, political and social framework in which meaning is produced. Postcolonial and decolonial perspectives have discussed translation in terms of epistemic violence and its ambivalent dynamic of domination and subalternity.[25] These perspectives have also insisted on the potential of translation, as Aniket Jaaware notes, as an "agent of social change,"[26] as "it would be counter-productive to restrict the meaning of translation to linguistic or even cultural equivalence."[27] In a similar manner, Mignolo and Schiwy argue for an understanding of the ambivalent character of translation as a tool of domination during colonialism, but also as a tool of building bridges of communication. While translation has been a tool of colonial governance "imposing the construction of hierarchical dichotomies that have imposed certain rules and directionalities of transculturation,"[28] it also facilitated communication between different languages, forging the possibility of cultural encounters in a space ruled by power imbalances. Introducing the angle of transculturation, Mignolo and Schiwy emphasize the productive character of translation as it enables an intense traffic of ideas and languages.[29]

The articulation of individual particularities, reflecting social positions, appears as a point of departure in an encounter that needs some translation to enable communication between different participants. As Mignolo and Schiwy state, languages are vehicles of global communication. In this regard, translation is a method that enables plurilingual communication. In my encounter with Carla and Dani, the diasporic Spanish language functions in a double sense as it is not only a signifier of colonial epistemic power, but also a transculturalized tool of communication. Transculturation reflects our positionalities, in which commonalities but also differences are made known. My assumption of a common identity as Spanish speakers, post/migrant and gendered subjects is challenged by the panoply of social positions that textured our encounter, resonating with legacies of a racist colonial and imperial past, European border and migration regimes, heteronormativity and the modern/colonial world order. In the micro spaces of the everyday we are embedded in this historical, political, social and cultural complexity, where encounters carry the simultaneous experiences of conflict and exchange. This is exactly the simultaneity of creative exchanges and social conflict that is implicit in Fernado Ortiz's concept of "transculturation."

In 1940 Ortiz published his groundbreaking study *Contrapunteo Cubano del Tabaco y el Azúcar*[30] on the specificity of Cuban's modernity based on the experience of transculturation. Through his analysis of the sugar and tobacco industries, Ortiz shows how different historical moments— colonialism, slavery, independence and industrialization—shaped Cuban society and informed a specific form of conviviality, emanating out of the (forced) encounters between African, Asian, European and Amerindian people. His analysis of the sugar and tobacco plantations situates cultural practices in the midst of capitalist production, thus negating an understanding of culture detached from history and politics.[31] Insisting on culture as an outcome of different historical layers and modes of production, transculturation goes beyond an idealized notion of culture, as the prefix "trans" denotes. Instead, Ortiz discusses its material consistency by defining culture as a social phenomenon. As Fernando Coronil argues, such a definition of culture implies an understanding of lived culture or everyday culture as a field of social negotiations or, as I would add, a site of hegemonic struggle.[32] Culture, thus, is understood as an outcome of a process of "double translation," through which material conditions are translated into the immediacy of life, as well as the creative and affective forces of life being translated into the social.

Ortiz's concept is extremely useful for the discussion of translation as a transcultural method in ethnographic and qualitative research because it leads us to consider the relationship between the realm of the symbolic and the material conditions of life. It also reminds us of the historical legacies, in particular the legacies of colonialism and slavery, that haunt our everyday encounters. When we think of situations of translation in research the perspective of transculturation frames our encounters within the tension of transformation and conflict. Going back to my conversation with Carla, transculturation is present in our encounter. Our languages and experiences in our German diasporic space have intermingled and created a new variety of accents and languages to understand our reality. Our conversation is an outcome of this exchange. Nonetheless, insurmountable differences inform our encounter. The translation project that emerges from transcultural encounters does not pursue the goal of articulating a universal commonality but rather attempts to find a language in "différance," a language that departs from the "very possibility of difference(s)."[33]

Transcultural translation engages with the "double bind" of abstraction and practices, tracing, and simultaneously contesting, the abstraction of the common through the "complexity and heterogeneity of the resistance that is lodged in the many languages—not only the many languages of the world but the many idiomaticities of those languages."[34] Mignolo and Schiwy use the Zapatista Movement, which acknowledges its constitutive heteroglossia while strategically operating with Spanish and English to transmit its messages locally and globally, to show that transculturation conveys the mixture of both languages and knowledges. As they note, transculturation "is here best described as a social conflict between languages and cosmologies in hegemonic and subaltern positions, respectively."[35] My conversation with Carla and Dani reflects the conflict between migrant cosmologies and the hegemonic and subaltern positions articulated in the German diaspora, where Fordist Spanish migration meets post-Fordist Latin American migration. In this space of transcultural translation commonalities are expressed and differences experienced. How, then, can we translate the experience of migration and gender?

TRANSLATING MIGRATION, TRANSLATING BECOMING WOMAN

Dani was not recruited by the German State, in contrast to my parents who arrived through the "guest worker program" in 1962. She had to find a clandestine way to enter Germany since the official doors of immigration were closed for her as a non-EU citizen. However, the doors of private households that demanded her labor and care were wide open. Dani told me about her experiences of sexism and racism and the police violence she faces on an everyday level in West Germany. How can her experience be translated into that of my parents? My parents faced many difficulties when they lodged in barracks on their arrival in Germany, when they struggled to overcome the inhumane conditions of factory work, when they were trying to find a way to reunite their family.[36] Despite the German State's constant demand of the "guest worker" generation to remain for a limited time, my parents became pensioners in Germany. Since the 1960s Spain has changed politically and economically. Today Spain is a "global player" in the international financial markets and in the development of the EU directives regarding the restriction and control of asylum and migration. In Berlin Dani faces the effects of EU migration policies. She was forced to return to Chile as she could not regularize her residency situation. Life in West Germany was exhausting and she wanted to continue the struggle she started for domestic workers' rights and access to legal residency back home in Chile. Some of her fellow political activists, who were also "undocumented" domestic workers in Germany, became ill due to their physically and psychologically draining everyday lives, which were affected by the search for stable working and living conditions.

Some of the aspects of my parents' experiences in West Germany may be reflected in Dani's experiences, but the picture that is projected is a broken one. It is one that does not allow for a translation of the original into a copy, it is one that requires a translation beyond the reproduction of the original. My encounter with Dani, determined by relationships of power, emerges through the attempt to translate our life situations. The impossibility of a commonality in identity becomes clear, ultimately revealing this encounter as one of radical difference. Deep division lines, articulating social inequalities, structured our encounter. Two opposing spaces are competing here with each other, resulting for a brief moment in the creation of a common space. These spaces do not automatically overlap as they are divided by the division of labor and other social boundaries. How then can these opposing spaces be translated? Does "Becoming Woman" offer a common point of reference?

"Becoming Woman" is coupled with specific working and living conditions. As the Italian feminist post-operaist theorists, such as Judith Revel, Antonella Corsani and Sara Ongaro, propose, "Becoming Woman" indicates a broader development in society coupled to the "feminization of labor." In Chapter 4 of this volume I will discuss this in detail. However, here what interests me is the translation of "Becoming Woman," considering the working and living conditions in which certain gendered abilities are produced and extracted through specific modes of production. In this regard, "Becoming Woman" delineates a set of practices and relations, partly shared by a group of subjects interpellated and identified as "woman." For example, domestic work and caring for others are two spheres of the "feminization of labor," in which "femininity" is interpellated, performed and enacted. Dealing with the different challenges of organizing and administering several realms of life—such as the care of others, profession and household—requires a flexible, resilient subject. Therefore, the "feminization of labor" describes a general tendency in the current logic of capital production.

At the juncture of the "feminization of labor," perhaps a commonality between the domestic workers and their female employers in the private households can be discerned. Both women tackle the fact that domestic work and care work, traditionally seen as reproductive labor, are assigned to them as "woman." Their "Becoming Woman" is realized through sharing these conditions of work, which is attached to the lack of recognition of women's work in general. As I will discuss in the following chapters, society is structured by the devaluation inherent in the feminization of labor. However, as I will show in the discussion of affect and affective labor, other coordinates configure and blur the contours of "Becoming Woman," making it an unstable category for identification of a "global gendered commonality."

Introducing the question of translation into this context demands what Spivak identifies as the "ways of resisting capitalist multiculturalism's invitation to self-identity"[37] through the attribution of a unifying identity like "woman." While the notion of "Becoming Woman" attempts to break with an essentialist notion of femininity by situating it as an effect of assemblage, it holds the traces of monolingual Eurocentric thinking. What if this presupposed assemblage of "Becoming Woman" is broken by a myriad of differences, embedded in different languages and historical, geopolitical contexts? What, if it emerges within the epistemic framework of "colonial difference" or the "coloniality of power"?[38]

As the example from my own research demonstrates, we mean different things when we say "woman." Thus the analysis of the feminization of labor always arises within a geopolitical and historical framework. As Samia Mehrez states in the Egyptian context, the "history of the concept of gender in the Arab context is a history of cross-cultural communication and translation of knowledge."[39] The differences marking my encounter with the domestic workers do not only indicate the asymmetries structuring our encounter, they also point to the plurilinguality of gender that cannot be enclosed in a monolingual framework claiming universal truth. Mehrez illustrates this tension by demonstrating that the Greek concept *genus* cannot be simply translated to the Arabic term *jins*, which defines gender as a grammatical category but also as kind, sort, species, category, class, sex and "race."[40] Both terms reveal that the distinctiveness of their historical context and social practices cannot be reduced to an identical, antithetical or complementary logic. "Rather they are different."[41] Consequently, she asks if in Egypt "gender" is understood as synonymous with "women," what would be the range of gender-related issues, problems and setbacks that are masked by equating gender with women.[42] Mehrez suggests an alternative translation that goes beyond the dichotomy man/ woman.

In order to transcend the binary logic inscribed in "literary translation," the politics of location focus on the moment of "untranslatability,"[43] which Derrida has described as the "supplement" of translation. The "supplement is neither a plus nor a minus, neither an outside nor inside as its counterpart, neither accident nor essence."[44] It is in the movement between the two poles of the translation that an overdetermination, a supplement, is produced. This movement, which Benjamin is also attentive to and which Spivak sees as the moment of "hearing-to-respond," is embedded in the moment of heterogeneity incited by translation. It is a moment that embraces Rada Iveković's attempt to create a "middle, or *queer* way to approach"[45] dichotomies in encounters of translation. In this research, this moment of encounter occurs in the exchange and circulation of affects in domestic work.

Translating Affect in Domestic Work

Our affective and material interconnectedness predetermines the interactions in domestic work in private households. As the accounts of the domestic workers and their employers show, their relationship is predominantly textured by structural constraints. It is not the benevolent or multicultural habitus that impels households in the middle-income range to employ a migrant woman, who whilst outside of their social milieux becomes the "manager" of their intimate spaces. Rather, as I will discuss in Chapter 3 of this volume, the lack of State provision for childcare as well as the care of the elderly and the societal devaluation of domestic work drive the households to outsource this labor. While the rationale is pragmatically determined by the question of how to cope with career and family, create work–life balance and neutralize potential conflicts regarding housework between the partners or household members, domestic work is imbricated with affection. The domestic worker does not only clean the bathroom and make the beds, but also provides empathy and compassion, at the same time that she represses her own sensations of disgust and anger related to the humiliation attributed to this labor by society.

Yet these affects shape domestic workers' encounters and become affective imprints on their bodies and minds, marking divided spaces of sociality and holding the effects of domestic work's lack of recognition. Thus, transcultural encounters between female employers and their domestic workers, whilst they might be circumvented by their employment relationship, are characterized by the immediate dynamics of interpersonal interactions. Affects, as I will discuss in the following chapters, while not always explicitly articulated, shape these encounters. However, while some feelings, sensations and intensities might be shared between these two groups of women, the meaning attached to them differs in respect to the sociopolitical context that they inhabit. While some employers describe domestic work as enjoyable as long it does not become a routine, the domestic workers emphasize the lack of recognition of this work. For example, Monika, one of the employers in Hamburg, Germany, a designer and mother of two told us:

> I don't find domestic work terrible at all. I am happy to cook, for example. At some point, however, one does not feel like it, for example, if one has cooked the entire day then for a long time, then I am not happy to cook anymore.

Monika relates to domestic work as individual choice. Later on she tells us that her husband cooks from time to time, but what she omits from the conversation is the fact that she has employed Denise to keep the house clean, cook and pick up the children. Denise, an Afro-Ecuadorian who arrived in Hamburg in 2000 planning to study but became "undocumented" after her tourist visa ran out, defines this labor thus:

And, I mean, imagine how you feel, it's just like—you feel like you are being used. You feel like being useless. And, I don't know, maybe because we are Black, I don't know, but it's not only Black people who are doing this job. So many people, I mean so many *Ausländers* [German term for foreigner] are doing these kinds of jobs. And I don't know if they are encountering the same experience I have encountered. I feel very bad and I don't feel like doing the household cleaning *again*.

The common affect that these two women might share is the revulsion regarding the imposition of domestic work. This commonality, however, is stripped away by the differences inscribed in this experience. While Monika can evade it by employing another woman and detaching herself from it, Denise is bodily and symbolically affected by it. Denise's body carries the affect of revulsion as she tries to make sense of the fact that there are Black or *Ausländer* bodies carrying the affect of disgust, personifying the devaluation of domestic work and the dehumanizing effects of racism. The affect produced by the symbolic power attached to domestic work as gendered and devalued labor impacts differently on these women's bodies. Thus this experience cannot be represented by unifying signifiers such as "women" and "women's work." Rather, this example makes us listen to differences and opens a process of translation in which differences are unleashed and plurilinguality revealed. As Spivak notes, translating thus becomes a "simple miming of the responsibility to the trace of the other in the self."[46] Translation in research requires the openness to learning to unlearn our own privileges, recognizing the "pluriversality" and "un-translatability" of our encounters. This is an important step in decolonizing migration studies.

DECOLONIZING MIGRATION STUDIES

The representation of academic knowledge is guided by a process of translation. This arises from the tension between "assimilation" and "resistance" to a dominant monolingual script. How we perceive and interpret the world is not an innocent practice, but rather it depends on social negotiations and hegemonic strategies of representation. Representation is an outcome of a process of hegemonic struggle, as Spivak argued in her seminal text "Can the Subaltern Speak?"[47] Introducing the twofold nature of representation as description (*Darstellung*) and delegation (*Vertretung*) of the world, things and people, Spivak discusses the hegemonic dimension of representation as an articulation of a dominant common sense. Academic, media and political discourses are characterized by contestation and power struggles. Dominant views become common sense and are thus normalized. Migration studies are heavily invested in a political framework of regulation, management and immigration control. In the social sciences migration research is very often guided by an applied research framework and research funding is provided by State programs immediately connected to policy making. Migration as a "real phenomenon" is presented in a managerial language, embedded in methodological nationalism, classifying and quantifying migrants and post/ migrants and targeting these groups as objects of governance. Thus, migration as a phenomenon is measured, circumscribed and regulated, whilst the communities and subjectivities touched by it dissolve behind a list of nationalities and obfuscating figures. How do we break with this dynamics of putting numbers to a "presupposed reality" that needs to be verified through the incessant production of more numbers, nationalities and social classifications? What if we leave the terrain of demographic governance and approach the phenomenon of "labor migration" from the perspective of transcultural translation? What if we start to dismantle its "social veracity" by demonstrating its "cultural predication"?

If we perceive migration from a transcultural translational perspective, migration as a social phenomenon is revealed as culturally predicated. As such migration as a social text, as an outcome of a dialogic system of representation that needs to be approached by different strategies of reading in the form of translation, requires an engagement with culture as contested, temporal and emergent. It is in this setting that the task of translating evolves as political cultural practice, drawing from the dynamics of the social and their textual interpretations. Translation in research reminds us that the transference and production of meaning is involved in hegemonic struggle over representation of migrant and diasporic communities. What language can we use to describe the legal status of a migrant that falls outside of state interpellations? It is exactly in relation to this tension between state interpellation and representation that the question of translation emerges.

Within the context of the modern/colonial world-system, "grounded in an ethnoracial, gendered, and epistemological foundation,"[48] the question of representation is related to hegemonic power struggle. Applying translation as a method in ethnographic research on domestic work requires that we consider the discursive order organizing this field. The academic and political representation of domestic work within the context of migration follows certain tropes of governance such as "migration policies," "migrant women" and "work–life balance" that denote the sociopolitical contexts of emergence. This codification evolves along "chains of value-coding,"[49] where the signifiers "woman," "migrant" and "domestic worker" not only reflect discursive constructions of reality, but are ingrained in human bodies. As such, these tropes do not just refer to the realm of symbolism, but to corporeal affective realities. We could say that this outcome is inevitable as it is immanent in the synthesizing logic of research that aims at "scientific objectivity." What about leaving migration as a denotation of "social conflict" and exploring it as a violent episteme, one circumscribed by the discursive framework from which it emerges? Focusing on the relationship of affect, domestic work and migration from a transcultural translational perspective counters the epistemic violence of discourses and governance technologies that regard migration as a source of "social conflict" and "societal fracture." Further, this perspective enables us to trace the principles of situated research and border epistemology in critical migration studies.

Situated Research and Border Epistemology

My own knowledge production as a researcher in Anglophone and continental Western European universities, competing in the global market of education, raises ethical and political questions related to the representation of migration in research. The close proximity between research and policy making means that an approach that engages on different levels of translation between theory and practice and institutional knowledge requires a decolonial ethical framework.[50] Focusing on the analysis of the modern/colonial world-system,[51] the decolonial perspective departs from coloniality as a vantage point from which to shift the "geography of reason."[52]

Through the discourse of modernity in Western philosophy and social sciences an "ontology of continental divides"[53] has been produced and a hierarchical classification of the world established.[54] This classification reflects the division of the world into, first, second, third and fourth worlds, rooted in Eurocentric interpretations of economic, political, cultural and intellectual development. Social sciences, and in particular Sociology, engage with this perception by situating the origins of modernity in Europe.[55] In migration studies this is translated into the "tradition–modernity paradigm," through which "non-European" migrants are projected as being in a "premodern" stage. This is reiterated through numerous migration policies targeting non-European migrants in "need of integration" or conveyed in discourses of "parallel societies" or "clash of cultures." This perception operates on the foundations of a "progressive modern Europe" and its "underdeveloped, traditional and backward" racialized, ethnicized and gendered Other, its "exteriority."[56]

In order to counter those assumptions that very often subtly underlie research on migrant subjectivities, practices and communities, migration studies needs to be read against its grain. To read it against its grain means destabilizing disciplinary boundaries and their Eurocentric paradigms by confronting them with "colonial difference," a goal that Walter Mignolo's border epistemology envisages. Border epistemology is a framework that emerges at the juncture of oppression and resistance. It is composed of the "plurisversality" of local colonial histories entangled with imperial modernity[57] and draws on Gloria Anzaldúa's analysis of *borderlands*.[58] Living at the borderlands for Anzaldúa is imbued with dispossession, persecution and violence, but also unleashes new strategies for coping with and transgressing boundaries. Anzaldúa's "borderland" and "border consciousness" invite us to situate our research at the crossroads between hegemonic paradigms and their crossing. This tension between the dominant framework of meaning and its shifting towards a new heuristic position enlightens the perspective of transcultural translation. As Mignolo notes in his further development of "border consciousness," "border thinking" accentuates the "de-linking from the colonial matrix of power."[59] It traces the threshold between modernity and coloniality as it acknowledges the centrality of Western traditions of thought for the development of modern sciences and the dominant conceptualization of the world. At the same time it also reveals the limitations and epistemic violence of this perspective.

While Anzaldúa and Mignolo elaborate border epistemology within the analysis of coloniality in the *Américas*, the translation of this analytical approach within the European context poses questions in regard to its "exteriority"[60] within its own borders. The exteriority of Europe within its borders is articulated by the presence of postcolonial and Eastern European migrants and refugees interpellated as the "Others" of modernity. The research participants in my study, living in Europe without residency permits and working as domestic workers in private households, are at the juncture between border and migration regimes and the crossing of these borders on physical, cultural, intellectual and affective levels. Under these conditions a new epistemology emerges, reflecting the existential experiences of the subjects caught in them.

Ontologizing Epistemology

As Anzaldúa states, while living at the borderlands is imbued with the experience of dispossession, persecution and violence, it also unleashes creative strategies of survival to cope with and overcome this situation. Anzaldúa refers to this as *la facultad*, "the capacity to see in surface phenomena the meaning of deeper realities, to see the deeper structure below the surface."[61] This "faculty" arises out of existential experiences of abjection and subjugation at the juncture of different systems of domination and it informs the "semiotic vector" of what Chela Sandoval defines as the "differential consciousness" in her methodology of the oppressed.[62] *La facultad* for Anzaldúa emerges out of an existential life situation, "when you're against the wall—when you have all these oppression coming at you—you develop this extra faculty."[63] *La facultad* speaks to a special faculty emerging out of the epistemic and ontological conditions of living at the borderlands between the United States and Mexico. Under these conditions a specific knowledge is produced through the struggle for liberation, a knowledge conditioned by the historical and material circumstances within this context. Knowledge is accompanied here by wisdom, as Patricia Hill Collins has observed in regard to subjugated knowledge.[64]

Black feminist epistemology, in particular, has insisted on the role of personal experiences and practices in the generation of knowledge. Collins differentiates in this regard between "wisdom" and "knowledge." While "knowledge" is perceived as occurring outside a historical and political framework, "wisdom" is immediately linked to the need to understand the world, to be able to maneuver within it and survive. In the case of subordinated women, Collins notes that "the intersecting oppressions" these women experience underlie the essential distinction between "knowledge" and "wisdom." "Knowledge without wisdom," she writes, "is adequate for the powerful, but wisdom is essential for the survival of the subordinate."[65] With this observation she insists on the need for standpoint theory, the heuristic position of embodied knowledge, thus countering assertions of objectivity in "scientific knowledge," which presupposes a historically and socially decontextualized approach to the production of knowledge. Instead, Collins demonstrates that knowledge is determined by an intersectional system of oppression through which access to the spheres of knowledge production is conditioned.

Following this tradition of contested knowledge and linking it to participatory action research of the 1970s and 1980s,[66] this research engages with Maria Mies's Participatory Action Research (PAR).[67] Pursuing the twin goals of dissolving the power asymmetries between researcher and research participant, and being attentive to embodied knowledge through situating our research within the geopolitical and historical context of emergence, the research process is considered a generator of collective knowledge. It is an educational process empowering all those involved to change themselves, their relationships with each other and their society. Collecting observations and arguments from different points of views, the project engaged with the wisdom of all the participants. However, while the aim of generating knowledge collectively was attempted, the social divisions structuring our research team impeded participation on equal terms. As I have discussed elsewhere, academic and political work with "undocumented migrants" is always affected by the fact that those conducting this work have citizenship rights and access to official representation, unlike those being worked with.[68] The relationship between researcher and research participants in migration research is already caught in the global North–South divide.

Thus, it is not a coincidence that the majority of research projects on migration within the Western European context are conducted by researchers who are White nationals and the majority of the research participants are racialized, minoritized subjects, struggling with the social barriers imposed on them because of their geographical background, gender, class, "race," ethnicity, sexuality or religion. This demands that we be attentive not only to an analysis of the social field and its epistemic foundations, but to the material conditions of knowledge production.

Knowledge Production

As Pierre Bourdieu emphasizes, entry to the academy, and thus to "authorized" knowledge production, is determined by access to social capital, social networks and resources.[69] Within the Western European context the production of institutionalized knowledge has been a field mainly defined by elite White men. As an outcome of the women's movement, since the 1980s the access of White women to leading positions in research and teaching has increased. However, scholars with a non-White European background are hardly represented, for example, in the UK, the Netherlands and France, and almost completely omitted in countries such as Germany, Spain and Austria.[70] While some countries' research ambitions have opened the doors to international competition, as in the case of the UK and the Netherlands, in most countries universities remain in the hands of national White elites.[71] Moreover, the geographical situatedness of institutional knowledge production and the hegemony of the English language in academic work[72] enable certain research to become global—and thus "universal" references of knowledge production. However, research and theory from the "global South" and in other languages are perceived as regionally situated with epistemological relevance solely for the region of study. Thus, knowledge production in higher education institutions is structured transversally by local and global inequalities. Who the researcher and the researched are is not mere coincidence. Thus, we need to inquire critically into research on "migrant" domestic workers in order to examine the power relations between researchers and research participants.

Within the Western European context, research on migrant domestic workers reflects the broader gendered and racialized division of work in society. The researchers conducting research on "migrant women" are mostly White European women. Meanwhile, "the researched" are racialized women from Eastern Europe or the "global South." Though some of my research participants have a university degree, they are unable to work in an academic institution or within the educational system in general. Different barriers are in place in the form of language proficiency and recognition of professional experiences and skills that are subtly textured by racism and restricted access to the labor market. The only avenues to employment that remain open, in particular for "undocumented migrants," are personal service, hospitality, care and cleaning.

This observation requires that we situate the production of knowledge and the encounter between researcher and research participants within the context of working conditions within and outside academic institutions. While this study has evolved within the methodological framework of PAR, connecting theory to practice and considering the theoretical contributions from all the participants in the research, hierarchies still shape the relationship between different participants. This is not only the case between the researchers and the domestic workers or between the domestic workers and their employers. Starting with the research team, the position of the different researchers is marked by professional hierarchies expressed in different academic positions.[73] Additionally, the research participants, working "undocumented" in private households, decided to be anonymized in this research as they feared that their "named representation" might put them in danger of discovery and deportation. Different employment positions created different long-term involvements in the research as the researchers were dependent on consecutive individual or project funding. A schism is thereby produced in which knowledge is generated through the dialogue between researcher and research participants, but on the level of academic representation it is the researcher who is acclaimed as the sole author. The lack of institutional recognition of dialogicity and interdependence in research requires a methodology that interrogates the institutional situatedness of knowledge production.

Precarious work, or *precarity* for *Precarias a la Deriva*,[74] is a common feature of current employment regimes. Precarity informs not only the working conditions of migrant domestic workers, but also the process of knowledge production, creating precarious and marginalized zones and positions. Thus access to academic debates is given in particular to those in "permanent authorized" institutional positions, while researchers in temporary positions need to divide their time between searching for new employment and finding some time to write. Precarious working conditions in the academic field sustain discontinuity and invisibility. Further, academic institutions, whilst promoting collaborative work, focus on individual outcomes when it comes to assessment and ranking criteria. This contributes to the structural dynamics in academia, mediated through the politics of funding and public recognition.

My writing of this book is an outcome of a collaborative and cooperative process of thinking, telling stories, arguing with funding institutions, encountering voices outside the academic setting and creating solidarity networks for a human and affective environment committed to social justice. In this regard, this project engages with "critical border thinking," as "a universal project of 'de-linking' from modern rationality and building other possible worlds."[75] It follows Anzaldúa's suggestion that we disengage with "the dominant culture, write it off altogether as a lost cause, and cross the border into a wholly new [. . .] territory."[76] Further, it connects decolonial ethics to what J.K. Gibson-Graham frame as "new ethical practices of thinking economy and becoming different kinds of economic beings,"[77] "emerging from the mutuality of our relationships and especially our interdependence with others."[78] Accordingly, transcultural translation represents a methodology of "transversal understanding."

CONCLUSION: TRANSVERSAL UNDERSTANDING

The perspective of transcultural translation entails a critical reading of the field of "transnational migration" and "paid domestic work." The proximity of migration studies to governance demands strategies for countering and undermining the effects of migration policies on research, reflected in rhetoric on how to control and manage migration. Further, some astuteness is required to be attentive to the adaptation and reiteration of classification systems produced within the logic of migration and asylum policies. For example, the legal statuses of "migrant," "refugee," "asylum seeker" or "illegal migrant" are effects of migration and asylum policies. Yet the strategy cannot be to avoid these institutional practices of naming in research as they codify existing realities produced by technologies of governing. Rather, cunning is required to reveal the effects of their domination and attendant subalternization. The task of transcultural translation guides us to a process of transversal understanding beginning with an understanding of "untranslatability." Research engaging with transversal understanding, while interweaving with a dominant script, resists the attempt at assimilation into dominant codes. This means understanding the gaps, the unevennesses and silences that do not repeat the imposed logic. Not repeating the imposed logic opens up a space for heteroglossia, contesting and challenging the disciplinary confines and rigidity of academic knowledge by marking the researcher's positionality and situatedness and her/his responsibility to produce critical thinking.

Theodor W. Adorno defines critique as the attempt to transgress what appears as given. In his dispute with quantitative sociologists at the University of Cologne in the late 1960s, Adorno insisted on the need for double reflection[79] as society cannot just be conceived of as an empirical given that needs to be measured and validated. Rather, society itself is an outcome of our epistemological understanding of the world. Such an understanding of society requires a critical analysis that goes beyond what is intelligible and inscribed in a legitimized and institutionally authorized text of representation. Society is not a reproduction of what is conveyable in quantifiable terms, so in order to grasp its *Gestalt* we need to understand the parameters through which it becomes an object of research.[80]

While I consider the need for an analysis of "empirical realities" in order to understand the effects of policies, this analysis needs to attend to the interpenetration between discourses, institutional dynamics and everyday practices. Considering the performative effects of our epistemological framework, the perspective of transcultural translation opens up an avenue to critically inquire about the representation of domestic work. An approach that critically questions the epistemological dimension of representation and its political implications requires a method that focuses on language as a system of abstraction of the data form. As Spivak notes, if "we are going to fight the data form we fight it through abstractions, we use it to reevaluate, recode, reverse, and displace value."[81] It is in this regard that the perspective of transversal understanding in terms of transcultural translation, of spelling out translation in difference and tracing the hierarchies in which communication occurs, becomes relevant in research. It is in the light of this perspective that this book engages with the affective dynamics between Latin American domestic workers and their employers in private households in Western Europe.

2 Coloniality of Labor
Migration Regimes and the Latin American Diaspora in Europe

> While they are invested in their personal development, we are getting sick, we are left with arthritis, with asthma and every time we are getting worse, we are getting old in this country, without social security without anything and this country is prospering. (Velma, domestic worker, Berlin)

Velma, one of the research participants and founder of the Latin American "undocumented" women's group *Mujeres Sin Rostro*, summarizes her life as an "undocumented" domestic worker with these words. As with the other women in my sample, Velma came to Berlin with the expectation of developing herself professionally and intellectually. Velma describes herself as a restless, active and unconventional person, driven by the aim of intervening politically and making herself heard when she perceives injustice. She told me that since her thirteenth birthday she has been involved in political organizing. First against the Pinochet regime, causing her family, particularly her father, some trouble as he was afraid his daughter would be detained by the police. Second, in Berlin she saw the need to fight for her rights and the legalization of "undocumented" migrant workers.

Velma told me that she always has taken responsibility being the oldest in a family of seven and raising her two children as a teenager. Life has shown her how to cope with difficult situations, how to prosper and not lose track of her own aims and goals. She separated from her husband when her children were still toddlers as he was not supporting the family or helping in the household. This meant that there came a time when she said, "I can't cope anymore, because I just don't like to constantly raise children, cleaning, changing nappies, this can't be all there is." The option of going to Europe appeared, "then every one tells you that there are no problems, just go, go to produce, then, they actually dismantle your life's whole framework, but at the same time you see as a woman that maybe there might still be a way out for you. I like to read, to create, I like art." The option of migrating to Europe, while it contains a destabilizing moment and the command of becoming a "productive subject," also promises Velma the opportunity for personal development. Velma's motivation to migrate is driven by her attempt to find a different space as a woman in which she can start to do things other than just being a housewife and a mother. She told us that she was able to do new things in Germany, and more significantly for her, to contribute socially to changing women's subaltern position. Thus, for her "the woman is not just born to clean." Whilst Velma engages in political activism and also works as an "arpillera"[1] artist in Germany, these activities do not provide her with an income.

After her three-month tourist visa ran out, Velma became "undocumented." Due to her engagement in different networks, she quickly found jobs and accommodation. She shared an apartment with two German women and worked on an hourly basis in different private households. Despite the structural constraints that Velma experiences as an "undocumented migrant" woman in a racialized and gendered segregated labor market, she considers that migrating to Germany has brought her nearer to her goal of living as an independent woman. This is an aspect also shared by other research participants. However, Velma's achievement of autonomy in migration is overshadowed by the effects of institutional and everyday racism that her treatment as an "undocumented migrant" reveals. Connected to this are the experiences of structural and everyday violence, affecting the bodies and minds of people living under the conditions of illegalization. Affect emerges here as the bodily expression of scars, wounds and sensations born from this experience, but is also fueled by the yearnings, passions and desires accompanying these thorny itineraries. In the private household where these women are employed as domestic workers, these affects are (re) activated or newly produced in the encounters with household members or infused by the energies circulating in it. In particular, encounters between female "undocumented migrant" domestic workers and their employers are inflected by the dynamics imposed by EU asylum and migration policies. In the overlapping of these two, an assemblage is created that I will discuss here in terms of Anibal Quijano's "coloniality of labor."

Velma's story tells us about the effects of European migration regimes in which non-European migrants including Latin Americans are degraded to the status of "unwelcome" migrants. This has not always been the case in regard to Latin American immigration. In the 1970s, on the basis of their asylum petitions, Chileans, Argentineans and Uruguayans found hospitality in the UK, Germany, France and Spain, for example. Nowadays the term "exile" has almost disappeared from public discourses and been replaced by policies attempting to regulate and restrict entry to European territories. Terms such as "asylum seeker"[2] and "economic migrant" connote an "illegitimate" claim for residence in Europe. The media exploits the refugee question through, for example, depictions of "overloaded boats" arriving on Europe's coasts or the "waves of refugees" trying to cross the English Channel to enter the UK. The imagery produced by the media and political debates codify refugees as "invaders," producing the "migrant body" as "body information,"[3] a body created through the affective circulation of media images, policy inscriptions and political discourses. Within this hostile climate, petitioners for asylum and the grounds for their asylum petitions are treated with suspicion by national policy makers. This is significant, as to apply for asylum represents one of the few avenues to achieve "transitory" settlement within the EU-zone. For non-EU citizens in particular, entering the EU with an asylum petition or a work contract has been increasingly difficult in the last two decades. This is due to the "harmonization" of national policies within the EU along the two pillars of "economic migration," targeting "high-skilled migrants," on one hand, and on the other, "migration control" pursuing the surveillance of European borders. Both sides are not driven by humanitarian goals and enforce the restriction of entry and settlement for non-European migrants, particularly women, as they are hardly the addressees of "highly skilled" migration recruitment geared more towards the male-dominated labor sectors.[4]

This logic of governing migration and asylum through control and surveillance technologies stands at the center of the modern/colonial world-system and shapes its modern expression of the coloniality of labor. In this chapter I will be attentive to the coloniality of labor within the context of EU migration policies and the appearance of Latin American immigration to Europe in the late 1980s. It is through these dynamics that "colonial difference" is discussed here within the European context. The creation of an "exteriority"[5] in colonial times, which Dussel situated outside European territory, is now also negotiated within its own borders. This "exteriority" within Europe is created in the interpellation and enunciation of non-European or Eastern European migrants and refugees as the racialized, ethnicized and gendered "Other" of the nation. An "Other" who is created through material living conditions, imposed by migration policies and configured within the logic of capitalism. Despite the actual end of colonial administration, a colonial logic of governing through ethnicity and "race" divides is still in place in contemporary societies. As Santíago Castro-Gómez and Ramón Grosfoguel observe, the transition from modern colonialism to global colonialism, a process that has certainly modified the forms of domination unleashed by modernity, has not altered the structure of the center–periphery relationship on a global scale.[5] This perspective entails perceiving current forms of governing not as a direct consequence of colonialism, but as entrenched in a social classification system departing from the colonial categories of "race" and "ethnicity." Whilst not explicitly spelled out in national EU migration policies, the divide between "EU" citizens and "non-EU" citizens subtly refers to this colonial classification system when it comes to migrants and refugees from former European colonies.

While not specifically denoting racial and ethnic differences, migration policies operate on the epistemic grounds of "colonial difference." As Mignolo asserts, "colonial difference" entails the hierarchical differentiation and racial classification of populations from "the" European perspective.[6] The interpellation and treatment of migrants and refugees as "invaders," "impostors" and "aliens" by migration policies invoke this population as the "Other" of the nation, codifying it as a body subjected to technologies of governance, information, surveillance and control. The "Other" of the nation is thus identified within and without the nation through the color line, religious beliefs and cultural differences. Within the nation, the "immigrant" postcolonial population becomes an object of control and management if they supposedly do not adapt to hegemonic norms and value systems, conveyed in the numerous public policies on "integration," or if they are identified as a "public threat." As an "outsider" to the nation, the postcolonial post/migrant and refugee are identified as a "potential threat" to social cohesion and security, an aspect that we will discuss next in regard to EU migration policies. "Outsiderness" operates on the basis of the continuity of a colonial gaze, classifying and identifying Europe's Other as a threat, in need of "integration," and as the stumbling block in "social cohesion." On the other side, it is this "Other" who subsidizes the economy, delivers the "unpleasant work" and thus contributes to the affective social and economic reproduction of the nation. Given this context, it is clear that European migration policies have to be approached from a decolonial perspective.

DECOLONIAL PERSPECTIVE ON
EUROPEAN MIGRATION POLICIES

From a decolonial angle, the continuity of European hegemony in the new constellation of global power and its place in neocolonial modes of production and capitalist accumulation is significant in order to understand, for example, on which epistemic foundations and historical legacies European migration and asylum policies operate. Departing from a decolonial perspective on transnational migration studies, and in particular on domestic work, drives us to consider what Marx coins "temporal incommensurability" (*Ungleichzeitigkeit*). That is, the parallel existence of two time periods, occurring in one and the same place, configuring a social phenomenon. Marx did not think about the imbrication of European modernity and coloniality[8] or the feminization of labor in terms of "temporal incommensurability." However, I would like to introduce domestic work in conjunction with migration regimes into this debate. This is the case as domestic work inhabits, but also challenges, the two temporalities of reproduction that Marx discusses as "real subsumption" and "formal subsumption."

For Marx, the analysis of "real subsumption" and "formal subsumption" is significant in order to understand the two levels on which the accumulation of capital and its reproduction operate. While Marx aims to give us a universal account of reproduction in society, his model is confined to the European context and precludes Europe's enduring colonial ties. In his discussion of "formal subsumption," Marx does not engage with the coloniality of labor or the feminization of labor. Both relations of production are obfuscated through an apparent chronological framing of "formal subsumption" and "real subsumption." Both terms define two different relations of capital accumulation with time. "Real subsumption" takes place when capital has "taken over control of production."[9] It is the moment when the labor process is directly subordinated to capital, to the mode of capitalist production. The production and the productivity of the worker as well as the relationship between worker and "capitalist" are submerged in this logic of production. In this case, as Sandro Mezzadra notes, a "synchronicity between the time of capitalist accumulation and the time of production"[10] emerges. This process is characterized by the flexibility of capital to incorporate new modes of production and strategies of subsumption. Through this capital invests directly in the process of production with the aim of incorporating new and resilient aspects of the social forces of production. In contrast to "real subsumption," "formal subsumption" describes certain specific forms of production in which capital has not directly invested. It is a process of production that "has not yet succeeded in becoming the dominant force, capable of determining the form of society as a whole."[11] "Formal subsumption" is thus the mode of production and productivity that already exists and is not related directly to the strategy of capital production. In other words, "formal subsumption" is based on people's spontaneous vital, creative, affective forces and intellectual activities that organize life. It is in this regard that work disciplined by the commands of capitalism encounters productivity surfacing from social life. For Mezzadra, these two temporalities represent the split of the world history of capital, its "double movement."[12] Translated into contemporary modes of production these two temporalities define both the dynamics of production in peripheral economies and in the centers of economic power. Thus, in the context of globalized economic relations, these temporalities are also connoted by the overlapping of different zones of production in one and the same location, an aspect that Aihwa Ong discusses in regard to "timescales" and "latitudes."[13]

Latitudes are "striated spaces of production that combine different kinds of labor regimes."[14] As she shows in the case of East and Southeast Asia, different modes of control such as the disciplinary and regulatory overlap, demonstrating that "contemporary transnational production networks are underpinned by carceral modes of labor discipline."[15] These produce "lateral spaces and enclaves on a transnational scale," governed by racialized and gendered labor segregation, where a heterogeneous space of global capital production is configured. Here "the geographical stretching of network economies is often accompanied by a temporal stretching, a regression to 'older' forms of labor disciplining epitomized by the high-tech sweatshops."[16] Ong's analysis of the industries in "East Asia" stresses the coexistence of disciplinary modes of production with the organization of labor based on the autonomy and creativity of the labor force. As she makes apparent, advanced capitalism has not overcome its "carceral modes of labor discipline."[17] It still operates on this basis, weaving it into new modes of production or just coexisting within a new script of production.

Ong's attempt to analyze productive labor within the neoliberal organization of capitalism introduces an analysis of gendered and racialized labor segregation and exploitation and the focus lies particularly on industrial labor or the "new economy." The classical sphere of feminized labor, domestic work, is not addressed in this perspective as it is not addressed in Marx's "real subsumption" and "formal subsumption." However, the analysis of domestic work within this framework shows, on the one side, the limits of this analysis, but, on the other, the possibility of understanding the productivity of domestic work within the framework of Marx's reproduction.

Domestic work emerges as a hybrid category. It stands at the juncture of modernity/coloniality or "formal subsumption" and "real subsumption." Domestic work represents an articulation of the diachronic relationship to time of the current modes of production, engaging on the one hand directly with prevailing modes of production, but drawing on the other, on forms of capital exploitation situated in other times: coloniality of labor; or outside the logic of production: feminization of labor. However, situating it within the framework of "real subsumption" and "formal subsumption," domestic work could be related to "formal subsumption" as it is labor that capital does not invest in or act directly upon, but that which it exploits. While capital does not directly organize domestic work, it extracts the productivity generated through this labor and its social relations. Relations of capital production fuse here with relations emerging from social practices, which are not always directly related to capital production as my discussion on affect in the next chapters will show.

Domestic work is situated in the privacy of the households indirectly governed by migration policies and family policies. As *living labor,* "the diversity of human faculties, of practices of cooperation often developing outside the direct command of capital, of 'forms of life' that make up that productive power,"[18] it becomes a constitutive part of "formal subsumption" by enabling the incorporation and realization of a flexible labor force in advanced capitalism. This is shown in the organization of flexible working arrangements and time in private households. While the employers interviewed for this study, journalists, teachers, lecturers, designers, architects, physicians or lawyers, increasingly share flexible working hours and the demand for more self-management in their workplace,[19] their domestic workers are subjected to the same demands at home. However, these demands within the working parameters of domestic work seem to be "naturalized," taken for granted. Thus, no extra conditions or income increase is tied in to their negotiations of flexible working hours or self-management capabilities. On the contrary, the domestic worker is expected to be an "independent" and flexible worker. Domestic work functions here on two levels, as support for the flexible working conditions in the "formal" organization of labor and as prescriptive of the incorporation of the quality of domestic work as *living labor* into a strategy of production. Thus, the accumulation of capital is not just a result of a clearly structured, organized and projected plan of production. Rather, capital is successful when it reacts to the spontaneous productivity created by peoples' activities and forms of social organization.

Capital needs to work on two levels: on an organized one and on a flexible one. On the flexible level, capital is interested in *living labor*. *Living labor* is based on the creative, subjective and social faculties of people to forge a common living and to organize life. As such, these are faculties that we might not find in a classical Marxist account of labor-power, but that have increasingly become relevant for the organization of the mode of production in advanced capitalism as we will discuss in Chapter 4 of this volume. Thus, the understanding of domestic work as "formal subsumption" becomes dubious, if we note that behind the supposedly "unorganized" character of this labor is a system of exploitation, rooted in a patriarchal and colonial system of the devaluation of labor and its translation to "unwaged" or "low waged" labor within the logic of capital accumulation. As such, domestic work, while relating to Marx's temporalities, also evidences their limits. This is so because the perception of domestic work as "simple labor," not embedded in the production and circulation of capital and emanating from "free-floating," feminized faculties of caring for others, attends to a hegemonic cultural script, perpetuating this labor as inferior and unproductive.

This is particularly so when migration regimes interplay with the feminization of labor and are articulated, for example, in "undocumented migrant" domestic work. Two temporalities, modernity and coloniality, are conflated here, articulating the inherent paradox of the modern/colonial world-system expressed through the local face of "undocumented migration" in advanced capitalism. These women, codified as "undocumented migrants," work without work contracts or entitlement to social security and social benefits. Their working conditions in the private households recall feudal and colonial times, while they embody the exemplary worker of the "new economy" through their self-governing abilities as autonomous workers. Further, their work sustains the welfare of the household and enables its members to pursue their careers or have good work–life balance.

As Quijano and Mignolo argue, the coloniality of labor is inherent to the logic of capital accumulation.[20] Modern forms of capital production have not replaced colonial forms of production; rather they conflate, articulating current forms of capital production. In other words, we could say that both temporalities relevant for economic and social reproduction, "formal subsumption" and "real subsumption," obfuscate the entanglement between modernity and coloniality by offering a clear chronological divide. This divide presumes that we overcame colonial modes of production. Thus, what these terms do not tell us is that the "already existing labor" is codified by a historical moment of appropriation as "available" and "disposable" labor due to its cultural predication. In other words, through its codification as racialized and feminized labor. Thus, the "already existing" productivity acquired from *living labor* attends a hidden script of disciplinary capitalism in which feminized and racialized subjects are targeted as "raw material" as their labor is codified as "natural," not in need of capital investment or pursuing a strategy of capital accumulation. In fact, capital invests in this labor insofar as it is artificially maintained outside of the circuits of capital accumulation by ignoring and negating its constitutive contribution to it. Domestic work in general and "undocumented domestic workers" in particular thus engender the place of "exteriority"[21] or "colonial difference."[22] Their presence remains dictated to by temporalities and conditions absent from a script of modern progress and prosperity. Symptomatically, this is exposed in the working conditions of domestic workers characterized by oral contracts, unregulated working times, unsafe and vulnerable working conditions and high dependency on the employer. Through domestic work capital absorbs the imprints of life, the biopolitical power of human social relations.

Therefore, while capital does not invest directly in domestic work, its productivity forms the basis for capital accumulation. Hence, while the temporalities of "real subsumption" and "formal subsumption" cannot explain the intricate quality of domestic work, the contemplation of these temporalities drives us to think about the temporal ambivalences in the logic of capital accumulation. It is in the interpenetration between new modes of labor organization and classical mechanisms of labor exploitation that domestic work emerges at the juncture of different temporalities. When applied to Western Europe, the local face of the spatio-temporal conjuncture of domestic work is framed within migration regimes, based on current EU asylum and migration policies. It is within these parameters and system of codification that *living labor* is disciplined and targeted as exploited labor. Thus, migration policies do not just account for the control and management of peoples's entry and settlement aspiration within the EU-zone, but also for the organization of the modes of production. Through migration policies niches of exploitation are created in which the coloniality of labor is revived alongside the feminization of labor. This is the reason why this chapter attends to the policies and mechanisms of regulating and codifying migration in the EU. Here the tension between policy measures in regard to the regularization of labor and residency become tricky set within a field marked by the exceptional character of "irregularity."

Between Irregularity and Regulatory

Perceived as a "natural given," domestic work is held in a state of "irregularity," as its working conditions are not covered by trade union agreements or international labor organization conventions. Set within the context of migration regimes, a spectrum of legal irregularity or regularity is created regarding residency and settlement rights, counterbalanced by mechanisms of irregularity and regularity regarding the legal coverage of the working conditions in domestic work. This regime uses a series of labels, codifying the "migrant" as "regular or irregular" and "regular" or "irregular" workers. Interestingly, while domestic work has been considered a "private matter," exempt from State regulation, the employment of "migrant" workers calls State regulation into the midst of private households. This becomes apparent in the case of the employment of "migrant" domestic workers in private households. Subjects working in private households without a residency permit become objects of regulation and control, appearing in research and policies as "data bodies," bodies constructed as ciphers through flows of information and technologies of control and surveillance. We need to be attentive to this power–knowledge dynamic when we enter the field of migration policies. Engaging with this "data bodies" rhetoric carries the risk of reproducing it. Therefore, this chapter tries to keep the balance between the dynamics of migration policies circumventing mobility, settlement and access to resources, and their power to reduce subjects to a homogeneous mass for the sake of being able to produce data for migration management. It is in this regard that the tension between "regulatory" and "irregulatory" measures in terms of "migrant domestic" workers reveals how different policies complement or disable each other, demonstrating the limits in their regulatory logic.

As Bridget Anderson points out in her research on domestic workers in live-in and live-out employment in Delhi, Catania, Bangkok, Malmø, Barcelona and London, the conditions and employment relations experienced by "migrant" domestic workers need to be analyzed, taking into account the interrelation between migration policies and the labor market.[23] Thus, focusing:

> only on irregular migration can take away our attention from important factors such as labour markets, the gendered division of labour, gendered employment patterns, and the role of agencies. It can mean that we look at immigration laws and practice as sole solutions to the difficulties experienced by migrant domestic workers, and divert us from common ground shared with indigenous informal and low wage labour. However focusing only on employment misses the crucial processes by which immigration status reinforces employers' power and control over labour.[24]

While Anderson warns us here against understanding "regularity" just on legal grounds and disregarding the intrinsic "irregularities" in employment relations, she concedes that there is a link between "irregular legal" status and "undeclared" labor. Nonetheless, "regularized legal" residency bound to a work permit can change to "irregularity" if the employment relationship is terminated. Thus, "legal" residency status based on a preexisting employment relationship does not guarantee permanent residency status or the ability to change employers in case of abuse, discrimination or just for reasons of prosperity and promotion. This is particularly the case in the UK, where domestic workers have entered the country with an "Overseas Domestic Worker Visa (ODWS)." The ODWS is based on a previous employment relationship of one year with the employer with whom the domestic worker enters the country. Her "regularized" residency status is thus bound to this concrete employment relationship. When this relationship is terminated, the domestic worker loses her residency permit. This visa can be renewed for one year, and after five years the worker can apply for an independent residency permit. Also in Spain the law of regularization (2005) prescribes the existence of an employment relationship in order to issue a residency permit. The coupling of residency permits to an existing employment relationship continues to foster domestic worker dependency on their employers. Balancing "regulatory" and "irregulatory" dynamics, we see how they intersect and how they can switch from one side to the other, revealing the field of migration policies and domestic work as a quite fragile legal area. This also demonstrates the contradictions between domestic work as labor organized in the privacy of the household and migration policies as a field of public regulation. Resisting the tension of recognizing domestic work as a profession and the demand for domestic workers as a fact, the policies of regulation of domestic work reveal their limitations. These limitations come to light every time this logic is undermined by an unprecedented appearance that stretches the division between "regulatory" and "irregulatory." It is within this logic that the terms "undeclared" labor or "irregular" labor, as well as "regular" or "irregular legal" residency, emerge. Through this, labor migration is constantly recreated as a field of exception.

Domestic workers employed by private households are caught in this logic and generally fall in a gray area between "regularity" and "irregularity." When it comes to "migrant" domestic workers, their status is partially regularized in countries like Spain and the UK, as I will discuss in the next chapter.[25] But even in countries like Spain where official agreements regarding minimum wages and health insurance exist, employment relations are largely based on private and individual oral agreements. Migration policies that attempt to regularize these "irregularities" do not diminish the power relations and dependencies governing the field of domestic work. While migration policies aim to regularize "irregular" employment relations, the measures and criteria they introduce in some cases produce confusing situations. For example, to regularize migrant workers on the basis of the conditions set out in a single work contract simultaneously carries the possibility of "irregularity" when the worker is made redundant or aims to change employment. In the case of the domestic workers in this study, "regularity" and "irregularity" take an interesting twist.

As Broeders and Engbersen demonstrate in their study on "irregular immigration" in Europe, the typologies of "irregular immigration" can be set around three criteria: "legal and illegal entry; legal and illegal residency; and legal and illegal employment."[26] The interviews with the Latin American research participants show that all of them entered Europe "legally" with a "tourist visa." After the visa expired, they found themselves with an "irregular residency" status coupled to "illegal employment." Though in some countries like Spain attempts have been made to regularize the situation of "undocumented migrant" workers,[27] paradoxically, the number of "irregularized" migrants is increasing due to the growing settlement and employment restrictions imposed by national migration policies, reflecting EU agreements in this area. It is within these dynamics that individuals subjected to the field of governance of migration are reduced to "data bodies" and stripped of their human rights. Paradoxically, while highly regulated through legal language, these subjects are kept in a state of uncertainty and exposed to the most vulnerable and exploitative working conditions and, in the case of "undocumented migrants," to subhuman living conditions. It is in this paradox between a rhetoric of regulation and the persistence of deregulation of working and human rights that migration policies evolve within the EU. These policies tacitly and indirectly circumvent the modes of production in the modern/colonial world-system.

EU ASYLUM AND MIGRATION POLICIES

> I usually ride my bike in my neighborhood, I know the people there, but I try to blend in when I go shopping elsewhere. (Carina, 26, domestic worker, Leeds)

Carina, one of our research participants who is an "undocumented" domestic worker from Chile living in Leeds, speaks about the (im)possibilities of movement when she tries to avoid being noticed by the police. The constant threat of deportation and detention appears in all the interviews with "undocumented" domestic workers in all four countries. Our research participants live in big cities, which offers them the opportunity of blending into the everyday bustle. However, some public spaces and being the focus of attention are avoided. All research participants, even those living in the UK and Spain where police raids in public spaces are less common than in Germany and Austria, comment on the increasing control that they face. The increase in police raids in public spaces goes hand in hand with the "illegalization" of migration in the EU-zone.

National asylum and migration policies are increasingly influenced by EU directives. The European Commission and the EU Member States have been engaged in the last decades in creating common principles and measures. In particular, since the Tampere European Council meeting in October 1999 and its confirmation through The Hague Programme in 2004, negotiations are leading to a new strategy on the governance of immigration in the EU-zone. Particularly since 9/11 migration policies have developed along the lines of what Antonio Negri has coined "guerra ordinativa,"[28] the integration of "war" as a principle of organizing the social order. Thus "war" is no longer a state of exception.[29] It is actually "the continuation of politics by other means,"[30] or as Nelson Maldonado-Torres asserts, the constitutive "underside of modernity."[31] Negri's observation of the "guerra ordinativa" and Maldonado-Torres's of war as the "underside of modernity" seem to inform the logic of asylum and migration policies within the EU. New migration policies within the European Union demonstrate how the specter of "terrorism" is mobilized to institute more restrictive policies of control and criminalization towards subjects codified as "migrants" and "asylum seekers," thus creating enclaves of exception, where universal proclamations of human and citizenship are deactivated. Such a field is represented by the increasing attempt of "illegalization" of citizens of former European colonies seeking work and better living conditions within the EU zone. It is within this logic that migration policies evolve as an ensemble of technologies of surveillance and control, organized along different areas of governing, covering security, economic migration and cultural integration.

From "Security" to "Solidarity"

The European Immigration and Asylum Pact adopted by the European Parliament on October 15, 2008, which builds the foundation for the five-year program in the Justice, Freedom and Security area initiated in 2009, has been developed along the lines of "migration management," "security" and "integration."[32] This program was preceded by different steps towards a consolidation of EU asylum and migration directives initiated, for example, in the European Council Summit in Seville in 2002. At this summit the four pillars for a European common immigration policy were discussed: (a) economic migration, (b) integration,[33] (c) "illegal immigration" and return[34] and (d) migration and development.[35]

The European Immigration and Asylum Pact has developed these pillars further. Its aim is to develop a common asylum and migration policy within the EU on four levels:

1. through cooperation with the countries of origin and transit in the form of development aid

2. a common European asylum system, in respect to the terms of the Geneva Convention and Member States' obligations under international treaties
3. integration policies
4. a systematic approach to the management of transnational migration movements

These goals should be achieved through (a) a joint visa policy; (b) cooperation and exchange of information to create a common data bank; (c) and creation of European border guard and police cooperation This latter process was initiated by the creation of a common border patrol, FRONTEX, in 2005.

Further, on the level of asylum, the EU aims to create common asylum procedures and a uniform status for those who are granted asylum or subsidiary protection, as well as strengthening practical cooperation between national asylum administrations and the external dimension of asylum. The "external dimension of asylum" is linked to the relationship between migration policies and development aid strategies. In the policy plan the EU envisages asylum as "an integrated approach," integrating financial support to "third countries" and "transit countries." This policy impacts on "transit countries," for example, Morocco, which received funding to implement internment camps, control its borders and organize preventive information training for "immigrants." Within this development "transit countries" are themselves becoming countries of immigration as the hurdles for crossing EU borders increase.[36]

Rhetorically, this pact is bound together through the three principles of "prosperity," "solidarity" and "security." These principles, reflecting a neoliberal humanitarian language and coupling "solidarity" with "security" and "prosperity," indicate where the accent lies in these recommendations. All these principles represent the political and economic interests of the signatory countries. By "prosperity" is meant the "integration capacities" of "migrants" in regard to their professional skills and "willingness" to integrate into the national culture and language. At the margins a note is also made regarding their political participation on the communal level. The principle of "solidarity" holds a twofold perspective addressing on the one side external cooperation, and, on the other, the control of Europe's internal borders by presupposing "burden-sharing (financial solidarity)" amongst the EU Member States and "solidarity and partnership with the countries of origin and transit of immigrants." In regard to external cooperation, the accent is set on the combination of migration policies with development aid. On this basis, different EU Member States have initiated political cooperation with countries in Africa, Asia and Latin America. Spain, for example, has renewed its cooperation with different African states. The second phase of "Plan Africa," an agreement on economic and political relations between Spain and five North and East African countries (Morocco, Mauritania, Senegal, Mali and Guinea Biseau) taking place between 2009 and 2011, aims to tie economic cooperation to political cooperation particularly in regard to migration and border control. The visit of the Spanish minister for foreign affairs, Miguel Ángel Moratinos, to Morocco in 2008 seems to have been focused on this issue. During his visit, Moratinos met the king of Morocco, Mohamed VI. They discussed the "integration" of Moroccan "migrants" in Spain in regard to their participation in communal elections. At the same time the enforcement of border controls on the North African coast and the displacement of European refugee detention camps to the North African border zones were stipulated. After visiting Morocco, Moratinos continued his journey to Mauritania. Here he visited the refugee detention camp built with Spanish funding, called by Amnesty International "Guantanamito," in Nuadibú in North Mauritania.[37]

On the level of "internal" solidarity, phrases like "the fight against illegal immigration," "zero tolerance for trafficking in human beings"[38] and "sustainable and effective return policies," addressing not only the control of "undocumented migrants" but also of "legal migrants" or "foreign nationals" have appeared on the EU agenda. So, the control of borders is not just applied to its physical delimitation but to the whole territory of the nation itself. Post-migrant citizens or "migrants" are targeted by anti-terror laws and reduced to "unwelcome foreigners." For example, they are asked for documentation when frequenting public spaces or waiting for a bus at the coach station. Another way of controlling the "foreign population" is through national policies in regard to "economic migration" and "integration."

Economic Migration

The principle of "economic migration" represents a major pillar in the governing of asylum and migration based on national labor market demand for regulated migration. Thus the adaptation and application of EU directives varies in regard to national political agendas and economic interests. For example, as I previously mentioned, Spain implemented a national program on regulation in 2005, promoting processes of legal regularization based on individual work contracts. In the same year Germany implemented its first immigration law, *Zuwanderungsgesetz* (Immigration Law), thereby recruiting non-European citizens based on the demand from certain sectors of the economy. In Austria new "Aliens Laws" comprising the "Settlement and Residence Act" (*Niederlassungs- und Aufenthaltsgesetz* [NAG]) and "Asylum Act" (*Asylgesetz*) came into force in January 2006, continuing the policy of the "quota system" established in the 1990s, aimed at recruiting designated numbers of "migrants" according to national labor market needs.[39] In Britain, migration policies have also been firmly shaped by the principle of economic migration, particularly the demand for highly skilled migrants. In 2008 Britain launched a new immigration system, the "points-based system," supported by economic interests and anti-immigration nationalist rhetoric. The "points-based system" is aimed at enforcing immigration control, facilitating the recruitment of "highly skilled migrants" and recruiting for areas in which there is demand for "migrant" workers. Based on this system, "migrants" are evaluated and advised regarding their skills, experience, expertise and age. This system has also been included in regard to non-European graduates, enabling "successful students" the possibility of staying in the UK for up to two years through a new visa category after finalizing their degrees. On the other side, non-European students are also subjected to migration control.[40] Further, Britain has opened the labor market for the new Eastern European EU Member States. In contrast with Spain, however, Britain has not introduced any amnesty for "undocumented migrant" workers and Germany has only opened the labor market for strictly regulated and selected labor sectors such as the IT industry.

Such legislation and policies reflect the specific migration dynamics in the different countries. While Austria, Germany and the UK are trying both to systematize their need for economic immigration and to restrict immigration, Spain's regularization program has enabled the settlement of people already working and living in the country. This aspect also reflects the different legal avenues for "migrants" entering these countries. Whilst family reunification is the predominant method of entry in Austria and Germany, in Spain and Britain entry is channeled through the labor market. This might explain Spain's interest in regularization and Britain's insistence on the recruitment of "highly skilled migrants."

With the exception of the Spanish regularization law, which guaranteed a residency permit based on a work contract and covered all employment sectors from agriculture to domestic work, none of the other programs consider domestic work a recruitment sector. If we take into account the increasing feminization of migration to the EU in the last decades, this situation reveals a paradox. While the demand for domestic workers is growing in these countries, State recruitment policies (although increasingly addressing care work) remain mostly silent in the case of domestic work. This lack of policies on regularization of "undocumented migrant" domestic workers also becomes evident in regard to the second pillar of EU migration and asylum directives, focusing on integration. Whilst this principle targets the economic, political and cultural integration of "foreign citizens," its application is mostly conveyed in cultural terms.

Cultural Integration

Integration policies within the EU are understood in terms of acculturation, the acquisition of the dominant culture by the minoritized group, leaving little space for the recognition of bi- and multilingualism or transculturation.

The effectiveness with which nation-states like Germany and Austria are reacting to this goal is remarkable. For example, in July 2007 Germany announced its National Integration Plan, which includes more than 400 measures and voluntary commitments relating to integration. Federal government officials, local authorities, associations of migrants and numerous other nongovernmental actors contributed to the plan. One target of this program is to require "migrants" to attend German language and integration courses. It also imposes financial penalties for "migrants" who are obliged to take the courses but fail to enroll. These measures are developed according to an integration discourse, the main aim of which is to "incorporate" the "migrant" population into a presupposed and "clearly defined" "core German culture."[41]

Britain has also experienced a revival of the rhetoric on "British identity" and the need for integration to "British culture" under New Labour. The establishment of the UK Border Agency (UKBA), an executive agency of the British Home Office that is responsible for managing migration and border policies, reflects this new political framework. In January 2009 the Borders, Citizenship and Immigration Bill was published. This bill replaces the ten acts of parliament and formulates five key aspects, "strong borders, selective migration, earning the right to stay, playing by the rules, managing any local impact."[42] These points involve restrictive border control expanding the power for UKBA officers at any border to cancel visas, penalties for passengers without the right papers, a new points-based system regarding residency permits, streamlined expulsion, English courses for "migrants," control of "civic conduct," possibilities of refusing reentry, criminalization of "illegal" work by targeting employers and the demand that "migrants" contribute a "little" extra to the cost of local services.[43] For the British context this is a noticeable shift from policies in the 1980s and 1990s, which were, at least rhetorically, "strongly supportive of multiculturalism."[44] Some critics have classified this position as a regression to the 1960s and 1970s politics of "assimilation."

Spain, due to its own heterogeneous cultural and language varieties, shows less consistency on a national level. For example, Catalonia's communal administration has been very precise in formulating integration policies promoting Catalan culture and language and effectively adopting them on the level of support of local migrant organizations.[45] However, the communal administration in Madrid, overburdened with demands to provide advice and consultancy to migrant groups, has adopted the EU directives as a way of supplementing their already existing services. Here, the implementation of integration policies has resulted in the provision of services that were needed but not implemented due to a lack of financial support.[46]

Significantly, these different implementations of the EU pillar of "integration" on the national level, demonstrate how rhetoric is not always immediately adapted to policies and how different geopolitical and economic frameworks in each country dictate transnational cooperation agendas.

However, all these approaches dismiss transculturation in Europe, insisting on monocultural and monolingual concepts of the nation-state when it comes to post/migrant groups. They also disregard the creative and productive input of post/migrant and diasporic groups to the "creolization"[47] of Europe. For example, on the level of popular culture what would "new German cinema" be without Fatih Akin, Yüksel Yavuz or Aysel Polat?[48]

The official call for "integration" addressed to post/migrants and newcomers is the culmination of retrograde policies, based on the European myth of Europe as the cradle of civilization,[49] "ethnic purity" and homogeneous religious beliefs. This fantasy is nourished by its collective oblivion about its multireligious and multicultural societies in medieval times, for example, in the Mediterranean, the misconception of its connection to a colonial past and the silencing of its imperialist ambitions. The ascription to "migrants" of "insurmountable cultural difference" by official discourses focusing on integration transmits the idea that social integration is only achieved when the newcomer blends into the "new culture" and is stripped of their cultural heritage. However, the necessary degree of "blending in" in some cases is never achieved because of the "racial epidermal schema,"[50] or the focus on non-Christian beliefs, through which subjects become suspected of failing to integrate or resisting integration. It is in this regard that the discourse on integration reveals its racializing and orientalizing effects as institutional practice, evoking what Etienne Balibar has defined as "neo-racism," operating on the epistemic predication of "insurmountable cultural differences."[51] However, these discourses have not only a policy effect, but they also become embedded in societal common sense, which is reflected, for example, in media representations of "migrants" as potential terrorists and "cross-cultural encounters" as sources of conflict.

Latin American migration to Europe in the last decade has become indirectly a target of these policies and discourses as non-European citizens' entry to Europe is highly regulated and set within fixed temporal and economic demand parameters. This results in the increasing "illegalization" of citizens coming from this corner of the world. Thus, as the tragic case of de Menezes in Britain shows, if they are in the wrong place at the wrong time, they risk becoming targets.[52] Latin American migrants to Europe, like other non-European citizens, are subjected to the parameters set out in national migration policies, restricting their freedom of movement and their access to the labor market in the EU zone.

LATIN AMERICAN AND CARIBBEAN MIGRATION TO EUROPE

The connection between Latin America and Europe goes back to colonial times, when Portugal and Spain colonized this part of the world after the fifteenth century. In the nineteenth century the British Empire also engaged in trade and entrepreneurial enterprises in this region. After the nineteenth century immigration to Latin America from Europe, in particular from Spain, Italy and Portugal, became prominent. For example between 1850 and 1950, 3.5 million Spaniards migrated to Latin America and the Caribbean (LAC).[53] In the second half of the twentieth century we witnessed an inverse movement from LAC to Western Europe. In the late 1970s some countries in Europe such as Germany, the UK and Spain hosted a significant number of political refugees from Chile, Argentina and Uruguay. In the last two decades a new movement from Latin America to Europe has taken place, predominantly directed to Spain, Italy and Portugal, but in the last five years also to other European countries like the UK, Germany and Austria. This migration has been largely motivated by the economic and political crises in some Latin American countries, European tourism, binational marriages and the quest for educational opportunities.

According to recent studies on LAC migration to Europe, Spain is by far the most popular destination for these migrants. Spain had 2.4 million citizens born in Latin America in 2009, a noticeable increase in a decade as in 1999 LAC migration was 400,000.[54] LAC migration to Spain is predominantly from Ecuador (471,425), Colombia (354,869) and Argentina (293,227). In 2004 LAC migration to Italy was estimated to be 205,000, to the UK to be 113,000 and to Germany to be 94,000.[55] Propelled by economic and political crises in the 1990s, migration from the Dominican Republic, Colombia, Ecuador, Argentina and more recently Brazil, Venezuela, Bolivia, Honduras and Paraguay is rapidly increasing. For example, in 1999 Ecuador experienced a severe economic crisis, brought about by the "El Niño stream," a drop in the oil price and the Asian financial crisis in 1998, culminating in the replacement of the Ecuadorian currency by the US dollar.[56] Income per capita fell by 9 percent and unemployment rose from 8 percent in the previous year to 17 percent in 1998. Urban poverty increased from 36 percent to 65 percent in the same year. In 2002 approximately 800,000 people left the country for the United States and Spain.[57] In 2001, *el corralito* (the economic crash) in Argentina, which led to the removal of President Fernando de la Rua and a succession of four different presidents in 12 days (between December 21, 2001, and January 2, 2002), forced a significant number of Argentineans to leave the country for Spain and Italy.[58] Civil war in Colombia and political conflicts in Peru, Bolivia, Honduras, Venezuela and Paraguay have led to migration predominantly to Spain and, to some extent, to Germany, Austria and the UK. Of course, the migration to Europe is very often preceded by inter-regional migration within the nation and between Latin American countries.[59] Migration from Peru to Chile or Argentina or from Colombia to Brazil, as Gioconda Herrera notes, are also very pronounced and in part exceed or equal the migration from these countries to Europe.[60] Interestingly, the EU is increasingly aware of the significance of these movements for their cooperation strategies with LAC.

In 1999 the first summit between the EU and LAC took place in Rio de Janeiro. This summit was aimed at creating political cooperation. In the second summit in Madrid in 2002, the agenda topics of this cooperation were explicitly formulated, with immigration, justice and the development of new immigration policies being prioritized. In the next summit in Guadalajara in 2004 and particularly in Vienna in 2006, migration was on the agenda of the *Summit Declaration*. This stated the need for migration control and the prevention of emigration in the countries of origin. This was followed up in the second meeting of experts between the EU and LAC in March 2006, where activities in the areas of treatment, rights and integration of migrants, new approaches to migration policies, "illegal migration" and "the fight against human trafficking" were proposed. This development reflects the aspects of "security" and "solidarity" already discussed in terms of EU asylum and migration policies. However, one of the crucial aspects debated in all those meetings was the management of and data collection on "remittances." LAC are among the main remittance recipient areas in the world. In Ecuador, for example, remittances are estimated to be the second largest foreign currency earner after oil exports and the remittance corridor between Spain and Ecuador is amongst the most significant globally. The significance of LAC for the development of the EU and its Member States is also manifest in growing research interest in this topic. Research in Spain on Caribbean and Latin American communities has been extensive in the last decade. In other European countries such as Austria, Germany and the UK this is slowly emerging.

Spain

To date, Spain's migration policies have been influenced by former colonial relationships with Latin America, the Philippines, Equatorial Guinea and Morocco. Spain's colonial legacies and massive emigration movements in the nineteenth century until the middle of the twentieth century to the Caribbean and Latin America propelled a reverse movement in the 1990s. Until the 1980s Spain was predominantly an emigration state. It formulated its first immigration policies with the introduction of the "Foreigner Law" (*Ley de Extranjería*) in 1985, and until that time Spanish- speaking Caribbean people and Latin Americans could immigrate to Spain without a visa.[61] Parallel to this law and its successive modifications from 2000 to 2003, Spain established an immigration policy designed to meet its demographic, labor and economic needs, stated in the annual quota system (CUPO system) for the household, construction and agricultural industries. This resulted in the provision of legal work and residency permits for a significant number of formerly "undocumented" workers in 1991, 1996 and 2000.[62]

In 2001 a new procedure was introduced that significantly raised the number of regularizations of Latin Americans.[63] In addition to the reforms on migrant labor recruitment, the attractiveness of Spain for some Latin

American nationalities was also driven by the prevalence of "dual citizenship." Some Argentineans and Brazilians, for example, entered Europe with their Spanish, Portuguese, German or Italian passports or applied for citizenship on the basis of their European ancestry in the respective countries.[64] In the same year, Spain also established a bilateral agreement with Ecuador based on national labor market needs. This led to an increase of Ecuadorian migrant workers in Spain from 115,301 in 2002 to 471,425 in 2009.[65] In 2009, approximately 52 percent of Ecuadorian migrants were women.[66] In a study conducted by Gioconda Herrera, the economic background of Ecuadorian "migrants" was classified as "middle class" (60 percent), "poor" (27 percent) and "extremely poor" (13 percent).[67] This attends to the hypothesis that it is the economically more affluent groups that can afford to migrate overseas, if the decision is not additionally propelled by family ties and transnational networks.

After the terrorist attacks in Madrid on March 11, 2004, the Social Democrats gained the electoral majority. In January 2005 Prime Minister José Luis Rodríguez Zapatero's Social Democrat government introduced the "law of regularization," which enabled employers to "regularize undocumented workers" in their companies. In the same year, 700,000 people applied for regularization, attending to the requirements of a work contract, police check and total registration on the local register (*padrón*) in Spain before August 2004. This program works on two levels: (a) as a response to the demands of the economy and (b) by aiming at a permanent integration into the labor market, if a work contract of at least two years already exists. This last point was criticized by advocacy organizations as it left out a large group of migrants that could not have been registered before August 2004. A new clause, therefore, was introduced that permitted registration based on other documentation such as a health card or other official documents. According to Herrera, one of the groups benefiting from this development were Ecuadorians. Herrera notes 31.7 percent of the applications accepted for regularization in 2005 were for domestic work; however, the regularization programs have not markedly changed the position of "migrant" women recruited into the labor market.[68]

Interestingly, 30 percent of regularized Ecuadorians, approximately 85 percent of whom were women, were also contracted in 2004 in the special social security regime of domestic work.[69] The majority of Ecuadorian female workers in Spain are registered under this social security regime. This regime, as Walter Actis notes, seems to represent a first step into the labor market as approximately 70 percent of the workers registered under this regime tried to move up to the general regime in 2004.[70] As I will discuss in the next chapter, this movement is due to the provision of social benefits and rights in the general regime that are nonexistent in the special regime of domestic work. Another statistic to note is that only 15 percent of Ecuadorian "migrants" are registered as employed full-time, while 85 percent are employed on a temporary or part-time basis.[71] These figures seem to agree with research on Ecuadorian women working in the domestic and care sector in Spain, illustrating the abundance of "patchwork" employment, as their working week is stretched between at least two or three different households. Nonetheless, the regularization of some workers does not remove the precarious legal conditions of "undocumented" workers, and domestic workers in particular. Regarding the situation of "undocumented migrants" in Spain, comparing the figures in the process of regulation with that of those registered on the communal level, reveals that in 2008 approximately 25 percent (455,854) of citizens with a Latin American passport were living in Spain in "irregular legal" conditions.[72] In particular, Latin Americans arriving in the last few years from Paraguay and Honduras (70 percent), Bolivia and Brazil (60 percent) and from Chile, Mexico and Venezuela (40 percent) found themselves in these conditions. Significantly, women make up between 55 and 65 percent of these communities.[73] Let us now take a look at Latin American migration to the UK, Germany and Austria.

The UK

While the UK does not maintain direct colonial ties with Latin America, it has a rich history of trading relationships brought about during imperial times and connected to the cotton export industry, for example, between Argentina and the UK, and entrepreneurial ventures, for example, the Chilean nitrate and Peruvian guano industries.[74] In the nineteenth century some British communities such as the Welsh opted to migrate to Patagonia.[75] The reverse movement from Latin America to the UK was small until the 1970s, when communities from Argentina, Chile, Uruguay and Brazil found asylum.[76] It would not be until the 1990s that a migratory movement, predominantly from Colombia, Brazil and Ecuador and driven by professional, educational and labor needs, would become noticeable in and around London. In order to understand the legal hurdles Latin Americans encounter today in the UK, a contextualization of this migration within a broader policy framework in regard to postcolonial migration in Britain is needed.

In the UK postwar labor migration was linked to the rebuilding of the economy and the anticolonial and independence movements in its colonies in the 1950s. Here, the term "postcolonial migrant" refers mainly to those who arrived from the British Caribbean and South Asia in the 1950s. These movements were promoted by the introduction of the 1948 British Nationality Act, which created a single imperial citizenship category, Citizen of the United Kingdom and Colonies (CUKC). This granted CUKCs statutory right of entry to the UK. The possibility of entry to the UK was used by substantial numbers of people born outside the UK.[77] The UK reacted to these movements from its colonies by instituting the 1962 Commonwealth Immigrants Act. This act was introduced to limit large-scale immigration from former British colonies such as India, Pakistan, Jamaica and other

Caribbean nations. This legislation instituted mechanisms of control that are foundational for the development of migration policies today. Postcolonial immigrants needed to show evidence of secure employment or have highly demanded professional skills. This act was met with distrust by South Asian citizens who were afraid they would not be allowed to settle with their families in the UK, leading to an increase in immigration from this region to the UK at this time. In 1968 the restrictions towards South Asian citizens became explicit when a new Commonwealth Immigrants Act was passed. This act was a response to increasing immigration of Kenyan and Ugandan Asians following the "Africanization" policy in these countries.[78] The act restricted entry rights, guaranteeing entry only to those who had a parent born, adopted or naturalized in the UK. With the Immigration Act of 1971 the "color filter" attached to this policy of entry became apparent as Commonwealth immigrants with UK-born ancestors from Canada, South Africa, New Zealand and Australia were explicitly favored over those from India, Pakistan, Bangladesh or the Caribbean. In 1981 the British Nationality Act brought a further sophistication to the principle of selection by replacing the 1948 British Nationality Act and introducing three citizenship categories: British Citizenship, British Dependent Territories Citizenship and British Overseas Citizenship. The right of residency for "migrants" applied only to patrial British citizens. In the 1990s, UK immigration policies started to be shaped by general developments within the EU. While Britain opted out of the Schengen Agreement, it took part in the implementation of the Schengen Information System (SIS), a system that archives information regarding border security and law enforcement. Since 1993 it has also used various measures to accelerate the asylum procedure and limit appeal opportunities.

In 2002 the Nationality, Immigration and Asylum Act was introduced, reflecting the EU parameters of recruiting "skilled migrants" and the surveillance of national borders. This act emphasized border security, the illegal employment of "undocumented migrants," human trafficking and fraud. In 2006 the Parliamentary Act on Immigration, Asylum, and Nationality (IAN) was passed. Focusing mainly on immigration (rather than asylum), it included restrictions on appeal rights, sanctions against employers of unauthorized labor and a tightening of citizenship rules. Sanctions against employers were followed up by the 2007 law against "undeclared" employment, which instituted a £10,000 fine for employers of "undocumented" workers. A year later, the British government announced the creation of a new detention camp for immigrants in Oxfordshire. As previously mentioned, all these different measures and policies of immigration management and control were included in the Borders, Citizenship and Immigration Act in 2009.

However, these different attempts at limiting migration have not led to a decrease in immigration as the British economy itself demands labor migration. Extraordinary efforts have been made by the government to promote the recruitment of "skilled" and "highly skilled migrant" workers from outside the EU. For example, the Highly Skilled Migrant Programme (HSMP), based on points, was introduced in 2002. In 2003 80,000 work permits were issued to "skilled" or "highly skilled" migrant workers. In addition, in 2003, about 30,000 non-EU workers entered the UK on permits for employment in selected low-skill occupations in agriculture, food processing and the hospitality sector. The UK has established specific systems of employment for immigrants (e.g., Seasonal Agricultural Scheme, Sector Based Scheme or Working Holidaymakers Scheme).[79] In 2003 migrants entered the UK on a variety of schemes such as "working holidaymakers" (47,000), "au pairs" (15,000), "students" (319,000) and "dependants" (87,000).[80] In May 2004 the goal of recruiting migrant workers was also demonstrated as the UK, together with Sweden and Ireland, granted nationals of the newly integrated EU countries—the Czech Republic, Estonia, Hungary, Latvia, Lithuania, Poland, Slovakia and Slovenia—access to the labor market. These different schemes have merged under the "points-based system" that came into force in 2008. The "points-based system" regulates the immigration and employment of skilled and highly skilled non-EU workers, and limits low-skilled immigration from outside the EU. It proposed a five-tier economic migration system. Tiers equate to categories: (a) highly skilled, (b) skilled with job offer, (c) low skilled, (d) students and (e) miscellaneous. Domestic work is found under the fifth tier, which also includes "private servants."

In the shadow of these policies of control and labor migration, the demand for workers for what Hsiao-Hung Pai calls the 3-D jobs—dirty, dangerous and degrading—has increased.[81] It is in these jobs that we find an increasing number of "undocumented migrant" workers, in particular, in the domestic and care work sector.[82] Some of the communities providing the labor in these sectors are Latin American. Most research in Britain on Latin American communities is based in London and, as Cathy McIlwaine notes, Latin Americans "are one of the fastest growing, but also one of the most invisible migrant groups" in the UK.[83] While Britain has longstanding historical and political relationships with Latin America, migration from Latin America to the UK has not been large. According to the 2001 Census, of the 76,000 people who were born in South America living in Britain, nearly 60 percent (44,000) were living in the London area.[84] Paradoxically, after the introduction of the visa requirement for Colombian tourists in 1997 the Colombian community grew from 8,000 to 18,000 in 2005.[85] Tourist visa requirements for the UK were set for Ecuadorians in 2007 and for Bolivians and Venezuelans in 2009.

The figures regarding these communities are not very reliable, as the number of "undocumented migrants," who represent a significant percentage, is not included. Due to the visa requirements introduced in 1997, entry to the UK for Latin Americans is very restricted. Scholars estimate that including "undocumented migrants" there may be 700,000 to 1,000,000

Latin Americans in the UK today. The largest group is Brazilians (around 200,000), followed by Colombians (130,000–160,000), Ecuadorians (70,000–90,000), Bolivians (15,000–20,000), and Peruvians (10,000–15,000).[86] These numbers are guesstimates from embassies, community centers and refugee groups; there has never been a precise census of Latin Americans in the UK.

The UK seems to be attractive for a variety of reasons, such as political refuge and economic and educational opportunities, but the social networks already in place are decisive factors in migration choices. For some, the UK represents the second place of immigration, after having lived in Spain for a while. LAC migrants have developed productive activities around their communities with the establishment, for example, of *locutorios* (stores that offer long-distance telephone and Internet services), *giro tiendas* (money transfer shops), cafés, bars, restaurants, corner stores and food markets.[87] But the Latino presence in the UK, particularly in London, was not evident until the end of the 1990s and has only begun to be reflected in scholarly work in the last few years. The studies conducted focus on particular communities such as Colombians, Ecuadorians[88] and Bolivians.[89] These communities find employment in the "low- paid" sectors, such as domestic service, catering, gastronomy, hospitality and cleaning.

As recent studies show, the Latin American communities are beginning to be part of "multicultural London." This is also reflected on the level of political organization, which in the 1970s and 1980s focused on issues of democracy in the Cono Sur. In the 1990s labor issues became more pronounced. As Davide Però discusses, Latin American labor mobilization has increased since the mid-1990s, when different political organizations like the Latin Front and the Latin American Workers' Association (LAWA) emerged.[90] LAWA, in particular, has actively cooperated with the T & G Union in regard to the "Justice for Cleaners" campaign. Through this campaign the Ecuadorian janitors in London became part of the global network of the Janitors' Movement. In 2008, 800 Ecuadorian janitors organized within the T & G & GWU Union at Canary Wharf and succeeded in getting the minimum wage of £7.40 per hour for the day shift and £8.70 per hour for the night shift, the recognition of entitlement to eight bank holidays, pension scheme and disability benefits, health insurance and recognition by the union. Nonetheless, the "Janitors for Justice" movement has been the target of policing. In June 2009, nine cleaners were taken into detention and six of them deported after a dawn raid by the immigration police in the London School of Oriental and African Studies (SOAS). The cleaners, working for SOAS for years, won the London Living Wage and Trade Union representation after a successful "Justice for Cleaners" campaign.

Despite the violence and setbacks, the Latin American allegiances in the UK are growing, although they remain marginal in public discourses on migration. The Latin American research participants that we encountered in the UK were part of a highly invisible and dispersed community in the

North of England. Family links and social networks, but also lower costs for accommodation and maintenance, led them to the North after first trying their luck in the South of England. Their presence in the North is only noticeable through the slight sprouting of an "ethnic economy" like *locutorios* or "ethnic food stores." Also in Germany and Austria the presence of Latin American social networks has been becoming more noticeable in the last 10 years.

Germany

In comparison to Spain and the UK, Germany's migration history is not directly linked to its colonial past. In order to understand Latin American immigration in today's Germany, it is useful to frame it within the broader context of migration. Germany's colonialism lasted for a short period (1888–1919) in comparison to that of Spain and the UK.[91] Little is known about the links between colonial history and nineteenth century and post-1945 immigration in Germany. However, this history needs to be related to the history of anti-Semitism.

While research at the moment does not show any correlation between the recruitment of seasonal workers from Poland and Russia for the agricultural estates of Eastern Prussia between 1871 and 1918 and colonialism, it does demonstrate that to some extent the racialized division of labor in the colonies was partly repeated in the way Polish and Russian workers were treated.[92] They were recruited for short-term jobs to avoid their permanent settlement, they earned less money than Germans and were treated as inferior to them. This treatment was based on "anti-Slav" and anti-Semitic sentiments, articulated at that time by the "popular fear" of the "Slavic invasion."[93] The recruitment of Polish and Russian seasonal workers continued throughout the Weimar Republic (1918–1932), for example, Polish workers were recruited as *Wanderarbeiter* for the mining sector in the 1920s. At this time "the German priority" principle was introduced, which prioritized German candidates and only considered foreign employees if no German could be found.[94] Also the temporal character of the recruitment of workers for the agricultural sector was reinforced through the *Karenzpflicht*, which was aimed at sending workers home in winter to prevent their settlement in Germany. In 1908 the introduction of *Inlandslegitimationszwang* bound workers to stay with one employer to obtain residency for the time of the work contract. This was a State reaction to workers changing their employers due to abuse and exploitative working conditions. During the first years of National Socialism, "foreign workers" from Poland and Russia were not recruited due to the anti-Semitic and anti-Slav ideology of "Germanization."[95] This principle could not be held to, however, as in 1934 there was a labor shortage due to the ongoing anti-Semitic and racist system of elimination, detention and persecution as well as the numbers of people escaping from Nazi Germany, the preparation for war and the introduction of military service. The first administrative reaction of the Nazis was to redirect workers from agriculture and small businesses to industry. However, this inner recruitment could not cover the lack of industrial workers and in 1934 the Nazis issued intergovernmental contracts with Italy, Poland and Yugoslavia. These workers were controlled by the Gestapo and kept segregated from German society. Immediately after the beginning of the war, Germany treated its occupied territories as a "massive reservoir for conscript labor. Young men and women were seized and deported to Germany by the SS,"[96] and forced to work as *Fremd- und Zwangarbeiter* (Foreign- and Forced-Labor) for the German wartime industries.[97]

Four years after Germany was defeated in 1949 by the allied forces it was divided into two states, the Federal Republic of Germany (FRG), influenced by the Western allied forces France, Britain and the United States, and the Democratic Republic of Germany (GDR), influenced by the Soviet Union. The FRG envisaged rebuilding its economy by recruiting "foreign workers" based on the "guest worker program," a temporary work model with one- to two-year contracts that targeted young, single and "healthy" men and women who were supposed to supply the booming car, manufacturing and mining industries with the labor force needed. The "guest worker program" was first launched in 1955 with Italy, and in consecutive years further intergovernmental contracts were forged with Spain, Greece, Turkey, Yugoslavia, Portugal, Morocco and Tunisia.[97] As industrial workers their previous skills were not recognized by Germany's education and professionalization system. They were deemed unskilled and placed at the bottom of the salary ladder. As their recruitment was considered provisional, the "guest workers" were accommodated on arrival in dorms and barracks and their interaction with German society was limited to the workplace.[98] However, in the mid-1960s the first signs of settlement were noticed and the government reacted to it by passing a new "foreigner law" in 1965. This law made it possible for migrants to apply for residency permits and receive unemployment benefits and health insurance. While men were mostly recruited for the car, heavy manufacturing and mining industries, women were employed for food manufacturing, the textile and utensils industries, hospitality, cleaning and the private personal service sector. Parallel to the recruitment of migrants, in the 1960s Western German society went through profound changes in gender relations. West German women were increasingly incorporated into the labor market, finding support for domestic and care work in "migrant" women.

In 1973, when 2.6 million "migrants" were living in Germany, the recruitment ban (*Anwerbestop*) was issued, removing the possibility of entering Germany to work. The only avenues for entry then became family reunification and political asylum. These avenues have become increasingly restricted through a variety of laws, limiting the possibility for asylum.[99] By 2000 Germany was "home" to 7.3 million *Ausländer*, that is, "foreigners."

While Germany's "migrant" workers' recruitment policy started in 1955, it did not introduce its first Immigration Act (*Zuwanderungsgesetz*) until 50 years later, in 2005. The Immigration Act is essentially made up of the Residence Act and the Act on the General Freedom of Movement for EU Citizens (Freedom of Movement Act/EU). The Act amended a number of other laws, such as the Asylum Procedure Act, the Act on the Central Aliens Register and the Nationality Act. Based on a points system model, the Immigration Act regulates the labor market's needs in regard to labor migration. This law has created new categories of "migrant" workers. It differentiates between "highly skilled" specialists with guaranteed permission to remain permanently, workers with limited work permits, people whose permission to remain will be unlimited or limited for political or humanitarian reasons, and people who for various reasons do not have legal status. Again, the principle of restricting potential settlement, which has been observed in different periods of labor migration in Germany, is at work here. This law does not include the recruitment of "low paid workers" or any regularization process for "undocumented migrants" living in Germany. Non-EU nationals working in the hospitality, cleaning, personal service and transport sectors are affected by this law and this is the case for the majority of Latin American citizens entering Germany today. As in the UK, the research on Latin American communities in Germany is research field emerging.

Similarly to the UK, in the 1970s Germany hosted a large number of Argentinean and Chilean exile communities.[100] They were largely from middle- and upper-class backgrounds and found a provisional "home" in Germany. Latin Americans, particularly from Cuba and Chile, were also living in the GDR. The relationship between Cuba and the GDR was based on mutual political recognition, reflected also in the 1978 treaty that permitted the employment of Cuban workers for training ("zeitweilige Beschäftigung kubanischer Werktätiger bei gleichzeitiger Qualifizierung im Prozess produktiver Arbeit").[101] Immigration from LAC to Germany in the 1990s was moderate in comparison to Spain, Italy or France. Due to restrictive immigration and asylum laws, the entry hurdles were higher than in the UK or Spain until recently. According to the National Statistics Agency (*Statistisches Bundesamt*), in 2007 there were 99,858 Latin Americans and 48.8 percent had lived for an average of nine years in Germany.[102] It is estimated that 65 percent were women.[103] From 1995 to 2007 the numbers of Latin Americans increased. For example, the number of Dominicans increased from 2,548 to 5,980; Ecuadorians from 2,055 to 4,546; and Peruvians from 6,216 to 8,947. However, the Chilean community decreased from 6,443 to 5,959. The biggest registered LAC group in Germany are Brazilians with 31,461 in 2007. In the case of the Chileans, a new immigration is taking place that overlaps with the former exilic communities who have lived in Germany since the 1970s. In other cases, however, the communities are recent and predominantly female. This is the case with the immigration of Dominican, Cuban and Brazilian women. In general, the increase in Latin American female citizens in Germany is linked to marriage or study. The biggest group of Latin Americans comes from Brazil and some of them have dual nationality, German and Brazilian. Of the 27,238 Brazilians in 1995, 19,989 were women.[104] There is a significant group of Caribbean women from the Dominican Republic. Most of them arrived as married women to Germany. This phenomenon shows the link between tourism and migration. Considering this, the figure of Latinos in Germany might range between 250,000 to 300,000.[105]

These figures only reflect persons with legal residency, which in this case are those with student visas, work contracts and/or residency gained through marriage to a European. The number of "undocumented migrant" workers is much higher and they are mostly based in urban areas with an extensive demand for personal and cleaning services. This figure was estimated in 2003 as being between 500,000 and 1,000,000.[106] "Undocumented migrant" women from Latin America find employment in the informal labor market, particularly in the hospitality, construction, agriculture and private personal service sector such as in cleaning, care work, domestic work and sex work. This development can also be observed in Austria.

Austria

While 10 percent of the population in Austria has a migration background, Austria refuses to publicly recognize that it is a country of immigration. In the case of Austria, Latin American immigration also needs to be situated within the broader framework of its migration policies. In the 1960s, due to a lack of workers in Austria,[107] the German "guest worker model" of temporary recruitment was introduced.[108] Workers were recruited for limited periods of time through offices of the Austrian government in their countries of origin. Similar to the process of settlement in Germany, the recruited "guest workers" did not return after finishing their work contract as their labor force was needed for economic growth. Alongside this new situation, family members joined their relatives and different migrant communities who had been living in Austria for more than 10 years in the late 1970s. In 1974, in response to this new development, the Austrian government issued a recruitment ban. This recruitment ban, however, did not cover all of the employment sectors, as the *Generalvorbehalt* clause was introduced. This permitted the employment of migrants if no Austrian worker could be found for the vacant position. The "Austrian first policy" was ensured through the *Inländerprimat*, which favored Austrian workers. In 1975 the Alien Employment Law (*Ausländerbeschäftigungsgesetz*) led to the exclusion of non-Austrians from specific social benefits and introduced work permits.[109] This regulation has been modified by new laws without losing its fundamental principles of exclusion and restriction, resulting in ethnicized segmentation of the Austrian labor market and intensified dependencies of non-Austrian citizens on their employers.¹¹⁰ Austria has since recruited "foreign workers" predominantly from Yugoslavia for the employment sectors for which no Austrian candidates could be found.

In 1993 the "guest worker program" was replaced by an annual "quota system," based on the demands of the national labor market. Through the "quota system," a "quota" for family reunification and residency permits was also included.¹¹¹ This meant that a work permit could only be issued in combination with a residency permit. This represented the only access to the labor market. The system of temporary recruitment was legally administered through two laws, amended in 1993, *Fremdengesetz* (Foreigner Law) and *Ausländerbeschäftigungsgesetz* (Foreigner Employment Law). These two laws, addressing on the one hand residency issues (*Fremdengesetz*) and on the other employment matters (*Ausländerbeschäftigungsgesetz*), formed the two pillars of the *Asyl- und Fremdenpolizeigesetz* (Asylum and Foreigner Police Law) introduced in 2006.

In 2006, Austria followed the same trajectory as other EU Member States, adjusting its migration policies to the EU directives of "economic migration," "integration," "security" and "control" of migration. Yet the Austrian model formulated in the *Asyl- und Fremdenpolizeigesetz* opted for the most restrictive and dehumanizing mechanisms of migration control. Amnesty International and the UNHCR denounced some aspects of these laws as violations of human rights, such as the force-feeding of migrants and refugees during interrogation and detention. Furthermore, these organizations claimed that the legislation reveals xenophobia, and that asylum is regarded as an "area of control" rather than of protection as prescribed by the Geneva Convention on Refugees. While this legal framework seems to have shifted the emphasis from employment to control, the economic demand for a "foreign labor force" still shapes Austrian migration policies.

This legal framework follows the division between two categories of "migrants." One category includes EU citizens and refugees with the right to demand asylum in Austria, and the other category is comprised of generally non-Europeans who depend upon visas and the demands of the economy. The law allows the issuance of short-term contracts for six months, which deny workers rights to employment, health and social benefits, while they are obliged to pay into the unemployment fund. They also cannot transfer into another regular employment and apply for a general work permit. Second, the 2006 law explicitly formulated the recruitment of "key skilled and professional workers." Paradoxically, the law operates within the framework of the demands of the Austrian labor market, preventing the settlement of the "recruited labor force." A residency permit is not automatically issued when a work contract is forged, but a work contract is needed to apply for a residency permit. The termination of a work contract leads to the loss of residency. This situation affects not only the employee but also her or his dependents. Further, this precarious employment and legal status can end in deportation. For example, the application for emergency assistance (*Notstandshilfe*) or social assistance (*Sozialhilfe*), both forms of social benefits, can be interpreted as "proof" of unemployment and thus become a reason for deportation.[112]

As Bettina Haidinger notes, the only way for non-EU nationals to receive a work permit and long-term residency status are:

> (a) to be accepted as a "key skilled and professional worker" if they possess a qualification or work experience that is in high demand in the Austrian labor market and can secure an income that guarantees 60 per cent of the maximum amount calculated for social insurance tax revenue; (b) to be employed as a seasonal worker in tourism or agriculture; (c) to be accepted as a refugee; (d) to work as a student in minor employment, that is, earning less than €333.16 a month and being employed without obligatory social insurance; or (e) to marry an Austrian or an EU-citizen.[113]

These laws drive "migrant workers" into illegality, while their labor force is in demand, for example, for the hospitality, care and domestic service sectors. This situation affects non-EU migrants and, as Austrian Latin American women's migrant support organizations like Peregrina, LEFÖ and MAIZ note, it impacts severely on Latin American migrant women's work and living conditions.[114] In the 1970s Latin American migration to Austria was motivated by political exile, predominantly from Argentina and Chile. However, in the 1990s the figures of Latin Americans registered in Austria showed a notable increase in migrants, particularly Brazilian and Dominican women.[115] These figures are due to marriages with Austrian men and the connection with Austrian male tourism to these areas. In 2005, the Austrian Statistics Agency stated that Brazilians were the largest Latin American group in Austria with 1,859 (in 2001, 1368); followed by Dominicans with 1,409 (in 2001, 810); Peruvians with 566 (in 2001, 471); Columbians with 533 (in 2001, 401) and Chileans with 334. In 2007 there were 13,000 Latin Americans living in Austria. As Luzenir Caixeta notes, precarious legal situations drive women to take up jobs in the submerged sectors as cleaners, domestic workers or sex workers.[116] Similar to the other countries, the figure for Latin Americans living as "undocumented migrants" is not included in the official figures and is higher than estimated. Women are to a larger extent more affected by irregularity as the regularization provisions in place concentrate on "skilled workers," excluding feminized work sectors such as paid domestic, care and sex work. Another avenue for women to enter the country is as "au pairs," with mostly women from Eastern Europe being recruited. The majority of women, nonetheless, enter the country via "family reunification." But this avenue also represents only an option for a few, as the applicants for family reunification need to live for more than five years in Austria, earn at least 1,019.14 euros a month and be able to pay the rent each month.[117] Current laws also create women's dependency on their spouses because on divorce they lose their residency.

CONCLUSION: PARADOXES OF CONTROL AND DEMAND

In general, the situation of LAC women in Austria reflects the living and working conditions of these women in other European countries. The immigration of LAC women within the EU Member States reveals how little the debates and policies around labor recruitment in the EU integrate the feminized "low paid" employment sectors such as cleaning, domestic, care and sex work. These sectors still remain highly unregulated, leaving the workers in these sectors without any employment and residency rights. Meanwhile, the demand for domestic workers is still on the rise. As Franck Düvell argues, "to stop or control migration and in particular its undocumented version puts the authorities of the destination countries in conflict with two very powerful forces: market mechanisms and the subjectivity of human agency."[118] While the State attempts to dampen migration flows, households need workers as professional women, single mothers or women that need to work to pay their rent are no longer able to organize this work alone. Their partners are too busy working themselves, the State does not intervene and at the end of the day a person needs to be found to clear up the mess. This is the scenario in which domestic workers and their affective labor emerge as a site of the (re)production of life, as a biopolitical force, governed by the absence of direct State intervention, as I will discuss in the next chapter.

3 Governing the Household
On the Underside of Governmentality

> I am already a bit of a conventional mother who feels responsible for the household and gardening. My husband is also not particularly practical. There are men who enjoy when they come home to start repairing something, but in this house I am the one that repairs everything that breaks [*laughs*] or that does the gardening. I am the one who divides the work because I cannot manage it alone [. . .] sometimes we fight about it. (Erika, employer, Hamburg)

Erika, a 43-year-old teacher living with her husband and three children in Hamburg, tells us a story that is shared by almost all of the female employers we interviewed in the four countries. The management of the household entails a rigid division of work around three areas: the cleaning and sorting out of the house, maintaining her relationship with her husband and last, but not least, responsibility for the children. As our interviews in urban middle-class liberal homes indicate, these households shared the view that domestic work should be evenly split amongst its members. However, despite this rhetoric, the traditional gendered division persist when it comes to domestic work.

Domestic work needs to be discussed in relation to gender inequality in the labor market. While women in Europe have gained entry into the labor market in the last decade by achieving a total of 57.2 percent employment in comparison to men's 70.9 percent, qualitative progress remains problematic.[1] The male–female wage gap in the EU has remained steady at 15 percent since 2003 and the gender-specific segregation in the labor market is not declining.[2] This latter is even increasing in some countries. A substantial decline in the employment rate of women with young children (down 13.6 points on average) and an increase of 76.5 percent in women working part-time, which represents three-quarters of all women employed, further indicates that women are primarily responsible for domestic and care work within the European Union. Recourse to temporary work is also more common among women, with 15.1 percent compared to 14 percent for men.

These figures do not only reflect the gender divisions in the labor market, but also the persistence of a gender ideology that attributes to women the responsibilities for the household and the care of children and "dependent" relatives. It is largely women who still opt to go part-time or take extended maternity leave. Even when they are employed full-time, these tasks rest on their shoulders. Conflicts arise from this as the time and attention that can be committed if one is employed full-time is limited. The reasons for the discordance between family and profession are sought out and tackled on the individual level, doubling women's responsibilities and singling them out as providers of care and organizers of the households. As Anne, a 38-year-old lawyer who lives with her three children and husband in Berlin, told us, the spheres of profession and family are not always easy to tackle:

> There is too much on my head, therefore, I'm on the brink of going crazy. For example, if particular circumstances come up, if I have an accident, then my husband will do almost everything. But not without being asked. This means that the regular division of work is classical, traditional. The twins [her eight-year-old children] can't do much yet. They try to help but this results in more work. And Peter [her elder son of 11 years], it should be said, does it actually quite well. That means he does naturally nothing in the sense of general housework. But, he clears up his own stuff. On the other hand, I tried to keep my husband away from cleaning as he creates more problems, because why does one place an empty wine bottle on the sink to be washed instead of packing it in the old glass sack, I don't know. And why does one put his cup on the dishwasher and not in it, I do not understand either. (Anne, employer, Berlin)

The governing of the household rests with Anne, although she is as absent from it as her husband, a university lecturer. Nonetheless, Anne is involved in organizing the different household tasks and delegating them to another woman, employed to take up the domestic work that she cannot deliver alone. This other woman is Graciela, a 45-year-old Chilean woman living with her family in Berlin. Anne employed Graciela to work three times a week for four hours a day. Graciela is in charge of Anne's household, she does the cleaning, washing, ironing and cooking. She also told us about her own balancing of paid and unpaid domestic work, "I always say I have been a paid servant and I am a servant at home."

Graciela told us about how domestic work continues for her when she arrives home. She is a single mother, her children live with her family in Chile and she shares an apartment with four other flatmates, three of them men. While they have a rota and they are supposed to split the duties evenly, the men usually handle it flexibly, cleaning when it suits them and less than necessary. As Graciela likes to live in an agreeably clean environment, she ends up doing this work. Subtly, the gendered division of work is reestablished even in a space that is not organized by family ties. Graciela told us that in a way that is what she is used to, men usually disappear when cleaning or washing is on the agenda. When she was living in Santiago de Chile with her daughter, who was 16 then, she used to help her, but as she told us:

She hates domestic work. She always says to me, Mama, when I grow up, then I wish for a woman who does things for me. No?! So, no! No! She is not born to become a housewife, I think. (Graciela, domestic worker, Berlin)

Graciela's daughter expresses a common feeling shared by domestic workers and their employers alike. The attribution of domestic work to women operates on the basis of an ideology in which women are naturalized as "housewife" and "mother." This ideology, however, is reinforced by policies that consider the household a private sphere governed by individual arrangements.

GOVERNING THE HOUSEHOLD AT A DISTANCE

Michel Foucault's concept of *governmentality* gives us some insights into how State policies impact on and shape the private sphere. Foucault's concept of governmentality points to the interpenetration between "governing" and "mentality." Situated in European liberal societies of the nineteenth century, governing appears as a "human technology" no longer attached to the monolithic power of the Church or a sole sovereign, but to the ability to govern the population through the population. Through a variety of institutional measures and procedures the population appears not only as an object of control and regulation, but also of knowledge. Thus, governmentality focuses not only on how perceptions are shaped by technologies of governing, but also how these technologies are carved by the rationalities of the people.[3] Mentalities, rationalities and practices of the population thus become the focus of governing, decentralizing the monolithic form of governing conceived in sovereign power. Therefore, power becomes multidirectional, involving different actors and governing entities. As Foucault notes, this form of governing is based at least on three levels: (a) the governing of a moral Self; (b) the art of adequate economic governing of the family; (c) the science of political governing.[4] Self, society and knowledge are discerned as fields of governing. In particular, the family as a small societal unit has received increasing attention as the link between the welfare of the individual and society by the emerging social sciences in France, Germany and Britain at this time.[5]

The family denotes the private sphere as privileged locus for the (re)production of social life, and also increasingly became an interesting object for policy makers. In fact, taking care of the family still stands at the center of liberal governing; however, policies in this area have always been careful not to interfere in the privacy of the household. Nonetheless, the public–private split has been an issue of contestation in the last three decades. This was brought about by the women's movement campaign on violence against women and children and the campaign in regard to wages for housework.

All these initiatives have challenged the perception of the household as the ultimate space of privacy. Despite these public and political interventions, State policies targeting care and domestic work rely on the presumption of the household as a sphere in which social relations, and in particular employment relations, are negotiated on a private level, beyond the direct intervention of the State. Paradigmatic for governmentality, the family is placed at the threshold between public and private spheres. The techniques of governing the family work through the self-managerial abilities of the household members. Governing, thus, is here immediately connected to the creative and relational capabilities of the household members to govern themselves, deployed within a framework of State governing at a distance. Therefore, while the family seems to function outside a State regulative *modus operandi*, it is actually regulated by it. The family is governed by the State at a distance as the State introduces itself into the family through the beliefs and strategies of its actors. It governs this sphere through the mentalities, rationalities and practices of the individuals.

Nowadays the welfare of the family is still a topic on the agenda of political parties. The private household and the family are the entities through which strategies of governing address the juncture between society and individual, transmitting a national consensus to the micro-level of the everyday. Hegemonic social norms and values enter the space of immediate lived experiences, offering different degrees of legal and policy frameworks recognizing or "de-authorizing" certain kinship models within a national State frame. In Western Europe the kinship model favored still remains the "national heterosexual nuclear family." This is the case despite the concessions made by some EU Member States in regard to single parenting and same-sex households. In the twenty-first century alternative kinship models are still marginalized or are absent from family policies. However, when it comes to the interpellation of families within migration and asylum policies, the duty of care for the family exposed by the State evolves in a different logic. The "welfare" of these families is overshadowed by the aims of the State to control and restrict migration. Family members in migrant families are subjected to policies of restrictive entry and settlement. Their familiar ties are scrutinized and put into question, and family reunification is affected by the national migration regulative mechanisms. In the last decade the possibilities to join family members within the EU zone have become more restricted. Migrants and refugees are, thus, put in a vulnerable position in regard to their universal right to family. But migration policies connect with family policies not only on the level of governing the "nation's Other," they also impact on the governing of national households when these households decide to employ a migrant worker.

In private households we encounter the immediate effects of migration policies as the majority of the "migrant" domestic workers are confronted with the restrictions imposed on them through these policies. The dividing line between citizen and "undocumented migrant" structures the mode of encounter between employers and domestic workers in private households. Further, domestic work is not considered by the majority of EU Member States as a field of direct State control. Domestic work is thus mostly handled as a private issue, negotiated between the household members or the employer and the domestic worker. The State governs this field at a distance through introducing family policies, mainly addressed to the "national population," and disregarding domestic work as worthy of policy intervention. As the household members develop their strategies, although not always consciously, within a framework of family policies, migration regulations and labor market dynamics, their negotiations around domestic work are "indirectly" or directly guided by State policies governing the family at a distance. Governmentality, in this sense, engages with the governing of the Self at a distance as it is not directly targeting the subject as such, but its focus of governing is aimed at the subject's ability to govern her/himself within the parameters set by the State. This form of governing at a distance creates the impression of individual choices, while these choices are provided within a clear political rationale.[6]

In this rationale, migration policies and the racialized and gendered segregation of the labor market represent the "underside of governmentality." While they implicitly complement the self-governing strategies of the household members, repressive migration policies aiming to restrict, prevent and negate the movement of non-EU citizens within the EU do not govern through the rationales or mentalities of the population on which these measures are imposed. Governmentality becomes significant only in regard to the policy makers. It is their concepts of the "alien" and "Europe's Other" reflecting the coloniality of power that shines through here. These colonial mentalities governing the projected racialized and gendered Other of Europe are mobilized. As we have seen in the previous chapter, migration policies codify a field of exception to European universal human rights by operating within the logic of "colonial difference," creating an "exteriority" within its midst of the project of European Enlightment, the celebration of emancipation and universal reason. In migration policies and in the lack of regulation of domestic work, what appears is Dussel's "underside" or Mignolo's "dark side" of this European project of rationality. As we will see in the following, the logic in which the "semi-governance" of domestic work is negotiated drives itself to its limits as it produces a permanent negative dialectic, constantly negating what appears as a principal of modern reasoning.

Family policies and managing societal issues, such as domestic and care work on an individual level, rely heavily on an informal labor market, marked by legal and social inequalities produced through migration policies. While the State is not immediately involved in the employment of an "undocumented migrant" domestic worker, it profits from the existence of this labor force kept in precarious and vulnerable legal and working conditions. The State and the individual households employing "migrant" domestic workers benefit from this situation because it makes the social reproduction of the household cheaper and creates productivity. On the one side, the incorporation of male and female subjects to the sphere of production is guaranteed, on the other, the productivity emanating from the affective labor produced by the domestic worker contributes to capital accumulation without producing any costs for the State or their citizens. Consequently, while the State operates within the framework of governmentality in regard to its citizens' households, considering their needs and desires, the needs and desires of the "undocumented migrant" domestic workers are not reflected in its governing strategies regarding work–life balance or individualized care provision. The tendency of the Welfare States within the European Union to move towards subsidizing care that families provide is a development in this direction.[7] In this regard, on the level of family policies the style of governing is a recurring rhetoric in which individual families, and in particular national citizens, are made responsible for the progress and well-being of their family members. On the other side, another part of the population excluded from citizenship rights, and in the case of "undocumented migrants" of universal human rights, are kept outside a governmental program of self-governing through a governing at a distance. Rather, they are subjected to the repressive power of the "underside" of "rational Europe." Considering this, the household thus becomes, on the one side, a primary locus of governmentality *par excellence*, a space of "micro-power," and on the other, migration policies drive this logic to its limits.

GOVERNING CARE BY SILENCING DOMESTIC WORK

As I previously stated, the State tries to avoid directly interfering in the sphere of the private household. Domestic work, thus, does not form part of the area of public provision outlined by social or family policies. Nonetheless, the private household is addressed in "work–life balance" programs.[8] Programs on gender equality and "work–life balance" are at the heart of EU *gender mainstreaming* policies. The aim of these policies is to reconcile two social spheres that seem to be in conflict, profession and family.[9] Among the measures proposed to combine family and professional life, the European Union engages in improving the framework agreement on parental leave by recommending incentives for fathers and proposing strengthening the rights of workers to parental leave as well as demanding a longer period. Though these initiatives are aimed at supporting gender equality and discussed on a national level, very few fathers are able to make use of this.[10] Structural gendered gaps in payment, with men usually still earning higher salaries than women, a pervasive "mother" ideology attributing to women "natural" maternal abilities and a postmodern middle-class discourse of choice lead to women largely taking advantage of maternity leave within the EU zone.[11] This inequality is further fostered by policies aiming to increase the national birthrates. Spain and Germany, for example, have introduced monthly subsidies[12] or money for parents (*Elterngeld*).[13]

Paradoxically, these incentives are not accompanied by policies around childcare.[14] Instead, an increasing privatization of childcare throughout the EU can be observed. For example, in the UK nurseries and crèches can hardly be paid for by medium-low or low-income families. Spain has introduced the French School model of the *maternelle*, providing free access to schooling for children from the age of three on; however, the deficit in childcare provision is found on the level of toddlers where families rely mostly on private funding and family-neighborhood networks. In Germany and Austria,[15] in comparison, prices for a kindergarten place are adjusted according to the parents' income. Nonetheless, in Germany the local governance entity, *Komunen*, decides about the amount of this contribution, which leads to disparities between the nursery offers provided by the *Länder*.[16]

In general, the response of the EU Member States in regard to care work is privatization. Not only is childcare not generally made publicly accessible and affordable, but also the care of physically and psychologically dependant persons is increasingly transformed into a private matter. For example, the UK has introduced "care for cash" and Austria "household cheques," a form of cash payment for households to subsidize the employment of a home-based care worker, while Spain (through the 2006 "law of dependency," *Ley de Dependencia*) guarantees the right to care to physically and psychologically dependant people and their families. In 2002 Germany also initiated a care workers scheme. All these different programs rely heavily not only on the individual management capacities of the households in regard to care provision, but also on a female migrant labor force.[17] The German scheme, for example, is based on the temporary recruitment of care workers from Poland, Hungary, the Czech Republic, Slovakia, Slovenia, Romania and Bulgaria.[18] While these policies aim at gender equality within the European Union, they result in a perpetuation of local gender disparities, sustained by global gender inequalities.

Feminist social policy and migration scholars have analyzed the withdrawal of the State from the sphere of care as symptomatic of the transformation of welfare regimes in the era of globalization.[19] In regard to childcare regimes, Fiona Williams and Anna Gavanas argue that the demand for "migrant" care workers epitomizes the changing character of the nation-state. Two different dynamics overlap here, "the (external) international geo-political context in which nation-welfare-states exist and (internal) processes of inclusion and exclusion."[20] Though some women might be able to continue with gainful employment and pursue their careers, this is only achieved by delegating their responsibilities as "mothers" and "housewives" to another woman.

The person employed to do private care provision is usually a migrant woman whose working and residency rights are limited and who has no provision for the care of her family or household, let alone "work–life balance" programs. Instead, she experiences a restriction of family life by encountering migration policies that hinder family reunification. As our interviews show, most of our research participants had to leave their children behind in their country of origin while they take care of other children in Europe. It is in this regard that Pierette Hondagneu-Sotelo speaks of the "new domestic world order" or Rhacel Salazar Parreñas of the "new international division of reproductive labor."[21] Furthermore, the option of family reunification is hardly given for "migrant" women living without "legal" documentation in Europe. While family policies indirectly address the private households of the nation, migrant households are excluded from these rights.[22]

The Welfare State focus on care work camouflages the fact that what is also covered by employing a care worker is domestic work. Moreover, the debate on care work singles out one of the aspects of domestic work without tackling its structural character as necessary societal labor. As Bridget Anderson argues, the demand for care workers "is only one of many factors shaping the labor market for migrant domestic workers. Domestic work involves cleaning as well as caring."[23] As she further notes with Julia O'Connell Davison, the demand for carers is differently constructed than for cleaners.[24] Regarding current debates on care work, it is also important to emphasize the fact that these workers very often also clean while they care. Thus, it is important, as these authors argue, to disentangle the sphere of care in three areas of work: childcare, care of the elderly and domestic work. However, while personal care work like childcare and the care of the elderly is being publicly debated, domestic work as a whole is still kept away from the limelight.

It is not only care workers' entanglement with domestic work that is neglected in the State focus on care work, but also the increasing numbers of "undocumented migrant" women doing this work in private households. Their contribution to the national economy is not recorded in any censuses or in any official household budgeting.[25] EU national migration policies, we could say, are in this case indirectly supporting their exploitation and making these workers invisible. Paradoxically, domestic work hardly figures within the official migrant labor recruitment sectors, but it is still subject to State regulation.

Regulating Domestic Work

While the private household's demand for domestic workers increases, the State is engaged in protecting its borders and its national labor market. In the meantime, the national labor market is supplied by cheap and "undeclared migrant" labor, which contributes to national economic growth without causing any additional costs to the State. Working in completely precarious conditions, these workers are excluded from any social benefits, unemployment and health insurance. Further, as this labor force was raised and educated in their countries of origin, European states do not cover the initial costs of their reproduction.[26] Last but not least, these workers do not only contribute to the European states' gross domestic products (GDP), but also to the circulation of international capital through their remittances to their countries of origin.[27] Further, they fundamentally support the career planning and personal development of more privileged women without significantly disturbing the classical gender arrangement in the households, in which predominantly the male's professional ambitions are prioritized. New global inequalities are thus formed, sustained by a gendered and racialized labor market and neoliberal technologies of governing proclaiming gender equality but simultaneously perpetuating "restricted or subordinated forms of citizenship."[28] These new global inequalities are locally expressed by the lack of or only partial regulation of domestic work in the EU, as my discussion of the UK, Spain, Germany and Austria will demonstrate.

United Kingdom

In Britain immigration policies have developed along the lines of managing migration but prioritizing economic competitiveness and the recruitment of "highly skilled" workers. As I discussed in the previous chapter, this is also the case for other European Union Member States. In most European Union Member States, and in the United Kingdom in particular, domestic work does not represent one of the areas of official recruitment. Nonetheless, migration policies have shaped this area. In 1979 work permits were granted directly to "migrant" domestic workers and in 1980 the recruitment of "migrants" for domestic work was tied to an employer. A concession, brought by the Conservative government, was that domestic workers could be brought into the UK to work but they had no status as a worker. This concession tied the residency status of the domestic worker to their employer's needs. No possibility was given to change employers as the domestic worker would then run the risk of deportation if such a change occurred. In 1998 Kalayaan conducted a survey, in which thousand of cases of mistreatment of domestic workers were uncovered.[29] Some domestic workers reported how at the moment of arrival their passports were confiscated by their employer, wages were withheld and they had no social benefits, health insurance or employment rights. After the Labour government was elected in May 1997, Kalayaan[30] and Waling-Waling, in cooperation with trade unions and solidarity organizations, saw their first result in their campaign for independent work and residency status from employers. In 1998 the "Overseas Domestic Worker's Visa" was introduced, through which the domestic workers in diplomat households obtained independent residency status and were officially recognized as "workers."[31] This status entitles them to a range of employment rights, benefits, health insurance, minimum wage, statutory holidays, maternity leave and sick pay. An important aspect is also the possibility to change employers as long as they continue to work within a private household. However, their residency status is tied to a work contract and the visa can be extended based on an existing work contract. Only after five years as a domestic worker in the UK will a worker have the right to apply for permanent residence. While the "Overseas Domestic Worker's Visa" seems to guarantee the same employment rights and benefits to domestic workers, this applies only to a small group of workers. This is also the case for the group of domestic workers affected by the new regulations, introduced by the "points-based system" in 2008. Under this regulation domestic workers in diplomatic households need to apply under tier five for a temporary work permit. As for the "Overseas Domestic Workers Visa," their contracts can be renewed up to 12 months at a time, up to a total of six years. After five years of residing in the UK they are eligible to apply for settlement. However, these concessions of the Labour government are limited as they do not structurally abolish dependency on the employer.

Despite the opportunity that the visa offers to employers to bring their domestic workers with them to the UK, in order to qualify as a domestic worker the worker needs to be an established member of the employer's staff. Permission is given for six months and it can be extended if the employer stays longer in Britain. If the domestic worker changes employer, she must advise the Home Office, explaining in detail the reasons for the change. Domestic workers, thus, remain extremely dependent on their employers. During their campaign in 1997–1998, Kalayaan remarked that while they were succeeding in some cases to disentangle residency permits from employment periods, the process of regularization was reliant on the collaboration of the employers because a passport and proof of current employment were needed. Furthermore, the applicants needed to prove that they were able to support themselves by showing rent books or a council housing application. This was done on a case-by-case basis with the Home Office. However, the success in individual cases did not lead to a general recognition of domestic workers as "autonomous workers." Anderson considers this campaign to have had limited political success, partly because of the lack of social recognition of domestic work, but also because dependency on the employer in most cases has not been removed.[32]

Despite these exploitative conditions, between 2002 and 2006 85,000 people entered the UK on a domestic worker visa.[33] The "Overseas Domestic Worker Visa" is one of the few ways of officially recruiting domestic workers. The other avenue to recruit domestic workers in Britain is via au pair arrangements with the EU candidate countries (Turkey, Romania, Croatia, Bulgaria) along with Andorra, Bosnia-Herzegovina, the Faroe Islands, Greenland, Macedonia, Monaco and San Marino for women aged 17 to 27 for a period of two years.[34] Britain has no amnesty programs to regularize "undocumented migrant" domestic workers.[35] Meanwhile, programs like "cash for care" promote individualized care for private households without specifying who is doing this work, obscuring the connection between migration control and labor market supply. In 2005 the UK launched a five-year strategy on immigration but domestic work does not appear in their projected international labor recruitment.[36] If reproductive labor was regulated, as Anderson notes, its economic cost would be extremely high.[37] Therefore, the employment of au pairs or "undeclared" domestic workers suits private households. While there has been some discussion about meeting the demand for this sector through immigrants from the new European Union Member States, the State ignores the fact that this demand is already being covered largely by "undocumented migrant" women.[38] Their situation of vulnerability, due to their extreme dependency on their employers and lack of legal cover in case of physical, psychological or sexual abuses, has not significantly been changed and is being aggravated by new policies.

New migration policies set the role of employers as a part of border controls as they are supposed to "report" and "denounce irregularities" if they are detected. As Anderson states, "structural, materialistic and mediated power [is] given to employers who, by withholding a letter confirming employment, can ensure workers are deported 'by default'. This power, vested in an individual employer with whom the migrant is in intimate contact, makes the migrant extremely vulnerable to abuse and exploitation."[39] Migrant domestic workers are thus caught in an undefined sphere of personal dependencies and uncertain formal employment regulations. Under these conditions employer abuse and poor working conditions are common. However, in comparison to other EU states, Britain has developed strong anti-discrimination policies.[40]

Nonetheless, "the household as a place of work remains exempt from the Race Relations Act as well as from much employee protection."[41] Domestic workers in private households are thus kept outside of a framework of anti-discrimination policies and officially recognized unionized working conditions. Significantly, this labor force reflects the regional racialized and feminized segregation of the British labor market. In Southern England, a considerable number of recent immigrants from West Africa, Latin America and Eastern Europe are working in the domestic and care sector.[42] In contrast, in the North of England the women working in this sector are predominantly from the postcolonial Commonwealth diaspora and poor white women.[43] However, as our study demonstrates, Eastern European and Latin American women are increasingly also opting for working in the North as the cost of living is lower than in the London area. In general, however, the situation of "undocumented migrant" domestic workers in the United Kingdom does not notably differ, irrespective of location, a situation that we also encounter in Spain.

Spain

Employing a domestic worker has long been a sign of social distinction for middle- and upper-class households in Spain. Before the 1980s poor women from urban and rural areas from Andalusia, Extremadura and Galicia used to work in these households. Until the 1980s Spanish domestic workers were largely employed as "live-in" domestic workers. In 1985 a specific social security regime for domestic work (*regimen de servicio doméstico*) regularized the working conditions of domestic workers. In the same year only 7 percent of Spanish domestic workers were registered in a "live-in" position.[44]

The regime for domestic work entitles domestic workers to compensation for dismissal and bonus payments. Though this regime provides domestic workers with some rights, it also has some disadvantages in comparison to the general social security regime (*regimen general*). For example, they are not eligible for unemployment benefit, receive lower seniority pay increments than ordinary workers and if they work in more than one household they need to cover their social security,[45] while their employers are exempt from such contributions. Whereas for other workers sick pay is received after three days' sickness, domestic workers receive it after 28 days. The maximum state retirement pension for domestic workers is 70 percent of their declared monthly income. In practice, this means that their pensions are far lower than those under the normal system. The maximum working week is 40 hours, but does not include agreed time for performing non-habitual tasks that require little effort, such as opening the door or answering the telephone. The working day is established by the employer, with a maximum of nine hours per day. "External" domestic workers must have 10 hours uninterrupted time off per day and "live-in" workers, eight hours. However, the regulation of the working time of domestic workers is flexible and abuses are common, particularly in "live-in" employment situations. In comparison to Germany, the UK and Austria, Spain has the most regulated domestic worker system. Nonetheless, these regulations are overshadowed by migration policies.

While, as I previously mentioned, having a domestic worker at home is a sign of social distinction in Spain, since the 1990s the demand for domestic workers has been channeled by additional factors. Not only have women been increasingly included into the labor market,[46] but also the precarious and uncertain work conditions in Spain pressuring women to prioritize their income, as well as individual career ambitions and needs, oblige women to use outside help. In particular, dual-earner households, embracing a gender equality discourse, have opted for employing a domestic worker in recent years.[47] Their demand is matched by a "supply" of "migrant" women with restricted entry to the labor market. This demand has made domestic work a national labor sector and it has been incorporated into the migration regularization programs. Since the 1990s domestic work has been an area through which a "migrant" can regularize their legal situation in Spain. This explains why a significant number of, in particular, female "migrants" have applied for the special domestic work regime. This regime is considered a stepping-stone into the Spanish labor market. In the 1990s, Dominican women were the largest group of domestic workers in Spain. In the following years, Romanian, Moroccan, Peruvian, Bolivian, Columbian and Ecuadorian women joined this group. The figures on non-Spanish workers registered in the social security system in December 2006 show that from the 18,770,259 persons registered, 90 percent were Spanish citizens and almost 10 percent were born outside Spain.[48] Of these, 76 percent were registered in the general regime, while there were approximately 2 percent in the regime for domestic work. In this regime about 38 percent Spanish women were registered, while 62 percent were not Spanish and 93 percent of them were non-EU citizens. Their minimum wage is from 570 euros up to a maximum of 800 euros per month. In sum, the domestic service sector is subject to a regulation regime that establishes a very low level of protection. A written contract is only obligatory when the job exceeds 80 hours a month. Thus the contract may be informal or verbal, leading to many abuses by employers. Ultimately, without a written contract, domestic work remains "undeclared work" and a process of "regularization" of residency cannot be initiated.

In 2001 Colectivo Ioé suggested that about 60 percent of domestic workers are "illegally employed."[49] This situation emerges as a result of immigration policies, but also of the predominance of "undeclared" labor in Spain. A 2003 study by the State Agency for Women (*Instituto de la Mujer*) and the Center for Economic Studies Tomillo showed that only 17.4 percent of women working in domestic work were registered in the social security.[50] The introduction of the *Ley de regularización* in 2005, attempting to regulate this situation, has reinforced the domestic worker's dependency on the employer. Similar to the "Overseas Domestic Worker Visa" in the UK, a residency permit is bound to a preexisting work contract on which basis the employer can apply for regularization by demonstrating that the worker is indispensable for the job. So access to a work contract and consequently residency depends on the good will of the employer. This law also requires the recognition of minimal workers' rights, such as a minimum wage and social benefits. However, regularization means higher costs overall, so not all employers regard regularization as a priority. Thus, the majority of domestic workers are unregistered. Workers' acceptance of this situation is structured through the constraints of migration policies because as "undocumented migrants" or non-EU nationals their access to the labor market is restricted. We encounter a similar situation in Germany. However, in this country no regularization process is in place.

Germany

In 2000, a report on "undocumented migrant" domestic workers by the NGO *Zentrale Integrierte Anlaufstelle für PendlerInnen aus Osteuropa* stated that two types of services exist within the German domestic work sector: the housekeeper (*Haushaltsangestellte*) service, which is regulated full- or part-time employment, and "housecleaner," which is based on two- to three-hour shifts, one to three times per week. While the "house-cleaner" is considered just a helper, the housekeeper is a profession that can be studied for three years within the dual model of professional training in Germany.[51] The professionalization of domestic work in Germany is an outcome of a long-standing struggle of the German Housewives' Association (DHB), which in 1955 succeeded in getting recognition for housekeeping as a profession. On the basis of a collective agreement the DHB laid down standards such as a 38.5 hour working week, two days off per week, two free weekends per month and holidays of 26 to 30 days a year. House-keepers work on the basis of social benefits and appear in official statistics as registered domestic workers. Germany had a total of 38,000 registered housekeepers in 2000.[52] Due to the Remuneration Agreement, a minimum wage and Christmas bonus for domestic service has been agreed upon. On this basis any domestic worker can claim the minimum wage. The same applies to pension rights. This does not only cover full-timers but also part-time workers, "mini-jobbers"[53] and trainees. Nonetheless, social insurance contributions for domestic workers are reduced and they are disadvantaged in regard to protection against dismissal and working hours, which includes working on weekends and/or holidays if needed by the household.

While they have recourse to these rights, hourly paid domestic workers have a much more complex working rights situation. As they work in different households on an hourly basis, they cannot register as housekeepers and are considered "cleaners" (*Putzfrau*) as long as they are not employed by one single household as part-time or full-time domestic workers. The profession of housekeeper is predominantly occupied by working-class German women, while "migrant" women tend to work as "cleaners." Cleaners usually take up the functions of domestic workers. In particular, the women that we interviewed in Germany were employed on an hourly basis.

Though the demand for and employment of domestic workers is difficult to quantify due to its location in private households, studies concur on their prognosis that the demand in this sector is growing.[54] In 2001 the Social and Economic Census Service documented 38 million private households, of which 1.3 million temporarily and 2.3 million permanently employed a domestic worker.[55] Jürgen Schupp also notes that in Germany, 3 million private households regularly employ "cleaning personnel and domestic workers," but only "40,000 employees are covered unequivocally by social insurance."[56] Further, as survey data from the Social Economic Census Service demonstrates, 9 to 14 percent of the households employing a domestic worker were inhabited by a "care-needy person."[57] Also 25 percent of the households demanding a domestic worker were composed of elderly people, 14 to 17 percent were full-time employed couples with children and 10 percent corresponded to single-person households.[58] These data suggest the immediate link between domestic and care work.

Between the 1960s and 1990s working as a cleaner in a private household represented gainful employment for the majority of migrant women of the "guest worker" generation. Some women of this generation combined cleaning in private households with their shifts in the factory; others had a range of households in which they cleaned. However, employment as cleaners did not provide them with social security insurance, nor did it guarantee unemployment, health or pension benefits. Nowadays, Eastern European, African, Asian and Latin American migrant and refugee women are replacing this "guest worker" generation. Job hunting in the domestic work sector is organized through diasporic-migrant networks.[59] Some of the women that come through the "family reunification scheme" or who are in the asylum appeals process are not allowed to work in the first few years of their arrival. Also women with tourist visas are not permitted to work. For these women domestic work in private households is one of the few sectors in which they can work unnoticed as it is exempt from direct State intervention. If employment is discovered they risk deportation and a restriction on travel to any of the countries covered by the Schengen Treaty. Thus, the precarious legal status of these women can be aggravated when their petition for asylum is rejected or their tourist visa runs out. In these cases, these women are officially deprived of their universal right of freedom of movement as they are drawn by these policies into a situation of "illegality," which prevents them from "legally" participating in the labor market. Their "undocumented" status puts them in an unprotected situation, earning five euros or less per hour, while an officially registered domestic worker might earn from 7 to 10 euros per hour.[60] "Undocumented migrant" domestic workers experience a high degree of insecurity and vulnerability, for example, sexual assault or nonpayment of wages.[61]

In April 2003 the German government attempted to regularize "undeclared" domestic work in order to tackle "illicit work" in private households, introducing "mini-jobs." With the slogan "You don't need to hide your household help," the federal government acknowledged the need for domestic and care workers in private households. On its home page it states:

> Many families, single people and single parents lack the time to take care of all the household work after returning home from a long day at the office, in the factory or in the school. Elderly people also sometimes require support. Shopping, clearing up, washing, cooking, cleaning, vacuum cleaning and ironing are more than just "a little housework". There should also be time for raising children. The mini-jobber undertakes these household service activities which would normally be taken care of by a family member. The employer pays a small amount of contribution as with commercial mini-jobs.[62]

However, this measure was aimed at persons with residency status who would gain additional untaxed money through these activities.

While the State acknowledges the social significance of reproductive labor and the "mini-jobs" system aims to regularize this employment, it does not diminish its discriminatory working and wage conditions. "Mini-jobs" regularize jobs only below 400 euros. From these 400 euros, the "mini-job" employee needs to cover social insurance, retirement and medical insurance and taxes. However, the employers should save on tax with up to 10 percent of the costs, a maximum of 510 euros per year being tax deductible.[63] Yet this regulation has not addressed the situation of "undocumented" domestic workers. Rather, it is focused on regularizing "undeclared" work done by nationals or persons with a residency permit. By June 2004, there were 67,400 legally declared domestic workers in "mini-jobs," which means of course that many more remained undeclared. Since only 13.3 percent of those declared were migrants, there must be large numbers of "migrant" domestic workers who remain unregistered. In general, the "mini-jobs" scheme has not improved the working conditions and social protection of domestic workers. Summing up, in regard to domestic work, Germany's policies share some common aspects with the "halfhearted" regulations in Spain and the UK. Policies addressing domestic work rely on the individual households to negotiate their time investment and abilities. While the State supports the households through programs like "mini-jobs" individually, these programs do not address the necessity of structural measures to regulate domestic work as a common good, with everyone in society being equally responsible for its accomplishment. Unfortunately, Austria also does not base its politics around this principle.

Austria

The "household servant" (*Dienstbotin*) became a marker of middle-class status and lifestyle of the bourgeoisie in Austria in the twentieth century.[64] In 1920 the Austrian Parliament created a law that regulated domestic helpers (*Hausgehilfengesetz*).[65] As MAIZ notes, "the ratification of this law was a socio-political milestone in addressing problems of domestic workers."[66] This law regularized working hours, limited the workday to 13 hours—previously domestic workers had to be on call 24 hours a day—guaranteed health insurance, retirement funds and entitlement to vacation, set a legal period of notice for termination of employment and called for decent standards for room and board. This progressive law left its imprint 42 years later in the 1962 federal law regarding employment agreements for domestic help and domestic workers, *HausgehilfInnen- und Hausangestelltengesetz HGHAngG*. In this law household work is defined as the services that can be provided for household members. This comprises the work of domestic helpers, housekeepers, nannies and babysitters, home care providers, caretakers, cooks, children's teachers and tutors, as well as household managers. The law regulates the terms of trade and the minimum wage on a regional basis in cooperation with the trade union. It also creates a legal framework for employment contracts, the regulation of working time, modes of payment, time off and protection of minors in employment. Also the employer's obligation regarding social benefits, holidays and the terms of contract termination are fixed by this law. The law also stipulated a 15th month bonus salary, which was introduced as a vacation bonus due to the exceptionally long working hours and unusual working conditions in private households. Nonetheless, these regulations do not protect workers from long shifts. The law fixed the maximum as 58 hours per week for "live-in" domestic workers, and 46 hours for "live-out" workers. Different attempts by the trade unions to change the working week to 40 hours have so far been unsuccessful. The average salary in Austria in 2001 was 1,859.70 euros but registered domestic workers earned 50 percent less than the average income of 932.70 euros per month for men and 806.80 euros for women.[67]

Similar to the German situation, domestic workers in Austria are predominantly employed as externals with the exception of the increasing group of au pairs who tend to live in the household. The Austrian migrant organization MAIZ observes that external "migrant" domestic workers are working for a variety of households simultaneously on an hourly, daily, weekly or monthly basis. "Migrant" domestic workers are employed as cleaners and work 60 to 70 hours per week. Others, mostly Austrian women, work for a few hours to earn additional money. Registered domestic workers are entitled to social security. The Austrian Social Security Agency (ASSA) estimated in 2002 that the number of domestic workers (with and without Austrian citizenship) was approximately 100,000 with 10,303 of them being "migrant" women.[68] This figure, however, indicates only full- or part-time employment. Domestic workers working on an hourly basis and under the part-time margin of 21 hours are not registered as such and do not appear in these statistics. Significantly, part-time employment in this area has risen from 39 percent in 1996 to 64 percent in 2002.[69] These figures, of course, are official and do not cover the increasing number of "undocumented migrant" workers. According to a study on informal employment in Austria in 2002, 10 to 20 percent (or 10,000) migrant women were working in the informal domestic and care sector.[70] As Bettina Haidinger notes, the number of "undocumented migrant" domestic workers was estimated to be 140,000 in 2006.[71]

In 2007 Austria took notice of the care deficit and reacted to it by introducing the "house support law" (*Hausbetreuungsgesetz*). This law focuses on persons in need of care in households. Similar to the Spanish law for "dependant persons," it provides individual care service in private households. Whilst it addresses care, it leaves domestic work out of the picture. Further, this system is coupled to a self-employment regime organized by a "service voucher for household activities" (*Dientsleistungsschecks*).[72] Only workers holding a residency permit have access to the "service voucher." The "service vouchers" can be purchased at post offices and convenience stores for part-time employees earning less than 341.16 euros per month. It covers accident insurance and in some cases health and pension insurance. This model, however, does not rely on a fixed salary. The salary is negotiable between the domestic or care worker and the employer, and it ranges in regard to the task from 8.50 to 15 euros per hour. Through these initiatives, the government aims to regulate working conditions and to integrate this work into the social security system by individualizing terms and conditions of employment and worker's security and safety. Thus, while private households might benefit from this measure, the temporarily employed care and/or domestic worker remains unprotected.

While the "house support law" rhetorically mobilized a "self-entrepreneurial" discourse, in particular targeting women and their "extensive expertise" as household workers and care providers, this initiative reiterates the classical gendered division of labor. It does this by individualizing and placing the responsibility for domestic work back into women's hands. As MAIZ emphasizes:

> Under the guise of progressive initiative and entrepreneurship, this policy develops patronizing measures that dismantle public care institutions in favor of privatizing caring labor. This would hardly create any changes in the gender-specific labor division within private households, for this proposition actually strengthens women's occupational ties to the private household and/or puts women in the position to (again, or continually) provide caring labor without remuneration.[73]

In common with other EU Member States, care work is also tax deductible in Austria. This measure, as MAIZ states, favors private households that can afford to employ another woman to do the "dirty" and caring work, in "this way, prosperous families can pass on their private expenditure to the public."[74]

In common with other countries in Europe, Austria also has an increasingly non-European "undocumented migrant" female labor force working in private households. As we have seen, Austria has well-systemized regulations for domestic and care work but they only apply to citizens and officially registered migrants. "Undocumented migrants" are kept outside a framework of legal protection. In regard to the regulated situation of "house helpers" and housekeepers, their working conditions are kept precarious and unprotected. MAIZ reveals, in their study on "undocumented migrant" workers in Linz and Vienna, that these workers are often subjected to physical, emotional and psychological abuse. Working hours and wages are very often negotiated within the privacy of the households and guided by local supply and demand, which means that the domestic worker is invariably paid less than the minimum wage. Precarious legal conditions of residency impact on negotiation strategies, leaving sometimes very little scope for claiming officially agreed-upon domestic workers' rights. In the case of withheld pay or unsafe working conditions, if the migrant worker decides to sue the employer, she risks being deported while the employer would not suffer any legal repercussions.[75]

All four countries discussed here depict a common scenario in regard to EU Member States' responses to the organization of domestic work. As I mentioned at the beginning of this chapter, while care work seems to be increasingly approached "halfheartedly," the new employment situation of domestic worker, which does not correspond to the requirements of the status of the housekeeper in Germany or Austria, remains untouched. On the other hand, when it comes to "undocumented migrant" domestic workers, we find that they are completely out of the loop, and they are only addressed by regulation programs as discussed in Spain or the UK. Though they do the work, they are kept invisible, out of reach of any legitimate worker's or human rights entitlements. Moreover, the policies in place targeting the need for care workers also camouflage the need for domestic workers. Further, while they promise societal solutions, the measures in place only offer individual solutions. They do not tackle the root of this problem constituted by the coming together of labor and migration regimes. This ensures that local inequalities are ameliorated by the incorporation of global inequalities, which results in the devaluation of the racialized and feminized labor of domestic work.

CONCLUSION: ON THE UNDERSIDE OF GOVERNMENTALITY

The overview of policies regarding domestic and care work in Spain, Austria, Germany and the UK demonstrates on the surface that State initiatives cover incentives for the individual organization of home-based care providers, but little attention is given to the arrangement of domestic work in private households. While political debates seem to focus on the demand for childcare and the care of "dependant" and elderly people, no long-term governmental strategies tackling the structural nature of this phenomenon have been undertaken. Domestic work still remains excluded from State regulation and is not broadly considered within the area of official migrant labor recruitment. Rather, through the omission of domestic work from official recruitment schemes, this area is still kept invisible, while at the same time, "migrant" and "non-migrant" women are doing this work paid or unpaid. Not even the Spanish amnesty program for "undocumented migrant" workers, where domestic work is seen as one of the employment areas through which regularization can be achieved, explicitly spells out domestic work as a migrant labor recruitment sector. Within the EU there is, thus, no recruitment policy for domestic workers in place. This is a tendency that can be observed in all of the countries discussed here. Further, as the discussion on family policies shows, the increasing incorporation of women into the labor market complicates the gender arrangements around domestic work in private households. While some liberal urban households are trying to find new ways of distributing childcare and domestic work by not perpetuating the classical gender roles, this balance can very often only be achieved through the employment of a third person. Progressive gender arrangements in private households are sustained by the exploitation of other women doing domestic work. Furthermore, the access of these women to the labor market is regulated and constrained by migration policies, keeping them perpetually in this "race-" and gender-segregated labor sector.

On an epistemological level, these policies represent a continuous reimagining and governing of the "underside" of European modernity. Considered a field related to "simple labor," naturalized as women's territory, this labor attracts little attention from policy makers and is avoided as gainful labor or even as everyday routine by those that can afford to escape it. No one likes to feel "inferior," to feel that the work she does is not socially recognized and poorly remunerated. This stands in no relation to the psychological, physical, affective and intellectual abilities that this job demands from its workers, as I will discuss in the next chapters. No wonder that this job becomes *almost* a *destiny* for people, in particular women, from former European colonies trying to find a living in Europe. The feminization of labor embraces the coloniality of labor, as I argued in the previous chapter, revealing the other face of governmentality. Domestic work is not only virtually unregulated, unprotected and unrecognized by official laws, it is also the field in which the "colonized Other," "Europe's Other," haunts its portrait of civilization, industrialization, civil rights and unionized rights. One wonders how societies within or at the fringes of the world's leading economic powers cannot afford to provide public care provision and to recognize the societal value of domestic work. But not only this, they also maintain the subjects doing this work outside of a script of humanity, by constantly codifying, classifying and measuring their presence, movements, abilities, creativities and labor. The lack of regulation of domestic work here goes together with a process of "illegalization" of human beings, resulting in a permanent reaffirmation of the devaluation of this labor and a dehumanization of the subjects doing it.

In sum, domestic work remains undervalued by society, in general, and by official policies, in particular, when it comes to public social and care provision. As I will argue in the next chapter, this is nothing new in the history of domestic work. Since the 1970s feminist activists and scholars have denounced the lack of societal recognition of this labor. In contrast, domestic work scholars have insisted on domestic work as a fundamental site for the reproduction of social relationships,[76] or as a field of the negotiations of gendered and racialized boundaries.[77] Domestic work has repeatedly been identified as societally necessary labor. I will go a step further in this analysis by arguing for the biopolitical quality of domestic work as affective labor in the next chapter.

4 Biopolitics and Value
Complicating the Feminization of Labor

As we have seen in the previous chapters, the decision to employ a domestic worker is shaped today by the effects of EU migration policies and the governing of the household at a distance. As J.K. Gibson-Graham argues, the private household is the site where capitalist and noncapitalist forms of (re)production meet.[1] From the angle of the household members, the household is perceived as a site untouched by the logic of the market. However, the moment a domestic worker is employed, employment relations are introduced into its midst. Further, when an "undocumented migrant" domestic worker is employed, the household is affected by migration policies. Overlapping with the heteronormative structure that we predominantly encounter in private households, domestic work is the social field, as Pei-Chia Lan suggests, in which gendered, class and racial boundaries are experienced and negotiated.[2] As feminist scholars and activists have insisted for decades in regard to gender relations, domestic work in private households remains one of the principal spheres in which "femininity" and "masculinity" are interpellated and performed. This is even the case in households where gender equality is prioritized or where gender relations are based on lesbian, gay or queer kinship models.[3] Thus, while the households may embrace gender equality, gendered divisions of work persist.

Domestic work has been central in understanding the epistemological and ontological dimensions of women's work. When in the 1970s, Marxist feminists demonstrated that domestic work is labor necessary for the reproduction of society, they were expanding Marx's understanding of "reproductive labor."[4] Almost 40 years later, we return to this debate. Despite feminist campaigns for "wages for housework" insisting on the "surplus-value" accumulated by this labor and evidence demonstrating the constitutive character of domestic work for societal reproduction, the devaluation of this labor persists in society. Little has changed since Marxist feminists demonstrated that the social devaluation of domestic work is intrinsically linked to the feminized and racialized character of its labor force.[5] Consequently, the question of value in domestic work needs to be readdressed.

MARX'S QUESTION OF VALUE

> Political Economy has indeed analysed, however incompletely, value
> and its magnitude, and has discovered what lies beneath these forms.
> But it has never once asked the question why labour is represented by
> the value of its product and labour-time by the magnitude of that value.
> (Marx, *Capital*, 50)

For Marx, value has a twofold character; it is abstract at the same time as
it is concrete. While its abstract value cannot be measured, it becomes measurable in its concrete form, the value form. Very often value is confused
with its value form, money, its most popular equivalent form. Money seems
to measure and connote value. The more we pay for a good or service the
more this good or service is considered to be of high quality. Our attribution of quality is thus related to our notion of value translated into the
money form, which represents and also leads to social recognition. Quality,
however, cannot be measured through quantity. Notwithstanding, the technology of measurement requires that we operate with entities and quanti-
ties, that is, with forms of materiality. However, as the last economic crisis
demonstrates, the correlation between quality and quantity has become
quite complicated since the emergence of financial and insurance capital.
For example, trading in derivatives means that the value attributed to a
paper form has been less about production than the exchange and circulation of derivatives themselves. Value is produced just through a complex
network of exchange activities attached to a framework of social and cultural meaning production. Value, at the end of the day, has very little to
do with its value form or its equivalent value form, money. As Marx suggests, it is a "social hieroglyph,"[6] a phenomenon socially produced and
culturally predicated, with material implications and effects that configure
an ontological predisposition. Considering this, and going back to a more
traditional side of the economy, we need to interrogate why domestic work
is set at the bottom of the value ladder, and how this is related to its quality
and to its labor force.

Domestic work is considered "simple labor" in terms of the skills
required. As Marx notes, "simple labor" is "the labour-power which on
an average, apart from any special development, exists in the organism of
every ordinary individual."[7] It is labor that emerges from the vital character
of human beings, which Marx calls, "labor-power in action, living labor,"[8]
the immediate expression of our diverse human faculties. Considering
domestic work "simple labor," largely arranged within private households,
means that the State does not invest in this labor. Though in countries like
Germany and Austria the profession of housekeeper exists, this profession
is clearly differentiated from that of cleaner or domestic worker. The cleaner
or domestic worker does not seem to need any specific qualifications to

deliver her labor and no social investment seems to go into her training or social reproduction. It is more through gender socialization that the training of women to do housework and "be mothers" takes place.

Not only is domestic work considered "simple labor," but also the outcome of this labor is perceived as standing outside of the production and circulation of capital. In contrast to the factory, in domestic work no commodities are produced for the market. Thus, the products produced in this labor are not consumed in exchange for money. They are free and immediately consumed by their producers. Their value lies not in their capacity to be exchanged with other products, but in what Marx would term their "use-value." Marx differentiates "use-value" from "exchange-value" and attributes the latter to the commodity. The commodity, for Marx, does not only hold "use-value," but also an "exchange-value" acquired through its exchange with other commodities. While "use-value" might be a concrete experience of value, covering immediate human needs (for example, a chair has a "use-value" as I can sit on it), "exchange-value" is a more abstract notion related to the concrete activity of "exchange." Nonetheless, the magnitude of value inherent in the exchange-value of a chair cannot be measured by its "use-value," but it is actually extracted from the circulation and the dynamics of exchange. Translated into its equivalent value form, the "exchange-value" attached to a chair can differ in regard to the movement in the market, while its "use-value" is clearly defined by activities and needs related to it.

While the products of domestic work have a "use-value," they are not traded on the stock market or in the consumer market. The products of domestic work are characterized by their "use-value" as their goal is to serve the immediate basic needs of their producers. It is only in those instances where domestic work enters the labor market that its products become commodities. Nonetheless, the products of domestic work do not form the basis for its valorization. So, the sweeping of the kitchen or the cleaning of the toilet are not seen as products, neither are the meal made or bath prepared for the children. The products produced and consumed in domestic work are not individually paid for. Rather, what is paid for is social valuation of the labor deployed to produce these products. Also when domestic work enters the labor market it remains "simple labor," and while its products are consumed they are not even perceived on the level of their "exchange-value."

As Marx emphasizes, the value character of a commodity is not natural but produced by social relations. Thus, while a product can emerge from the most skilled labor, if this labor is considered "unskilled labor" by the society, its products are devalued and perceived as naturally given. As Marx notes, the "different proportions in which different sorts of labor are reduced to unskilled labour as their standard, are established by a social process that goes on behind the backs of the producers, and, consequently, appears to be fixed by custom."[9] Within this logic, the service and products of domestic work are taken for granted and not individually considered in terms of remuneration. Feminists suggested in the 1970s and early 1980s that to pay the actual costs for the value generated in domestic work would exceed any national or private household budget. The cultural and social perception and standing of domestic work is enforced, but also produced, by the dynamics of value within the accumulation of capital. For the accumulation of capital, Marx argues, "use-value" is not interesting as it does not generate "surplus-value." It is the "exchange-value" attached to the commodity that keeps capital going[10] as it is created through the exchange and circulation of commodities. The dynamics of value, therefore, need to be unpicked in terms of domestic work.

Dynamics of Value

In order to understand the production of value, Marx differentiates between "expanded relative value form," "particular value form," "the total and expanded value form" and the "equivalent value form"—money.[11] The "expanded relative form of value" defines the relational dimension of the value form. It addresses the general value produced in the exchange of commodities. It is value extracted in the exchange "of numberless other elements of the world of commodity."[12] Domestic work, though, because it does not produce commodities, is exempt from this basic circulation. But as feminists have demonstrated, the reproductive character of domestic work is constitutive of the production and circulation of commodities. It is in the household where the labor force is produced, and the "original accumulation"[13] of value, as will be discussed later, takes place. So, where do we set the starting point of the production of value?

Marx argues that there is a further level to the translation of value into value form, the "particular equivalent form."[14] The "particular equivalent form" denotes the substantial character of value, which represents the elements included in the production of a commodity, for example, the ingredients of a cake: sugar, flour, eggs. These ingredients have their own value within the cake as end product. But the value form attached to the outcome of domestic work is not just general ("relative") and concrete ("particular"), it is also inscribed in an "interminable series of expressions of value."[15] Thus, the "total or expanded form of value" indicates the symbolic character of value evolving from the cultural perception and societal codification of value itself. These three levels, relational/general, substantial/particular and symbolic/cultural ultimately result in the equivalent value form—the societal manifestation of value: money.

While through the equivalent value form value is translated into a thing, money, the conceptualization of value and the magnitude of value are outcomes of historical processes, social relations and cultural negotiations. The value of domestic work is thus not abstracted from its concrete labor, nor does the magnitude of its value correspond with the labor-power or labor-time invested in it. Rather, value changes domestic work to a social hieroglyphic because:

> when we bring the products of our labour into relation with each other as values, it is not because we see in these articles the material receptacles of homogenous human labour. Quite the contrary: whenever, by an exchange, we equate as values our different products, by that very act, we also equate, as human labour, the different kinds of labour expended upon them. We are not aware of this, nevertheless we do it. Value, therefore, does not stalk about with a label describing what it is. It is value, rather, that converts every product into a social hieroglyphic. (Marx, *Capital*, 45)[16]

Consequently, the attribution of low wages to domestic work is not accidental; the classification of this labor as "less valued" is tied to a social process of meaning production. The social value attached to domestic work is thus an outcome of hegemonic struggle. As Judith Rollins argues in the case of the United States, domestic work holds the historical traces of colonization and enslavement.[17] Thus, it represents the continuum but also transformation of the "slave"—indentured servant—servant—domestic system encrypted in the racialized and feminized bodies of its labor force.

Labor Force and Cultural Codification

The societal devaluation of domestic work has less to do with its concrete reproductive character than with its cultural codification. Neither the concrete labor-time nor the concrete labor-power defines its value. For example, if the labor produced by the worker is socially characterized as "unskilled labor," then its value character is socially considered inferior to "skilled labor." In short, the devaluation of the productive character of labor does not depend on the concrete quantity of time expended on it, but on the quality attributed to it by society. The value assigned to this labor is compounded by gendered colonial legacies, expressed in a hierarchical epistemological system that favors rationality and discredits corporeal, emotional and sustainable qualities. The value of domestic work is thus preset by a cultural system of meaning production based on historical and sociopolitical systems of gender differences and racialized hierarchies. This correlates with its female labor force, particularly the racialized, feminized subaltern.

The value form of domestic work is thus inextricably attached to historical genealogies and social processes of hegemonic struggle. Therefore, the value form and its equivalent monetary value refer to "a relation constantly changing with time and space."[18] The social value of domestic work results from the dynamics of production, distribution and consumption. Value is thus a historical, social and cultural outcome. The value attributed to products and produced in their exchange and circulation is not just "the material receptacles of homogenous human labour."[19] Rather, it is an expression of a system of equivalence resulting from a specific historical moment, situated in a concrete geographical and political context and evolving out of situated cultural practices and the dynamics of social institutions. Serving as inscription and indicator of a specific historical social order, value has a twofold character as, on the one hand, it relates to material conditions of production, and on the other, to a cultural script of production. It is from this ontophenomenological perspective that domestic work simultaneously operates as inscription and corporeality, manifested in its affective qualities, but also in the gendered and racialized inscription of its labor force. The labor force invested in producing goods remains the same in principle. However, this labor force is codified in different historical, geopolitical and national contexts. In particular, in domestic work the labor force is characterized by feminized faculties, correlating with the coloniality of labor. Domestic work, thus, is configured within and through a field of contextualized social practices and situated meaning production related in particular to processes of feminization and racialization, as I will go on to discuss. It is in this regard that domestic work remains a primary locus of societal reproduction.

Reproduction

As Marx notes, reproduction intersects with production as the "conditions of production are also those of reproduction. No society can go on producing, in other words, no society can reproduce, unless it constantly reconverts a part of its products into means of production, or elements of fresh products."[20] Every worker needs food, clothes and other essentials to be able to function and to be productive. Production is immediately connected to consumption and thus to reproduction. Capital invests in the needs of its producers to guarantee their productivity and ability to consume. As Marx argues, both production and reproduction have a capitalist form:

> If production be capitalistic in form, so, too, will be reproduction. Just as in the former the labour-process figures but as a means towards the self-expansion of capital, so in the latter it figures but as a means of reproducing as capital—i.e. as self-expanding value—the value advanced. (Marx, *Capital*, 317)

Reproduction and production are two expressions of capital accumulation. While production for Marx addresses the capacity to produce capital, reproduction focuses on the circulation of this capital as value. While the first reveals the material character of capital accumulation, the second stresses its social and cultural codification, through which, ultimately, value is attributed and circulated. Without the circulation of the cultural codification of capital, capital will not be related to value. Through reproduction the cultural predication of capital, its value, is configured.

Attending to this process, Marx distinguishes between "simple reproduction" (*einfache Reproduktion*) and "expanded reproduction" (*erweiterte Reproduktion*).[21] "Simple reproduction" describes the direct consumption of the products by the producers. While "simple reproduction" addresses individual costs that go into the sustenance of the labor force, "expanded reproduction" focuses on the transformation of "surplus-value" into capital. The latter is not determined by the needs of the workers, but by the logic of exchange and multiplication of capital.[22] Thus, the producer's immediate consumption is mediated by an extensive network of social relations of value exchange. As Marx notes, social relations produce value, thus, in the instant the consumer enters a broader social network, social relations become part of the production and circulation of additional value, "surplus-value," and the radius of reproduction is extended (expanded reproduction), as it leaves the locus of immediate and singular reproduction (simple reproduction). In the interchange between the two, "surplus-value" is generated.

Domestic work has been discussed as an ambivalent side of "simple reproduction." On the one hand, this labor forms the pillar of the reproduction of the labor force, from giving birth to caring for individuals. On the other, from a Marxist perspective, no "surplus-value" is created in this labor as it generates "use-value" and not "exchange-value." Paradoxically, as feminists have argued, the conceptualization of domestic work as nonproductive has led not only to the lack of its societal recognition and fair remuneration, but also to the silencing of its societal contribution as a side of "expanded reproduction." Domestic work is not only fundamental for "simple reproduction," but also for the "expanded reproduction" of capital. Its biopolitical character sets this labor in the midst of societal reproduction and negotiations of gendered and racialized boundaries. This perspective drives us to rethink domestic work beyond reproductive labor.

BEYOND REPRODUCTIVE LABOR

Feminist critics of Marx's conceptualization of "simple" and "expanded reproduction" have highlighted the omission of domestic work in his analysis. Mariarosa Dalla Costa and Selma James, for example, insist on the fundamental role of domestic work in the production and reproduction of society.[23] As they note, the "housewife" is the pillar of capitalist production. Her labor-power is absorbed by capital without receiving any recompense in the form of money or social recognition. The costs for the "simple reproduction" of the "housewife" or "domestic worker" are omitted from the equation of capital accumulation and silenced in Marx's analysis. But, it is exactly on the basis of this omission that domestic work supplies the chain of capital accumulation, producing additional value that is immediately absorbed into the reproduction of the household and society as a whole. Through unwaged or low-waged household work, mostly done by women, society saves reproduction costs. Domestic work supplies the production chain with an original accumulation, based on the free absorption of this labor. But it does more than this. It also contributes to the cultural codification of domestic work as racialized feminized labor.

It is exactly this appropriation of domestic work, coined in Marxist theory as "reproductive labor," that produces "surplus-labor," through which "surplus-value" is acquired.[24] "Surplus-value" is produced on four levels. First as labor deploying labor-time and labor-power, thus creating things and investing in activities, domestic work creates value. Second, as a fundamental part of the circuit of production-consumption-reproduction, this labor contributes to the exchange of value. Third, the specific quality of this labor as corporeal, emotional and affective, essentially contributes to value production. Last, the hegemonic cultural codification of this labor as nonproductive enables the tacit appropriation of its value. Value is produced on these four levels flowing into the accumulation of capital, but without any reward to its producers. It is thus that additional value is extracted. In short, capital can be accumulated because feminized racialized subjects do domestic work but the value of their labor is extracted and reproduced without reward.[25]

Domestic work is perceived in society as a form of "raw material." It is extracted as something that is a "natural given" without considering the labor-power and labor-time that actually goes into it. This perception of domestic work as naturally given is a social outcome. Why rearing a child, caring for an elderly person or sweeping the floor is considered less valuable than designing a house or lecturing students is an outcome of social and cultural negotiations. Nonetheless, domestic work is constitutive for society's reproduction. Feminists have asked many times what would happen if one day the food was not cooked, the beds not made, the children not fed, the shirts not ironed. Who would do this labor and at what cost? Feminist activists have often imagined a scenario in which domestic workers go on strike, stopping cooking, doing the beds, picking up the children from school and taking care of the elderly. This would halt the whole cycle of production and show the intensity that goes into the production of our everyday lives. The productivity of a society would immediately be seen as linked to its "simple reproduction."

In the 1980s a group of German feminist scholars, Veronika Benhold-Thomsen, Maria Mies and Claudia von Werlhof, aka the *Bielefelderinnen*, broadened the view on reproductive labor by linking the situation of domestic work in the "global North" to subsistence farming in the "global South." In their book *Frauen, die letzte Kolonie* (*Women, the Last Colony*), they refer to domestic work as the "last colony," a precapitalist mode of production. Relating it to subsistence farming, the *Bielefelderinnen* traced local conditions of the gender division in the household back to colonial racialized labor segregation. Comparing the situation of the subsistence farmer in the "global South" to that of the "housewife" in the "global North," the *Bielefelderinnen* agreed on the "subsistence" character of these two modes of production, demonstrating the interpenetration between colonial legacies and the modern labor market. In Marxist terms, they framed the "housewife" and the "subsistence farmer" as primary resources of capital exploitation, demonstrating the gendered and racialized character of labor. They wrote:

> Therefore, the hierarchical and gender-based division of work that gives women the label of housewives and makes them accessible as unpaid and poorly paid workers, has nothing to do with crises, economic changes and similar reasons that gloss over the facts. It has to do with the structure of production methods as well as the massive unemployment and impoverishment in the third world, the plundering of the survival capacities and activities of these people. (Bennholdt-Thomsen et al., *Die letzte Kolonie*, 84)[26]

Thus, the *Bielefelderinnen* considered domestic work another mode of production of subsistence labor connected to conditions of survival in the "global South" and the transformation of labor in the "global North." Unemployment, impoverishment and the plundering of survival strategies are different faces of an expanded logic of capital accumulation, extracting its "primary accumulation" from the labor of the "housewife" and the "subsistence farmer." Both demonstrate the features of what Marxism has coined the "industrial reserve army," a group of "dispensable" people who are subjected to economic conjunctures—needed in times of economic prosperity and dismissed in times of recession and inflation.[27]

The process of "housewification" thus describes the increasing precariousness of employment. While it connects to a colonial legacy of racialization, the aim of this approach is to emphasize the gendered character of reproductive labor by centering the "housewife" of the global North and in her shadow the "subsistence farmer." At the time of the publication of *Women, the Last Colony*, the analysis presented by the *Bielefelderinnen* was considered a radical feminist proposal for understanding the intersection between racism and sexism and its relevance for a critique of capitalism. However, this approach can be critiqued. For example, while the framework of "housewification" tries to identify this process as a global phenomenon and subtly enunciates the dynamics of a modern/colonial world-system, the paradigm of the "housewife" of the "global North" subsumes quite disparate, geopolitically distinctive situations, as Chandra Talpade Mohanty remarks.[28] As Mohanty stresses the use of "woman" as an undifferentiated, essentialist, ahistorical and decontextualized identity category in this approach, omits not only the inequalities between women, but also the dynamics of an interlocking system of oppression. Hence, to single out gender relations as its predominant feature obfuscates the fact that gender relations are historically produced and geopolitically contextualized, and so evolve in a dynamic relationship with other systems of domination.

Whilst they attempted to produce a common moment of solidarity between women and the racialized subaltern of the "global South," the *Bielefelderinnen*, as Mohanty noticed, glossed over significant geopolitical differences and asymmetries, thereby obscuring the power relations between women. Though their point of departure is "triple oppression," the consideration of sexism, racism and capitalism flattens out significant national and local differences and drives the *Bielefelderinnen* approach into another theoretical pitfall. Dynamics, movements and complexities within different systems of oppression are not attended to through this model because it departs from a monolithic category of power. Black feminist analysis of the interrelational and intricate character of power relations seemed not to have been attended to by the *Bielefelderinnen*. Therefore, the perspective delineated by the Combahee River Collective of a simultaneous interlinking system of oppression is absent in this analysis. The Combahee River Collective argues, in their 1977 "The Combahee River Collective Statement," for a perspective that relies on the observation that it is "difficult to separate race from class from sex oppression because in our lives they are most often experienced simultaneously. We know that there is such a thing as racial-sexual oppression which is neither solely racial nor solely sexual."[29] This perspective shifts the focus from a model of oppression based on additionality and instead looks at simultaneous, interlocking and fluid relationships of power and domination. The focus is on the complexity and fluidity of power, decentralizing a monolithic notion of power and insisting, instead, on its productive and dispersed character.

Further, the analogy between women and subsistence farmers in the "global South" disregards the enduring colonial legacies that continue to forge the relationship between the "global North" and the "global South." To nullify the singularity of locality by equating the conditions of life of the poor worldwide detracts from the fact that the dismantling of the Welfare State in the "global North," as Spivak notes, cannot reflect the complete lack of a Welfare State in the "global South."[30] In these parts of the world "the poor" are completely excluded from any potential sustenance by the State, for example, in terms of education, housing and health care. This dimension of poverty is connected to the legacies of colonization, immediately linked to the wealth of the former colonizing countries and current hegemonic political and economic global powers.

Despite the problematic implications of the *Bielefelderinnen* approach, one of its least discussed ideas becomes relevant for the biopolitical dimension of domestic work. The *Bielefelderinnen* approach stresses the sustainable character of domestic work as it is immediately related to the provision, creation and recreation of life. The recreation of life is connected in this theoretical framework with the biological possibility of women to give birth. As Claudia von Werlhof notes, the "potential to give birth is the condition for the production of human beings [. . .] surplus-value can only be extracted from the living human being."[31] This perspective relies on Engel's perception that:

> the determining factor in history is, in the final instance, the production and reproduction of immediate life. This again, is of a twofold character: on the one side, the production of the means of existence, of food, clothing and shelter and the tools necessary for that production; on the other side, the production of human beings themselves, the propagation of the species. The social organization under which people of a particular historical epoch and a particular country live is determined by both kinds of production: by the stage of development of labor on the one hand and of the family on the other. (Engels, *The Origin of the Family*, 71–72)

In order to understand the logic of reproduction, Engels introduces the "family" as its privileged site. The reference of the *Bielefelderinnen* to this argument reflects the societal circumstances at this time as reproductive technologies were nonexistent. However, this argument also falls into the ideological trap of reducing reproduction to compulsory heterosexuality and biologism. However, for our discussion here, this argument is interesting as it focuses on the dimension of "life" in domestic work, in other words, its biopolitical quality.

BIOPOLITICS

The analysis of the organization of labor in the "new economy" has highlighted the incorporation of communicative, conceptual and affective labor into the process of production. Antonio Negri discusses this process through the example of the revolutionary movement in the Veneto region in Italy in the 1960s and 1970s. As he comments:

> the duration of this crisis, its depth—these things made up the revolutionary movement, action became *bios*. [. . .] I am one of those who think that 1968 brought about a new relationship between action and life that implies a fundamental and long-term change of paradigm, one that modified the relationship to life, to history. Nineteen sixty-eight was not a revolution—it was the reinvention of the production of life. (Negri, *Negri on Negri*, 22)

Negri relates here to the old Greek term *bios* to express the fusion between life and work. He thereby introduces a post-Marxist perspective that takes into account "life" as a crucial aspect in the accumulation of capital. "Life" lies at the heart of the production process, constituting the mode of production, thus evidencing its biopolitical character. Following this observation, Negri develops his hypothesis of the "subsumption" of *living labor* into the modes of production in Post-Fordism. Departing from the observation that the accumulation of capital does not end at the front gates of the factory but glides into all spheres of life, Negri focuses on the quality of labor as one connected to the sphere of life and its productive power relations, yielding people's creative and relational skills. As such "life" itself becomes a locus of capital accumulation as it is a site of struggle.

While this argument, as we have seen in the discussion of Dalla Costa and James and the *Bielefelderinnen*, is not new in feminist analyses of reproduction, Negri uses it for its analysis of the biopolitical quality of labor in late capitalism. In his work with Michael Hardt on *Empire*, they state that the incorporation of new technologies and production of "immaterial goods," information, knowledge, images and languages, require other faculties of the labor force than the ones demanded in the Fordist manufacturing industries.[32] The subjective, creative, communicative and affective faculties of the labor force are salient for the quality of labor required in this reorganization of labor emerging in the late 1980s.[33] Incorporating the practices that people develop outside of the logic of capital production, the "new economy" integrated organization principles deriving from cooperative movements and alternative industries or even from the dispersed practices of resistance of social movements to capitalism, as Negri discusses in regard to cooperative projects of the 1970s in North Italy. Importantly, capital is not just interested in what is produced within its confines of production, but it is increasingly focused on the practices and activities emanating from reproduction. Reproduction thereby becomes a continuum of production as it is turned into a sphere of capital accumulation. It is here that the biopolitical quality of labor in advanced capitalism lies. It appears at the juncture produced in the porosity of the boundaries between production and reproduction. The role of "life" or the immediate engagement with "life" here becomes pivotal on two levels. On the productive level, the engagement with "life" promises the expansion of capitalist logic and thus economic growth, on the other side, however, "life" also represents an ethical principle of care and conviviality. It is this double character that interests Negri in his consideration of biopolitics as a sphere, not just of production, but simultaneously of resistance. Accordingly, the appropriation of "life" by capital carries resistance as its inscription as "life" itself is an expression of collective, heterogeneous and, in some instances, subversive practices. Following Foucault's twofold character of power as "potestas" (oppressive) and "potentia" (productive), biopolitics evolves in the tension between life and power. Thus:

> One must be clear about the concept of biopolitics. It literally means the intertwining of power and life. The fact that power has chosen to

place its imprint upon life itself, to make life its privileged surface of inscription, is not new: it is what Foucault called "biopower" [. . .] But resistance to biopower exists. To say that life resists power means that it affirms its own power, which is to say its capacity for creation, invention, production, subjectivation. This is what we call "biopolitical": the resistance of life to power, from within—inside this power, which has besieged life. (Negri, *Negri on Negri*, 64)

Biopolitics thus indicates for Negri the locus of resistance. It is the place where capital's attempt to appropriate life is resisted. While this approach is attentive to the absorption of subjectivity into the biopolitical dynamics of production, it does not engage with the power dynamics through which social relations and the access to "autonomous" spheres of production are conceived. This perspective, however, disregards Aihwa Ong's analysis of "latitudes"[34] that was discussed in Chapter 2 of this volume. That is, the coexistence of traditional forms of production that rely on "carceral modes of labor discipline"[35] and modes of production occurring within cyber networks and conceptual labor. Further, it also ignores the racializing and feminizing processes in the organization of work, and as such the persistence of a "coloniality of labor" and the logic of "colonial difference." But, in particular this perspective, although it attempts to relate to feminist theory, does not conceive the significance of the feminization of labor for the organization of labor in today's societies.

FEMINIZED LABOR, PRECARIOUS ZONES AND *TRABAJO DE CUIDADOS*

Intervening in the post-Marxist debate on biopolitics,[36] the Madrid feminist collective *Precarias a la Deriva* argues for a broader understanding of women's work as symptomatic of the new quality of labor.[37] *Precarias* formulate a feminist critique by attending to the corporeal and affective character of feminized labor. In reference to the debate on the creative, conceptual and affective dimension of labor in the "new economy," *Precarias* examine the exploitation of feminized skills as symptomatic of a general development in the reorganization of labor in post-Fordist societies characterized by precarity.[38] Precarity is seen by *Precarias* as fundamental for and constitutive of societies confronted with the privatization of state institutions, the reduction of public services and the dismantling of social policies and welfare. Precarity also impacts on individual self-perceptions, social relations and strategies. In 2003 *Precarias* conducted militant research on the circuits of feminized precarity, composed by video-drifts,[39] collecting various accounts of women's living and working conditions characterized by the negotiation of mobility, flexibility, creativity and affects. Precarity in these women's accounts represents the sociopolitical context in which the transformation of labor takes place. This is determined by axes of time (stress, excess, instability, impossibility to plan), axes of space (mobility, locations of life, borders, migration and settling down), axes of income (badly paid jobs, lack of resources, support through family and friendship networks), of relationships (working groups, social structures, affective relations), axes of conflict, of hierarchies, of risks and of bodies.[40] While *Precarias* show that precarity is connected to work insecurity, economic instability and future uncertainties, they also focus on its impact on subjectivity, body, time, social relations and agency. To be *precaria* thus does not only mean that one has no job or just a panoply of bad, hourly paid, unsafe and temporary jobs without any kind of entitlement to social benefits, but it also means that one needs to create new survival strategies and solidarity networks in order to navigate through life. Precarious working and life conditions can only be handled for *Precarias* if there is a network of support and people that care for each other. It is in this regard that *Precarias*'s concept of *trabajo de cuidados* (care work) becomes significant, not only in relation to the factual care work that women do, but also as an ethical principle of conviviality, as we will explore in the last chapter of this book. Important, nonetheless, for *trabajo de cuidados* is its interrelationship with the feminization of labor. Precarity is here connected to relations of labor marked by feminization, impacting on the lives of subjects interpellated as feminized by society.

In regard to domestic work, the feminization of this labor is not only given by the high percentage of women doing this work, but by the quality attached to it. Considered as "unskilled labor" this labor is generally perceived as "naturally given," intrinsically related to women's socialization. No training or education seems to have been invested in this labor. Perceived as women's natural faculty, domestic work is naturalized and taken for granted in society. Yet the feminization of labor is not specific to domestic work. Rather, it is indicative of a broader development as we discussed in Chapter 1 of this volume in reference to Italian and French post-operaist feminists Judith Revel, Antonella Corsani and Sara Ongaro. In their diagnosis of "Becoming Woman" as the ontological feature of relations of production, they emphasized the appropriation of feminized faculties as the salient moment in advanced capitalism.[41] Referring to Deleuze and Guattari's idea of becoming that is a state of flux, evading the binary logic of identity, "woman" stands for both what is and what is not.[42] It indicates a mode of existence that is empirically linked with women's life situations and refers qualitatively to a general mode of being in society and work conditions, shaped by the feminization of labor. According to Tiziana Vettor, from the Milan group S/Convegno, this phenomenon underscores two aspects:

> the presence of more women in every sector of the labour market and having all types of contracts (not only insecure jobs); and that in work

today, in the so-called post-Fordist era, female attitudes have been shaped by production, in which—according to Deleuze—there are traces of the symbolic and female as a corporeal entity. The expectations, desires and presence of women have indeed been one of the main reasons for the transformation in types of production in the transition from Fordism to post-Fordism. (S/Convegno, "A Snapshot of Precariousness," 105)

So, the feminization of labor is not related to the quantitative aspect of work, but its qualitative dimension. Features like low wages or no wages and the integration of emotional, communicative and creative faculties, which have been discussed in the past as specific features of women's work, have become general characteristics of the subjectivities demanded by the new modes of production. The feminization of labor, thus, refers to a general tendency, one that the *Bielefelderinnen* understood in the 1980s as "housewification." In contrast to the *Bielefelderinnen*, however, the feminization of labor relates to Foucault's concept of power as "potentia" and "potestas." So, power is not solely perceived as a system of oppression and exploitation, but also as a transformative and productive force. Power in this sense is not one-directional, but multisited and dispersed, empowering subjects to counter the mechanisms and logics of subjugation. Going back to Negri's notion of biopolitics as both oppression and resistance, the feminization of labor, while it denotes increasingly precarious and exploitative working conditions, also represents a site of resistance. In this sense while feminization refers to a process of subordination, as we have discussed, in which labor is codified as "simple labor" and devalued, it also bears a different understanding of a living together based on the will and the disposition to care about ourselves and our environment. Stressing the connection of feminization to the care and sustenance of our lives, *trabajos de cuidados* involves not only personal care but all the feminized areas of work like sex, cleaning, care, personal service, education and translation. In all these areas, specific feminized skills are demanded. These are skills acquired by women through socialization into personal care, their ability to be attentive, communicative and sensitive as well as to be able to express and work with emotions. Studies on emotional labor have stressed the significance of emotions in feminized labor but I would like to suggest that we should go beyond emotional labor.

Beyond Emotional Labor

Caring for others, attention[43] and communication are three fundamental activities embedded in domestic work. While engaging with physical household tasks, domestic work provides an agreeable environment for the household members by producing "the proper state of mind in others."[44] As feminist critics like Arlie Russell Hochschild have highlighted, domestic work is intrinsically linked to emotional labor. Further, Christopher Carrington, in his study on domestic work in gay-lesbian households in the United States, asserts that the "emotion management" in domestic work "involves the management of feelings, both of your own and those of others. For example, it involves efforts to soothe feelings of anger in another or to enhance feelings of self-worth when someone feels down."[45]

Placed at the center of the private household and the family, domestic work is immediately linked to emotions and desires. As our study shows, female employers are engaged in managing the household and in supervising the emotional investment in caring for the house, the children and other dependent persons. When another woman is employed to do domestic work, however, an interesting sharing of emotional tasks can be discerned. Due to the perception of the household as a private sphere, a safe haven, an intimate space, in which emotions can be explored and expressed, the domestic worker is confronted daily by the emotions of the household members. For example, Mónica, an Ecuadorian domestic worker in Leeds, told us:

> Yes, and then, I saw her sitting at the kitchen table crying. First, I thought I should ignore it as I was just working for a month in this household, but then I asked her, if she would like a glass of water. She just nodded and I continued with my work. (Mónica, domestic worker, Leeds)

Due to the privacy of the household Mónica encounters a situation in which her presence is ignored, but in which she intervenes in intimate moments of desolation. However, she is not a friend of the female employer and as she told us in the conversation with her, she hardly sees the employer. On this day, though, she finds herself in an unprecedented intimacy that she has not chosen but that she needs to confront and manage. By asking her employer if she would like a glass of water she continues her task of serving the household, while at the same time her attention to the employer demonstrates the emotional character of her work.

For the families employing a domestic worker, the private household represents the possibility of emotional restoration. The private household is "suffused by positive emotions, naturally wishing to have and to cherish its children, the site of self-realization for mothers and of mutual regard and protection of family members."[46] This ideology of the family, and in a broader sense the household, as the site of personal and emotional reassurance is in stark contrast with both the commodified relationships introduced through the employment of a domestic worker and the persistent gendered division of work that is in place within it. As previously mentioned, in the households we interviewed, while both partners were professionals, the women were in charge of organizing, employing and managing the domestic workers. This outcome coincides with the findings of other studies.[47] Thus, the idyllic image of the family as the locus of love and care is disrupted by the structural inequalities that determine this sphere.

Women do the work, but research in this area shows that domestic work is more than an expression of the gendered division of work.[48] It is also a field in which hegemonic cultural meaning impacts and in which this meaning is reified or challenged through practices. Notions of "femininity" and "masculinity" are subject to interpellation, performance and enactment through the gendered distribution of household work. Further, colonial legacies of racial classification and categorization, while not always explicit in this field, organize it through the presence of a workforce largely from former European colonies. These social inscriptions and hierarchies inform the setting of domestic work in private households, revealing it as a locus of intersection between the feminization of labor and the coloniality of labor. Value is produced in this context, not only through the immediate contribution to the regeneration of the labor force but through the emotional and, as I will argue in Chapter 6 of this volume, affective sustenance of all the members of the household. However, domestic work as *trabajo de cuidados* is a site of contestation where the immediate investment of "life" clashes with the exploitation of "life." Thus, as a site of biopolitics, it is not irrelevant who does this work. The feminized and racialized character of this labor is not a coincidence, but its social disposition and cultural predication through which the devaluation of this labor is predetermined and reified. It is always clear then who does the cleaning.

Who Does the Cleaning?

In the dual-earner households we interviewed, while the female employer was fully engaged professionally, she still kept a constant eye on the family household. Even in some cases where the male counterpart was working at home and spent more time in the household than his partner, women were central to household management. The arrangement around domestic work in the households contrasted with the self-perception of the household members in regard to egalitarian gender relations. When some of the female employers describe the division of work in the households a kind of familiar image was presented. For example, Petra, a physician in Hamburg, told us that in her household the "man does all the carrying and I cook, wash and iron." This reminds us of what Erika in Chapter 3 told us:

> a bit of the conventional mother who feels responsible for the household and gardening. My husband is also not particularly practical, so, there are men who enjoy housework, when they come home, they start repairing things or dig in the garden. In this house, rather, I am the one who also is in charge of repairing things. In any case also domestic work is a bit divided. I am the one who divides the work because I cannot manage it alone. Sometimes we fight about it. (Erika, employer, Hamburg)

Erika is aware of the uneven distribution of domestic work in her household, but she does not classify it in traditional terms. As she notes, she is the one "in charge" of repairing things. So, she even does the household work that might be seen as "male work." In order to cope with all the responsibilities in the household, she opts to divide them. Erika's self-reflexivity demonstrates that the gendered division of work in her household is perceived as an expression of gender inequality. She tries to overcome it by managing the work. Thus, Erika's story is not that of the classical "housewife" who stays at home and is dedicated to cleaning the house and caring for her husband and children. Rather, Erika's role is that of a manager. She is managing the household in which gender divisions persist. What Erika doesn't tell us in this extract is that she is not managing the domestic work alone as she has employed a domestic worker. Erika is fully aware of the gender asymmetries governing the household and identifies them as imposed by society, but instead of formulating collective claims or opting for a transformative practice, she tries to tackle this social conflict on an individual level. Brita, an IT programmer, also insists on the equal distribution of domestic work in her household, but admits that after dividing the work evenly, she will be the one doing what remains:

> Yes, and I don't know, but there are relatively few fields where one can say so, for this type of work one of us is responsible. For example, the washing machine is mostly *me*, but this is not always the case. The washing machine can also be used by the others. Insofar as an actual division of work exists, cooking can also be done by all and then everyone can take the vacuum cleaner in their hand. And the division of work is actually that I do the washing on the weekend and during the week my son and my husband cook and on the weekend in reality I cook or we go out to eat when I don't feel like cooking. This is our division of work. And the clearing up is also divided, the clearing up is done by the one who has seen the work and it can well be that I do it sometimes. But I very often clear up the apartment, when I arrive. One cannot pin it down, as far as there is, there is no specific role model or division of work but the work is done by the one, yes the one who sees the work. (Brita, employer, Berlin)

While Brita's account gives us the impression that in this household all the family members are involved in doing domestic work, it seems that she supervises and manages it. She also does the work when the others forget it. Also the model displayed here is that of individual choices. Individually, these accounts seem to tell us domestic work can be tackled in an egalitarian way. Factually, however, these two women opted for employing a domestic worker to avoid conflicts around domestic work at home. Thus, the person who is not mentioned in both accounts is the woman that is doing the work, the domestic worker. Nonetheless, while the female employers are silent about the domestic workers, as women they cannot escape the constant interpellation, assignation and reproduction of "femininity" attached to this labor. In particular, when they are mothers, this becomes unequivocal and is unceasingly reiterated in their everyday lives. As Arabella, a designer in Berlin, told us, society singles you out as the only one responsible for children. She draws attention to the fact that while both parents are around when the child needs something, it will be the mother who will react first and who will be reminded by others to react immediately to the needs of the child.

While these accounts show the persistence in private households of asserting equality, they demonstrate that unequal gendered divisions still govern the private sphere of the household.[49] Liberal discourses on alternative gender arrangements, albeit integrated in the household members' self-perception, are in stark contrast with the arrangement of routines in which femininity and masculinity are reiterated through the clear or even fuzzy gendered division of household tasks. As Carrington notes, doing household work reflects the production of gender identity.[50] Domestic work is thus a crucial field for gender performativity. This is even the case in social milieus in which a feminist or gender liberal awareness of the distribution of household tasks and childcare predominates. For example, Carrington notices in lesbian and gay households how femininity and masculinity are marked in space through the division of households tasks visible to everyone in the "frontstage" and other tasks that happen in the "backstage."[51] The "backstage" denotes the invisible work that happens in the kitchen, while the "frontstage" relates to the public, visible tasks like being the host of the party.

However, the moment a third person is employed to do the "backstage work" the female or female-identified subject of the household appears in the "frontstage," sometimes replacing her male counterpart who is then completely absolved from any household duties or tasks, or in some cases also complementing him. This situation becomes more complex when the female employer is mostly absent due to professional demands and it is the domestic worker navigating on both fronts. Nevertheless, as our research shows, the female employer remains present in her absence as she becomes the manager of the household, supervising the domestic worker at a distance.

Domestic work, thus, is negotiated between these two women who are constantly interpellated as "housewives" and "mothers" by society. The domestic worker reminds the female employer of the inevitable correlation between domestic work and woman. Though the female employer might choose when to do the household work, "at weekends," "sometimes after work," she is still stuck with it. Not even the best plans on how to distribute the work in the household seem to work and at the end of the day she is the one reminding the household members what needs to be done or even doing it herself. As Brita says, "I very often clear up the apartment, when I arrive." Governing the household at a distance, as we have discussed in Chapter 3 of this volume, is supported by family policies that promote individual options instead of tackling the structural inequality rooted in this phenomenon. Policies like work–life balance allude to the idea that social inequalities can be tackled individually, again leaving female household members with the decision of shifting to part-time work or employing a domestic worker. As should be clear, domestic work as socially necessary labor is devalued through its connotation with "femininity."

Nonetheless, while the feminization of labor is based on a common feature imposed on feminized subjects, it needs to be set within a historical, geopolitical and intersectional context of power relations. Thus, feminization takes place in relation to other social relations in a specific geopolitical and historical context. So the expressions of feminization are not just delimited by gender relations. For example, as the discussion on the negotiations of "femininity" between domestic workers and their female employers will show, it is striking how "femininity" is not just configured by heteronormativity, but always also mediated by other social relations and moments of oppression determined, for example, by class and "race." Set within these overlapping systems of differentiation, "femininity" ceases to be the sole cipher in the devaluation of labor. When a domestic worker, in particular an "undocumented migrant" worker, is employed, however, the inscription of "femininity" is altered, if not destabilized.

Destabilizing Femininity

The employment of a third person adds a further aspect to the persistence of gender asymmetries in private households. This is so as instead of transforming established gender relations it perpetuates them. To employ another woman to clean the house enables the female employers to "avoid the tensions and conflicts that can arise when they push their husbands toward more equal participation."[52] However, it does not eliminate the social inequalities informing gender relationships in private households. Rather, the employment of a domestic worker introduces a new division in domestic work. Differentiating the household tasks between more and less agreeable duties, the domestic worker ends up doing what Anderson has coined "dirty work," the cleaning, washing, sweeping.[53] However, the time the female employer spends in the households is regarded as "quality time," special time dedicated to caring for the family. Of course, this division is more artificial than real as sometimes the domestic worker is asked to pick the children up from school and to put them to bed, just as the female employer might be obliged to clean the toilet if the domestic worker is unable to come.

As previously stated, domestic work relies heavily on interpellating and performing "femininity." Normative notions of "femininity," while destabilized through the pursuit of a professional career by the female employers, are reestablished through the employment of a domestic worker. Even the accounts of the female employers demonstrating an awareness of gender asymmetries and insisting on alternative equality models in the division of household work turn out to be irrelevant in view of the classical feminized role that the domestic worker needs to deliver. The employer's professional success or egalitarian household model is only achieved through delegating the classical inscriptions of "femininity," for example, cleaning and sweeping, to the domestic worker. Paradoxically, while in regard to the employer classical attributions of "femininity" seem to be destabilized, in the case of the domestic worker they are reinforced.

The employment of an "undocumented migrant" domestic worker confronts the households not only with their own individual personal conflicts, desires and emotions but also with the profound societal antagonisms that structure their lives. This stands in contrast to the perception of the household as private retreat, where the household members can relax and be themselves. Instead, as feminist scholars have argued, while the household "functions according to a logic distinct from that of the capitalist mode of production,"[54] it interacts with and is pervaded by this logic, as it holds normative and hegemonic forms of gendered and racialized inequalities.

The desires of the household members to have an agreeable and functioning private environment are only fulfilled by employing another person. One who might not have the possibility of living with her own family, one who might live in a household "in transit," waiting to achieve secure legal and work conditions in order to realize her dreams of an emotional haven. Under these conditions, in which employment relations cross private arrangements and in which social groups divided by migration policies and citizenship regimes are compelled to share intimate spaces, the household becomes more than just the locus of reproductive and emotional labor. It is the field *par excellence* in which the expression of domestic work as a site of biopolitics becomes tangible. Thus, domestic work is more than an expression of the gendered divisions of work. It is the field in which the gendering of labor is confronted with the logic of "colonial difference." Domestic work as a site of biopolitics is more than just a new quality of labor. It represents the constitution of the common shaped by the modes of production, but also by the struggle for a better life. However, in contrast to a "disembodied" common that tries not to fall into the trap of anthropology by avoiding identifying the relations of power and exploitation that determine its own constituency,[55] I insist here, in reference to *Precarias*, on an embodied moment of societal formation and resistance. The common, thus, is intricately connected not only to the "Becoming Woman," but to the logic of "colonial difference," as my discussion of domestic work shows. It is in this regard that I would like to conclude this chapter with some thoughts on the feminizing and racializing character of biopolitics.

CONCLUSION: RACIALIZING AND FEMINIZING BIOPOLITICS

Pei-Chia Lan notes that unpaid and paid domestic work are not two separate entities. Rather they are "structural continuities that characterize the feminization of domestic labor across the public and private sphere."[56] This observation, as we have seen, is shared by *Precarias* when they insist on the continuum between production and reproduction in the *trabajo de cuidados*. This perspective extrapolates the locus of "care work" from the privacy of the household and situates it at the midst of society as a field not only of capitalist production, but of resistance to the logic of capital accumulation. Addressing the biopolitical character of care work, as labor engaging with the immediate pulses of life but also as a locus of resistance, *trabajo de cuidados* signifies a transversal, hybrid category featuring the precarious and informalized character of the feminization of labor as well as a new "potentia," a new will to life.

Challenging Marxist debates, *Precarias* refuses to reproduce the division between reproductive and productive labor. Rather, they attempt to conceptualize *trabajo de cuidados* within the tension of precarious, exploited feminized labor relations and the struggle for a better life. Partially resonating with Enrique Dussel's "politico-material principle"[57] of the will to life, but locating it within the autonomous, creative and affective potential of feminized subjects to build vital circuits of livelihood, *Precarias* attends from a different angle to Dussel's maxim of a will to life as "the production, maintenance, and enhancement of the immediate lives [. . .] of all citizens [. . .] of humanity."[58] Dussel connects the "politico-material principle" of the will to life with the Zapatista Movement's principle of "obediential power": "[T]hose who command must command by obeying"[59] the demands, claims and needs of the community with a "normative demand of democratic legitimacy" by proposing a "subjectified State," driven by the "normative responsibility of each citizen towards the others."[60] However, *Precarias* emphasize "vitality" that relies on the power of the people. Striving towards a society based on what seem to be libertarian principles, *Precarias* are interested in the activities of the dispersed movements, networks, allegiances and affinities brought about and shaped by current regimes of production and struggle within the common.[61] *Trabajo de cuidados* represents one of the incarnations of the common, configured by the basic and fundamental social practices and relations, language, habits and convictions, shaped by modes of production, but also deriving from the feminized potential inhabiting everyday resistance. The common as envisioned through the lens of *Precarias* is not a virtual force, but an ontological presence, one determined by the misogynist logic of society and "colonial difference." As such it unites the ambivalence of biopolitics at the same time that it is a product of the destructive powers inherent in a reckless, exploitative and dehumanizing logic of capitalism, discussed by Achille Mbembe as "necropolitics."[62] It is in this tension that attempts to racialize those designated Others in the household are resisted, as we will see in the next chapter.

5 Symbolic Power and Difference
Racializing Inequality

> The operation of the value-form makes every commitment negotiable, however urgent it might seem or be. For the long haul emancipatory social intervention is not primarily a question of redressing victimage by the assertion of (class- or gender- or ethnocultural) identity. It is a question of developing a vigilance for systemic appropriations of the unacknowledged social production of a *differential* that is *one basis of exchange* into the networks of the cultural politics of class- or gender-identification. (Spivak, *Outside in the Teaching Machine*, 63)

As I have discussed in the previous chapter, value is socially produced and culturally predicated. The value attributed to domestic work in society does not represent its genuine and immanent character or quality. Rather, as we have seen, the elements of the value form of domestic work are "social hieroglyphs." Thus, the devaluation of this labor is symbolically produced through chains of value coding, which situate it at the bottom of the social ladder. Bearing the traces of servitude, colonial and indentured labor, this work is characterized by: (a) the lack of State protection; (b) its social devaluation; (c) the attribution of "inferiority" to its labor force. In the interrelationship of these three levels, domestic work is configured as "simple labor" and its labor force as "unskilled labor," unwaged or poorly paid. In the previous chapter, I asked how such a societally necessary and constitutive labor could be treated as irrelevant. I asserted that the value attached to it has much less to do with its societal function than with the cultural perception and codification of this labor and labor force. Mutually configuring each other, the labor force and its labor are both codified by processes of hierarchical differentiation, conveyed in the feminization and racialization of its labor force. "Femininity" and "raciality" work here as signifiers of inferiority, expressed, assigned and negotiated in the private households, particularly when an "(undocumented) migrant" woman is employed.

While not directly addressing the field of domestic work, Spivak's quote incites us to be vigilant of the identitarian codification of the value form. Though not in opposition to identity politics, but conceiving its limitations if the incorporation of its logic into a system of capital production is disregarded, Spivak points to the risks of a reification of identities. Indeed, as Theodor Adorno and Max Horkheimer point out in *Dialectic of Enlightenment*, the logic of capital operates within identity discourses in order to create an imaginary relationship between commodities and consumers, engaging with their desires, fantasies, yearnings and emotions.[1] In other words, Spivak's observation leads us to thoroughly interrogate identity politics as the cultural predication of capital accumulation. As the development of identity claims from the 1980s to the governance of diversity in the 1990s in the United States and some European countries demonstrate, identity politics can be incorporated in forms of global governance and strategies of capital accumulation without disturbing the system of exploitation or putting an end to social inequalities.[2] The symbolic social and cultural script in which value is produced becomes significant if we are to understand how differences and hierarchies are invoked, performed, enacted and reified in domestic work.

Domestic work, as I have repeatedly argued, is the social field *par excellence* in which what Pei-Chia Lan conceptualizes as "gendered and racialized boundaries" are negotiated.[3] As Lan notes, the "construction of social boundaries—drawing lines between 'us' and 'them'—not only requires the political-legal regulation of citizenship and national borders but also involves symbolic struggles and local negotiations in the daily interactions between employers and workers."[4] As I will argue in this chapter, the relationship between the domestic workers and their employers is suffused with symbolic power,[5] a cultural framework of power relations, exercised and stipulated through communication and interaction. It is in this regard that this chapter will focus on the negotiations of "femininity" between domestic workers and their employers and the racial codification of the domestic workers. Further, domestic workers' strategies for coping with and resisting this logic will be traced, inserting them into Gloria Anzaldúa's framework of *la facultad*. But first, let us take a look at the dynamics of symbolic power in domestic work.

SYMBOLIC POWER

As I discussed in the previous chapter, the relationship between domestic workers and their employers does not only hold a common moment of identification as women, but it is also determined by the legal divide between "national citizen" and "undocumented migrant." The negotiation of these signifiers of social inequality demarcates the space in which these two groups of women meet and in which their "social boundaries" are expressed and negotiated within a framework of *symbolic power*. According to Bourdieu, *symbolic power* defines power relations negotiated on a symbolic level. For him, language becomes the privileged locus of symbolic power. Drawing from Ferdinand de Saussure's theoretical framework of structuralism and language,[6] Bourdieu develops a "structural sociology of language," contrasting Saussure's conceptualization of language as a system of arbitrary differential relations between signs, with a sociological definition of language as a "structured system of social differences."[7] From this perspective, power relations are negotiated in language, revealing the role of "symbolic power" in the performance, enactment and negotiation of social hierarchies. However, Bourdieu, in contrast to the poststructuralist approach to language, stresses that language is a cognitive structure of social knowledge, a cognitive map, interwoven and reproduced in our everyday practices. This cognitive structure of social knowledge underlies the interactions between domestic workers and their employers. "Forms of classification" and "mental structures" of social distinction are expressed, enacted and exchanged in their encounter, appealing to and reproducing social classifications. These are conveyed, for instance, in the attribution of identity features and assignation of difference. In the field of domestic work, these ascriptions evolve within the symbolic framework of "femininity" and "raciality." Identity and difference are, thus, textured by the structures of social inequality based on gender relations and the institutional and cultural dynamics of racism.

The interactions between domestic workers and their employers are submerged in a discursive matrix of power relations, embedded in a field of *symbolic power* in which social differences of class, gender, "race," nationality and sexuality are organized and negotiated. In their encounters, social conventions are articulated through their "habitus."[8] The concept of "habitus" denotes the bodily mimesis of feelings and experiences of social distinction, ingrained in the body like a "memory-jogger," an amalgamation of complex gestures, postures and words related to social, economic and cultural belongings.[9] The "habitus" is thus the bodily inscription of social difference through which social inequalities are performed and expressed.

EMBODIED DIFFERENCES AND SYMBOLIC VIOLENCE

While social boundaries are individually invoked in the private household, the question remains of how social differences are embodied. While Bourdieu considers the "performative" force of embodied social differences and inequalities through his concept of *bodily hexis*,[10] the bodily incorporation of language articulating social structures, he refuses to understand "performativity" within a merely linguistic framework. Contrary to Austin's concept of "performative utterance," which relates to a specific context of enunciation by an authority,[11] Bourdieu insists that it "is the facility of structural class power and trajectory effect on cultural classifications, which authorize an individual utterance in the first place, rather than any particular contextual circumstances *per se*."[12] For Austin, performative utterances are inscribed in a speech context in which an utterance holds not just a descriptive aim, but inscribes itself on a thing. It acts upon it as a "performative utterance," as a "doing things with words."

Bourdieu challenges Austin's framework by situating the speech act within a social context of inequalities and power relations. So, which "performative utterance" will be successful in leaving its imprint on the body depends on the social status of its speaker. In the interactions in the household, the communication between domestic workers and their employers are mediated through power relations. In this regard, the utterance of a domestic worker addressing her employer will not have the same effect as vice versa. For example, if a domestic worker says to her employers, "I am leaving," this utterance implies at least two meanings: (a) she is saying good-bye for the day or (b) she is leaving the job. The employer might react to this by exercising her authority and negating her right to leave. On the other side, if an employer says to her domestic worker, "I am leaving," no further reaction is expected by the employee as this is just an ordinary good-bye. The meaning attributed to these utterances is related to the authority embodied by the different speakers. While the "leaving" of the employer is almost irrelevant for the worker, the "leaving" of the worker could challenge the authority of the employer and so indicate social conflict. The effectiveness of a "performative utterance" depends on the power status of a social actor and her context. An utterance becomes powerful through its structural sociohistorical predication. Not all speech acts carry the same authority as the authority assigned to a specific speech act or enunciation relies on the social positionality of the speaker. How it is received by the addressee is also determined by power relations. This observation is relevant when we consider the asymmetrical relationship between domestic workers and their employers in the private household. Communication and interaction do not evolve here in a power-neutral space. They are textured by power relations, in which the social meaning of an utterance is prescribed by the sociopolitical and historical subtext that the positionality of its speaker or addressee enunciates. Even in the instances in which the employer attempts to interact with or portray the domestic worker in a more egalitarian way, the utterance is underlain by a *habitus* that reveals the structural social inequalities of the speech act. For example, Sybille, an IT specialist who is married with two children and lives in Vienna, shares her discomfort regarding the naming of the domestic worker as a "cleaning woman" (*Putzfrau*):

> My child hasn't learned to clean up his own things or his dirt, if you will. I am not in favor of the derogatory image he has of cleaning ladies. Well, I am not sure where he gets this from, since I am really not one who would use the term "cleaning lady." This is really important for me that he at least sees that we can be thankful that we have someone. And the disadvantage is maybe also that the men don't—well, that then there really isn't a fifty-fifty division. That men are again able to dodge out of responsibility is a big disadvantage. (Sybille, employer, Vienna)[13]

Sybille's observation regarding the attitude of her son to their cleaner reveals how domestic work is not just tied to the completion of household tasks, but to a system of social distinction. As Bridget Anderson states, a "domestic worker, then, is not just a person who does a job: like the 'mother' and the 'wife' she is performing a role within the family. In the final analysis, domestic work is not definable in terms of tasks but in terms of a role which constructs and situates the worker within a certain set of social relationships."[14] The domestic worker within the family setting represents the position of "servant." Even the change of the name that Sybille suggests here would not change her status. The power of naming, as this example demonstrates, does not rely on a single word but on a system of meaning production, composed of different levels of interpellation and practices of articulation. In order to change the status of the domestic worker it is not just a change of a term that is needed, but rather a change of the system that creates subordination. Interestingly, while Sybille is aware of the social differences articulated in the household through employing another woman, she tries to neutralize them by first attempting to rename the relationship of exploitation, voiced by her son, and second, by presupposing the existence of women's solidarity between the worker and herself in relation to men's lack of responsibility for the household.

In this extract, gender identity is mobilized as a signifier of unity, interrupted by the naming of the domestic worker as a "cleaning lady." Social conflicts in the household are thus articulated on the level of gender relations and employment relations. However, in order to overcome the second dimension of the conflict, Sybille privileges the focus on gender inequality. Sybille's extract illustrates a *habitus* of an urban professional milieu, characterized by self-reflexivity and progressive ideas on gender relations and awareness regarding social inequalities, but an inability to structurally overcome the inequalities within the household. Employing a domestic worker is not perceived by Sybille as a sign of distinction, nor explicitly inscribed in a form of servitude. However, structurally, the relationship of the household members to the domestic worker is one of exploitation, as expressed by her son. As Lan notes in reference to Bourdieu, "class boundaries are not fixed lines defined by the possession of economic capital but sites of conflict that take shape in the form of symbolic struggles—different social groups deploy cultural capital and symbolic capital to impose their visions of social order as legitimate."[15] Drawing on their social and cultural capital, the employers self-reflexively assess and value their employment relationship, showing critical awareness, at the same time that they profit from the global and economic inequalities in which employing a domestic worker becomes affordable. Sybille's comment illustrates gender equality as one of the discursive strategies legitimizing the employment of a domestic worker, operating on an apparently rational script. Another strategy is invoked by Maria, a journalist living with her three children and husband in Madrid:

> Once she went to the doctor, and they did something to her, poor thing, she was hurt, and then she didn't come back. And this is one of

the things that happen, they don't give you any notice. Well, this might be a little Ecuadorian, I think. She goes to the doctor and she doesn't tell you that she is not coming and you are there, waiting, well. It happened so many times. It happened once that there was a general strike and the buses weren't running. So they took the train and I went to pick them up at the train station, but they weren't there. Then you arrive home and there they are. A friend gave them a ride. This is a mentality that, well, a person is a person, and if I had an appointment with you, although I might have other things to do, I would come to our appointment because that is what we agreed on. And in these things, very often they do not explain very much, for example, the other day there was this thing in the nursery, this has happened a couple of times, sometimes my mother just went to pick up our daughter and sometimes she doesn't. So, all of a sudden we get a call from the nursery, my mother—well—she [the domestic worker] just didn't tell me a thing. And then my mother, "She told you, no? About the event?" And no, no, she didn't tell me a thing. She has a way of communication, well, it's different. She might be embarrassed or I don't know. And if she goes to the doctor and he hurts her, well she should tell me, no? But no, she doesn't say a thing. (Maria, employer, Madrid)[16]

Maria's account uncovers the contradictions informing the relationship between domestic workers and their employers. Proceeding in a racializing logic by first reducing her domestic worker to a homogenous group of "poor things" and "they," and then rationalizing her attitude as employer towards "them" by invoking herself as benevolent and a culturally sensitive person, Maria reduces the conflict with her worker to the lack of intercultural communication. While Maria does not use this exact terminology, she alludes to it by constantly rehearsing and attributing "cultural difference" to the Ecuadorian worker. Similarly to Sybille's account, Maria does not assert the social inequalities within the relationship between the domestic worker and herself. Rather, her strategy of rationalization defers the point of tension revolving around structural differences by flattening it to individual problems of cross-cultural communication. In contrast to Sybille, her "memory-jogger" does not refer to gender difference, but to a universal principle of "personhood," in regard to which she defines the "mentality" and particularities of the person working for her. A universal discourse on personhood is mobilized here to legitimize the attribution of difference. Maria seems to expect the domestic worker to be a friend who is prepared to share personal matters with her, thereby forgetting that she has "employed" this person to clean the house.

Both Sybille's and Maria's accounts are characteristic of a *habitus* expressed by an urban, progressive, professional and self-reflexive milieu. Aware of global inequalities and gender asymmetries, this milieu integrates a progressive multicultural and gender-sensitive discourse into their analysis of individual situations in their households. While Maria and Sybille attempt to rationalize their positions as employers, their assessment of their domestic worker's social position is limited and perceived only through the angle of their own needs. Here social meaning is produced on the basis of a matrix of social inequalities. This not only reiterates an existing framework of hegemonic perceptions of norms and values, but also articulates a range of social and economic interests attached to the needs of the household members. Sybille's and Maria's comments illustrate how "symbolic violence"[17] is expressed through tacit and normalized modes of social domination, reiterated in everyday social habits in which social distinction is performed and subtly legitimized. Hegemonic categories of thought and perception are thus imposed on subordinated subjects, attributing to them a deficit or abnormality, while the dominant subject reaffirms her power by rationally legitimizing her acts and thoughts. In contrast to this, Marga, a Peruvian domestic worker in Berlin, is quite clear about her relationship to her employer:

> I think that one should not lose the point between employer and worker [. . .] *because*—there can't, there can't—who said that, Marx? There can't be a friendship between employer and worker? I believe it is *possible*, yes, but it is very difficult. (Marga, domestic worker, Berlin)

The assumptions of "solidarity" or "friendship" articulated by Sybille and Maria are put here in a different light. As Marga says, friendship is not given just by the fact that two women meet or that their encounters happen in the privacy of the household. While these two women, employer and domestic worker alike, share the social correlation of "femininity" with domestic work, they tackle this interpellation differently. While Sybille and Maria can delegate some of the household tasks to another woman, Marga is the one at the other end doing this work. The possibility that these two women will become friends is on quite shaky ground as at the end of the day the employment relationship can be terminated by Sybille or Maria at any time. On another level, the association of domestic work with "friendly" servitude, reflected in the popular imagination of an always smiling cleaner or a domestic worker who is completely submerged in the needs of the household members, represents a constant expectation that domestic workers need to face in private households. For example, domestic workers reported that "friendship" can be easily exploited, especially if they are asked for favors that are not then paid for. Of course, in some cases, real friendships can emerge. For example, some employers supported domestic workers in acquiring legal residency status. Others supported the domestic workers in finding schools for their children, advising in regard to health care and helping them to look for accommodation. In a very few cases, the employer supported the domestic workers by paying a form of health insurance and giving them holiday pay. Unfortunately, these acts of solidarity and fair wages are unusual. The majority of the domestic workers expressed their discontent in regard to the exploitative conditions that they frequently encounter, in particular, when the employer exercises her control over the household.

IMPOSING SUPERIORITY

> Men are not as, what I mean, how can I say it? Men are not as hard as women. Women they have got *so many* restrictions and *so many* do's and don'ts. For men what matters is that you clean their house and that's it. There are not so many cosmetics, there are not so many things which you have to take care of, there are not so many, it's only one go and clean their house and that's it. That's all. I mean women, I tell you, if you work for a woman, you need to make sure that you clean the mirror; and you know—women with mirrors—and you have to clean the mirror, you have to make sure that the lipstick goes back where it was. (Rita, domestic worker, Hamburg)

Rita deploys gender stereotypes to describe how her relationship with her employers is inscribed in gender differences, played out in a set of rules and orders. As MAIZ notes in their study on domestic workers in Austria, through the monitoring of tasks hierarchies are established and questions of ownership and authority in the household are addressed.[18] For example, Mafalda, one of the research participants in Austria, reported that she was timed when she was changing her clothes so that her employer could deduct this from the time she worked.[19] These orders and rules imposed a constant surveillance on the domestic workers, conducted sometimes at a distance, through phone calls, messages and/or Post-its. At the same time, they are constant reminders of ownership. Paradoxically, while the employers refuse to be the main addressees of domestic work and have employed a domestic worker to accomplish their duties, they continue orchestrating the household in the background. In some cases, they vehemently reappropriate the household as their terrain of governing, which is still attributed to them by society and other household members as the privileged space of femininity. Though the female employers are absent, their presence is reinforced and reestablished through different strategies of control. In particular, the female employers seem to insist on surveying the whole process of cleaning and taking care of the house, as Natalia observes:

> Women they can come, she can come and she starts looking. I mean, somewhere which has never been cleaned before and she'll say, "You haven't cleaned here." You see what I mean? Just to make you feel, who am I? A cleaner, you see what I mean. (Natalia, domestic worker, Hamburg)

Natalia's extract stands in absolute contrast to Sybille's and Maria's accounts of solidarity and friendship between women. Rather than experiencing identification, Natalia perceives estrangement. Irritated and scandalized by the behavior of the female employers, the majority of the domestic workers consider solidarity between women a farce. Men as employers, on the contrary, seem to be absent or just at the margins. As numerous scholars on paid domestic work have shown, domestic work is socially perceived as the exclusive terrain of women. Thus, when the domestic worker enters their terrain of governance, one way of keeping the reigns in their hands is to keep a constant track of the work delivered by this other woman. Through this surveillance, social boundaries are newly traced, marking class and racial differences between them. As Natalia makes clear, the attitude of her female employer is supposed to make her "feel" that she is the cleaner. Thus, "superiority" is addressed in interactions by affectively reestablishing the position of the employer and affirming the position of the domestic worker as one of "inferiority." The transmission of feelings evolves here within a matrix of racialized and gendered power relations reinstating the coloniality of labor into the midst of private households.

COLONIAL DÉJÀ VU

While research on domestic work has focused on how "femininity" and class distinctions are established, performed and reiterated in private households, research on Black and Latina domestic workers[20] and "migrant" domestic workers[21] has drawn attention to how through racialization hierarchies and differences between women are played out. For example, Rina Cohen illustrates, in her study on live-in domestic workers in Canada in the 1980s, how household tasks were divided along color lines.[22] While "lighter" skinned women were favored for childcare, Black women were employed as cleaners. Anderson also shared this observation in the European context. In her study on migrant domestic workers in the 1990s, she observed how certain ethnocultural or racial-cultural explanations of personal abilities are used by the employers to legitimize a downgrading of the working tasks and low wages.[23] Within the EU context, racialized and ethnicized differences are articulated in regard to national histories of exclusion and current migration and asylum policies. In the case of Latin American "undocumented migrant" domestic workers, while some of them have a White European background, they experience a gendered racialization coupled with their irregular legal status and the social devaluation of their labor. For example, one of the employers interviewed by MAIZ, Eva, a teacher, expresses this in an obvious way. She emphatically told the researchers about the ability of her Ecuadorian indigenous domestic worker, Marta, as she sees "the dirt, which is unusual for an Indio!"[24]

Interestingly, Eva invokes a colonial understanding and naming, which seems to be quite removed from the Austrian context. Eva's example illustrates how colonial mechanisms of racialization are still evoked in the twenty-first century. As Quijano reminds us, the coloniality of labor,[25] related to the coloniality of power and global capitalism, has not ceased to exist after the end of colonial administration. This logic still lingers in the contemporary organization of labor, expressed in particular by a gendered and racially segregated labor market, narrowing the options for non-European women to access well-paid and secure jobs. "Race" as a colonial category, while not always explicitly pronounced and camouflaged by terms like "asylum seekers,"[26] "undocumented migrants" or just "migrants," is still at play in the organization of the European labor market. Within the confines of European households this logic is reiterated in the negotiations of racialized and gendered boundaries between "undocumented migrant" domestic workers and their employers. Some comments made by employers on the "ethnic" characteristics of their domestic workers seem like déjà vu, a flashback to a colonial logic that is thought to lie in the past. It reminds us of the everyday nature of racism in the organization of labor, in general, and feminized labor, in particular, bluntly uncovered here by Eva's further description of Marta:

> This Asian, level-headed, quiet, modest manner—I mean that—I've often traveled to Asian countries or it exists in South America, too, that the people are simply satisfied in their humility and are level-headed and are always nice and friendly.
>
> Q: And you believe that this could change through globalization?
>
> No—no, I don't think so [laughs]—for me, this is in those people's genes. (Eva, Vienna, employer)[27]

Eva's description of Marta as having "this Asian" manner is presented as an objective observation that arises from the firsthand experience gained from traveling to these countries. Her observation is firmly set in categories of "cultural differences," supported by the discourse of genetics. The bluntness of this racism is self-evident and Eva does not seem to care about the political correctness of her description. Her assumption is not challenged even when the interviewer situates her observation within the framework of globalization. Rather, a new variation of the rhetoric of racism appears: "people's genes." Interestingly, through racialization Marta is naturalized as a "genetically" preconditioned domestic worker. The colonial category "race" operates here through an apparently objective scientific category, "gene," normalizing racism by bringing back an old racist social classification system in a new vocabulary.[28] Not only does this perception allude to domestic work as inherent to woman's nature, but it also recreates the racist discourse of Black women and women of color as "genetically" attuned to and destined for this kind of labor. Racism is not always so explicitly expressed in the households selected for this study. Rather, the urban, liberal, middle-class households portray themselves as antiracists and their speech is guided by the parameters of political correctness. However, forms of downgrading the labor of the domestic workers and degradation of their persons are enacted through more subtle forms of attributing "inferiority." As the examples of Sybille and Maria illustrate, hierarchies are not perceived as social outcomes, but negotiated in cultural terms. Negotiations around working tasks and conditions are set within an "ethnocultural" script and identified as cultural communication problems, instead of perceiving them as conflicts of interests between two parties in a work relationship. But, another way that the employer can assert her authority and mark her difference to the worker is by directly exercising control, as Tony from Peru told us:

> *I am a woman*, and some women have got this attitude that "Somebody is working for me, so I have to treat her as a worker," you see what I mean? She can leave anything around, although she could easily pick it up. She just leaves it for the sake that you should pick it up. Men have sympathy. Let me tell you, they say, "Do what you can do with the four hours you have, if you can't do it—it's not a problem, you can do it next time." But a woman can tell you that "You have four hours and I'm paying you for four hours and you have to do the job for four hours." You see what I mean? But the job is not even possible to do in four hours, it's more than four hours you are supposed to work for, you know. (Tony, domestic worker, Berlin)

As Tony indicates here, the relationship to her employer is clearly discerned within employment parameters. Her employer addresses her as "a worker," scrutinizing her tasks and the time spent on them. Men, Tony notes, are more laid-back. Of course, the designation of the household as women's terrain, a previously discussed aspect, is newly stressed. Men, in general, do not compete for the control of the household; they usually relegate this control to the feminized subjects in the households. The domestic worker is exposed to these gender dynamics. The frustration and the lack of balance of household work are addressed by, one, employing her, and, two, by projecting onto her the accumulated energies of frustration and control. As a reminder of what is not working in the household, the domestic worker is made individually responsible for the mess, an attitude that is further channeled through the commodified character of her work. Buying the labor force of the domestic worker not only entitles the household to relinquish their social relations concealed in domestic work to her, but also to restore the hegemonic gender order. On the other hand, the domestic worker's presence signifies the devaluation inherent in domestic work as feminized, racialized labor. Paradoxically, whilst the employment of a domestic worker enables the female employer to get closer to the promise of gender equality, the need to employ another woman to do this work speaks to the failure of this promise.

The employment of another woman does not put an end to the social devaluation of domestic work. On the contrary, it extends and deepens the social degradation inherent in it by redesigning the line between appropriation and exploitation. This contradiction is absorbed by the employers by incorporating it in a rational script, simulating recognition of the conflict but at the same time negating it. As Bourdieu asserts, "symbolic power is a power which presupposes recognition, that is, misrecognition of the violence that is exercised through it."[29] A cosmetic separation between delegating and doing domestic work is established, alluring to the female employers because it marks the end of their "feminine condition"[30] while other women seem to be condemned to it. Nonetheless, the violence exerted through symbolic organization of power in the households impacts on people's bodies and minds. It circulates in the household, leaving its imprints on things and conditioning the energies in the space. Through this circulation of attitudes and feelings, energies are mobilized, conditioning the quality ascribed to domestic work. This is an aspect that Bourdieu's perspective on "symbolic power" is unable to capture as the focus lies on cognitive maps, not on what happens when they circulate and impact on people's feelings. This is an aspect that I will discuss in the next chapter in regard to affect. Further, Bourdieu is interested in practices of domination, focusing explicitly on the dominant subject, but the feelings of the subjects experiencing this violence are not present in his analysis. However, the question of how people cope with injuries and wounds caused by physical and symbolic violence is necessary in the analysis of domination.

EFFECTS OF DOMINATION

Though most of the domestic workers have educational qualifications, in some cases a university degree, and worked as professionals before coming to Europe, once they arrive in Europe all their educational and professional achievements are reduced to zero. Their education, skills and professional experiences are considered insufficient to pursue their careers and educational projects in Europe. Further, their lack of a residency permit restricts their access to the labor market. One of the few areas to which they have access is the private household. Here, they find employment as cleaners, domestic workers and carers. As Eleonore Kofman notes in the global and transnational migration literature, migrant women are frequently represented as "unskilled workers."[31] While in fact this is an effect of the international gendered and racialized division of work, the notion of "unskilled labor" is a complex one. Marga from Ecuador, who works in different households in Hamburg, told us what it meant for her to experience deskilling:

> For me to do the work here in Germany, well, it didn't matter to me, because no one knows me, no one knew what I had done in Ecuador. And, therefore, for my spirit, for my spirit within, so for my spirit it was quite depressing. I felt quite sad because I thought that this is a waste of my university degree from Ecuador. And I came here to another country to clean other people's dirt. But above all, I felt completely humiliated as I had to clean other people's toilets. That made me completely crazy, but okay, I had to do it. The money must come from somewhere.
> (Marga, domestic worker, Hamburg)

Marga's experience of devaluation is connected to her feelings of "depression" and sadness. "Cleaning the toilet" epitomizes the symbolic, but also factual, violence Marga faces as an "undocumented migrant." This violence affects her well-being and leaves her feeling humiliated. It is not the unpleasant task of cleaning someone else's toilet that causes her detriment as such, but its symbolic degradation for someone with a university degree. "Cleaning the toilet" represents the social misrecognition of feminized labor, and the reactualization of the coloniality of labor signified by the social position of the "undocumented migrant." As the "Other" of Europe, the lack of recognized educational and professional qualifications are stamped on her body and soul. She is reduced to the projections of the hegemonic society, seeing in her a "social parasite," an "invader" and a hindrance to "social cohesion." Thus, as she cannot convert her university degree into an asset, she must resort to domestic work. This is the field in which she is, though not officially, allowed to apply her "skills" in cleaning "people's dirt." It is this subtext that informs the social misrecognition of her labor. Consequently, her labor is classified as "unskilled" and doomed to be unwaged or low-paid labor. This makes her "depressed."

The social devaluation of domestic work is impressed on Marga's body as the feelings surrounding her everyday routines in the household affectively transmit "inferiority," expressing a process of subalternization, in which the domestic worker is forced corporeally to inhabit the devalued space of racialized, feminized labor. The symbolic attribution of "inferiority," but also her actual devaluation and misrecognition of her skills, is thus felt bodily, affecting her sense of personhood, but also driving her to act against humiliation. The process of deskilling is affective for Marga not only because it deauthorizes subjects in terms of their personal skills and abilities, but also because it evolves within the logic of the coloniality of power. The process of deskilling coalesces here with an institutional and social classification system, departing from the notion of "privileged" and "subordinated" zones. For Quijano, this logic primarily surfaces in the "intersubjective relations of domination between Europe and the

Europeans and the rest of the regions and peoples of the world, to whom new geo-cultural identities were attributed."[32] In this process it was not just minerals, resources, land and the labor force that were exploited and expropriated. "[C]olonized forms of knowledge production, models of the production of meaning, and models of expression and objectification and subjectivity" were also forged.[33]

Within the logic of migration policies, as we have discussed in Chapter 3 of this volume, this logic is reactualized and circumvented in the division between "national citizens" and the "nation's Other," categorized through a series of terms like "ethnic minorities," "migrants," "asylum seekers" and "refugees." These different terms assert the position of the "outsider" to the nation, the one whose presence needs to be explained and legitimized, the one whose knowledge, beliefs, convictions and cultural practices are suspect, carefully scrutinized and thoroughly screened through different technologies of control and surveillance or appeals to integration. As Santiago Castro-Gómez and Ramón Grosfoguel note, this logic attends "to a transition of modern colonialism to a global coloniality, a process that certainly has shaped the forms of domination displayed in modernity but which has not transformed the structures related to the center periphery relationship on a global scale,"[34] articulated in the local face of feminized, racialized labor in Europe. In the figure of the Latin American "undocumented migrant" domestic worker, the intersection between old and new forms of gendering and racialization are newly assembled, articulating old patterns of gendered racialization in the disguise of affective value production in advanced capitalism. In order to counter this logic we need to engage with a theoretical framework that takes into account, on the one hand, the effects of migration and border regimes and, on the other, the strategies of subjects to cope and resist them. Such a theoretical proposal is offered by Gloria Anzaldúa's border epistemology. I would like to conclude this chapter by discussing the strategies of my research participants within this framework.

CONCLUSION: RESISTING DEHUMANIZATION

Though Gloria Anzaldúa's analysis of *borderlands* is based on the specific history of today's border region between the United States and Mexico, its epistemological implications are useful for understanding the colonial subtext and the mechanisms of exclusion inserted in EU migration and border regimes. In her proposal of *borderlands*, Anzaldúa underlines the epistemic condition that arises out of experiences of exclusion and dehumanization.[35] Though *borderlands* emphasizes the repressive and oppressive character of border regimes, the United States' imperial power and the coloniality of power, Anzaldúa is particularly interested in the strategies of resistance created through living and juggling with the border's constraints.

Through these practices rigid boundaries, unshakable norms and cemented ideological barriers can be destabilized and new ways of understanding ourselves, the world and the cosmos emerge. An "in-between space" surfaces, "Nepantla," a "liminal state between worlds, between realities, between systems of knowledge."[36] "Nepantla" is the space inhabited by the subject at the borderlands, a subject that Anzaldúa metaphorically conceives of as the "borderwoman"—the *mestiza* who embodies *mestiza consciousness*. *Mestiza consciousness* embraces the ambivalences created at the crossroads of simultaneous systems of domination, in which divided but entangled belongings and the ambiguous position of insider–outsider are configured. It is this state of consciousness that Anzaldúa defines as the epistemic condition of the borderlands. This consciousness is caught in the paradox of the border as the site of rigid boundaries and the trespassing of them at the same time. In juggling with this situation, *la facultad*, an "extra sense,"[37] emanating out of the experience of social and individual suffering is developed. *La facultad* is the experience of being caught "between worlds" and finding creative and pragmatic ways to survive it. *La facultad*, as Anzaldúa asserts, is a way of finding the energies, forces and spirit to fight back against the oppressive mechanisms of exclusion and subjugation. As she notes, it is a way to be "healthy," "to awaken a sense of who you are and keep it strong and assert that you're OK, that you're not sick, that society—religion, political systems, morality, the movies, the media, the newspapers—that they're all wrong and that you're right. It takes tremendous energy, courage, and perseverance to keep that awareness awake."[38] While Anzaldúa relates this faculty to the people that "can't be straight," to the *mestiza*, the queer of color, the poor, the disabled, the persecuted, I would like to adopt this analysis in regard to the Latin American "undocumented migrant" domestic workers in Europe.

Translated in the context of late capitalism and EU migration regimes, the analysis of *borderlands* might give us some insights into the contradictory and ambiguous forces emanating from the effects of dispossession and persecution, on the one hand, and escape and transgression on the other. Entrenched in the divisions between "citizens" and "migrants," an old system of colonial classification of the population, reminding us of Quijano's coloniality of power, is revived. This results not only in a restriction or negation of citizenship rights, but also in the stripping away of "objectified intellectual knowledge"[39] of those neither considered nor recognized as citizens of Europe. Further, in the case of "undocumented migrants," the right of settlement is in constant denial, with the threat of detainment or deportation being a daily possibility. Latin American "undocumented migrant" women find themselves in these living conditions, trying to maintain their migration project and fighting against the abuses tied to this dehumanizing situation. In this regard, we could identify these women as struggling with migration and border regimes, forging a new consciousness through which they define their strategies of coping with and resisting the constant devaluation of themselves and their labor. While the domestic workers are constantly confronted with acts undermining their personal integrity and dignity, they refuse to internalize these feelings, although as affects they impact on them. As the extracts from the domestic workers show, they resist the attempts of subordination by not letting themselves conform to the expectations of their employer, but also by developing a "faculty" to emotionally distance themselves and analyze the power relations they encounter in the households. As such they learn to juggle between the demands of the households and their own goals, following their aims of educating themselves, sustaining their families and living their lives in a "global migration space."[40] In this transnational space of transcultural conviviality, economic, communicative and mental transatlantic networks are built, emanating from the strategies of survival and suffering, but also from the creativity to handle them.[41] Social networks are formed, undermining in some instances the restriction imposed by migration and asylum policies, as I will discuss in Chapter 7 of this volume.

The focus on Anzaldúa's *facultad* and these networks and practices demonstrate that subjects targeted by both the policies and habitus of oppression and dehumanization do not just succumb to them, but find ways to resist and counter them. This is an aspect that we do not perceive if we reduce our analysis to the dominant instances of power. It is in this regard that the limits of Bourdieu's model of "symbolic power" and "symbolic violence" are revealed. While this model offers a theoretical framework for analyzing the relationship between the symbolic and the economic, or culture and society, it remains on the cognitive level of practices, giving very little space to what is not inscribed in the discursive fabric. Thus, it does not give credence to affective dynamics and agency. Hence, in order to understand how practices become sensed and embodied, we need to engage with affects, as I will discuss in the next chapter.

6   Affective Value
Ontologies of Exploitation

A commodity is therefore a mysterious thing, simply because in it
the social character of men's labour appears to them as an objective character stamped upon the product of that labour; because the
relation of the producers to the sum total of their own labour is presented to them as a social relation, existing not between themselves,
but between the products of their labour. This is the reason why the
products of labour become commodities, social things whose qualities are at the same time perceptible and imperceptible by the senses.
In the same ways the light from an object is perceived by us not as the
subjective excitation of our optic nerve, but as the objective form of
something outside the eye itself. But, in the act of seeing, there is at
all events, an actual passage of light from one thing to another, from
the external object to the eye. (Marx, *Capital*, 43)[1]

As Marx notes here, a commodity is a "mysterious thing." While it seems
to have an "objective character," detached from its producers and emanating out of its relationship to other commodities, it is conditioned by the
perceptions of its producers. The social quality of a commodity, thus, is on
the one side "perceptible" and, on the other, "imperceptible by the senses"
if we disregard the affective relationships from which this product emerges.
When the question of how products are also related to our "subjective"
side, to our "senses," to the circulation of affects, is disregarded, we cease to
understand the cultural and social fabric of capital production. For Marx,
production is linked to our "senses" and cannot be reduced merely to a
thing, "the commodity." Behind the commodity is hidden not only its productive force and labor time, but also its *living labor*. This latter is intrinsically connected to the productive and creative character of workers, to their
senses and affects. Further, the perception of a commodity as something
useful or value generating is not merely a social outcome. It also results
from the object's potential to affect and to be affective, emerging from or
resulting in a "subjective excitation" of its producers and consumers. It is
through this sensation that the relationship between commodity and pro-
ducer/consumer is forged. Through "subjective excitation," the relationship
between producer/consumer and commodity becomes affective. What lies
behind the commodity is not only a complex web of social relations or a
cultural script of codification of value. Rather, there are a range of sensual
experiences related to the labor force and its ability to feel.

Translating this observation to the relationship between domestic work and value, we come back to the biopolitical quality of this labor, discussed in Chapter 4 of this volume. As we have seen, the analysis of domestic work in private households demonstrates that this labor is not just a primary reference for physical reproduction; rather, it is through it that social relations are culturally negotiated. Further, domestic work, as I will elaborate on in this chapter, is infused with the expression and circulation of affects in the households. Domestic work holds the emotions and feelings of its labor force, connecting them to other energies and sensations in the household. Domestic work, thus, reveals the affective dimension of labor by connecting its value production to the circulation of feelings and emotions. Through affects notions of value, translated into gestures of "superiority" and "inferiority" in the households, are expressed by women's bodies and impressed on other women's bodies, leaving a corporeal sense of devaluation or estimation. This is an aspect that, while addressed in the previous chapter through Bourdieu's notion of "symbolic violence," has not yet been looked at in detail. In this chapter I will attend to the sensorial corporeality of the devaluation of domestic work. What makes the social misrecognition of domestic work effective and normative, I will argue here, is not the character of its labor-power *per se*, but its quality as affective labor. Paradoxically, while this labor is perceived as nonproductive, it creates value attached to its affective potential, affective value. Drawing from this perspective, I will argue that while feminist researchers have insisted on the prevalence of domestic work as a site of social reproduction, a focus on affect and affection reveals the corporeal and sensual dimensions of apparently "emaciated and emotionally spare categories" like labor and value. In the interpersonal relations between domestic workers and their employers, these categories become "animated and animating," releasing the "performative and interpellating potential"[2] that I will look at here in regard to affective labor and affective value. Thus, the value produced, exchanged and accumulated in domestic work is not just an articulation of the "bodily intensity of performing surplus labour," it is the expression of "the affective intensity associated with exploitation."[3] However, before I look more deeply at this question let me clarify what I mean by affect.

EMOTIONS, FEELINGS AND AFFECT

And above all, to clean this apartment for someone who is almost never there. So, therefore, this apartment was simply lifeless or unlived in and that often made me mad. This—this huge apartment just for one person. Therefore, I mean, four rooms for one person, who is there maybe for two or three hours in the day, if at all. And that is simply, therefore, such, such lavishness. This often means, obviously, it means that above a certain monthly income, there is nothing more left or the

> path is lost. And others live with three persons in two rooms, that's it.
> (Elena, domestic worker, Hamburg)

In comparison to her employer, Elena lives with four others in a small two-room apartment. The "lifeless" atmosphere in her employer's apartment makes her "mad," she says. She poses the question of how to deal with the constant experience of inequality, how to digest it emotionally and bodily if it has no rationale. This unlived in "huge apartment" makes no sense to Elena. She responds to this irrationality by feeling angry. Her statement, "above a certain monthly income, there is nothing left or the path is lost," seems to convert the inexplicable into some kind of moral sense. Feelings and mind are summoned to find a response to the fundamental inequality that sustains the content and context of Elena's domestic work. The energies released in the apartment, described by Elena as "lifeless," have an impact on her. They are affective and they affect her. Elena's extract speaks to the absurdity of an everyday life organized within empty spaces. Nonetheless, while the apartment seems absent of "everyday life," life is infused into this space through Elena's presence and attention.

As Cristina Vega Solís affirms in her study on Latin American care workers in Catalonia, "attention" or "being attentive" are specific skills that unfold in the orientation towards another person.[4] She notes:

> To be attentive is to orient oneself towards the other and this implies a communicative activity in which emerges a position from which to speak and to affect. To notice, to approach, to understand, to balance, to anticipate, to contextualize, to support, are ingredients of the relational work of attention to people.[5]

For Vega Solís, "being attentive" is a perceptive disposition that emanates out of the intensity of information flows as well as an ethical disposition, based on affect.[6] Thus, the person who is cared for is not just an object of care. She or he is a person, vulnerable and receptive to the emotions of others. To be attentive to somebody means the recognition of the other person as a complex subject. It also implies the recognition of the difference between one's perceptions and the other's feelings. Thus, as well as entering the world of the other, the disposition of "being attentive" is linked to giving support and reinforcing security. "Attention" addresses the recognition and well-being of the other.[7] It is in this sense that Vega Solís understands "being attentive" as an affective force. As such "being attentive" is related to the transfer of information, but also emotions. The impact of "attention" on somebody leaves an imprint, a trace. However, the skill of attention, as for other transmissions of affect, is absent when we list the physical work made visible in the cleaning of the household.

While Elena's attention does not directly address a person, as her employer is absent, she is attentive towards the latter's environment. The objects she cleans and arranges are infused with her employer's energies. These energies are affective and affect her. They leave imprints on her body and mind. It is in this transmission of affect that social and economic inequalities are sensed bodily and perceived as sensation. In this case, Elena relates the lavish waste of space to madness when she says that above a certain income there is nothing more left or the path is lost. This madness impacts on her feelings, leaving her "mad" in regard to the inequalities she needs to face daily. Daily encounters are infused with emotions. However, whereas affects are driven by emotions, it is worthwhile distinguishing between feelings, emotions and affects.

As the Latin word *affectus* suggests, *affect* addresses the impact a feeling or emotion leaves on a person's body or mind. It is a pre-personal intensity, a relational moment, emerging out of the contact with others. While also attached to an interaction and transaction, the focus of emotions and feelings is on individuals' bodily reactions rather than on the relationship in which a sensation is created.[8] Relating to debates on emotions in occidental philosophy that depart from the mind–body split,[9] the focus on emotion tends to erase the relational aspect between body and mind when it comes to the senses. Going beyond this mind–body split, Baruch Spinoza suggests departing from affect.[10] He differentiates between three life drives: joy, sadness and desire.[11] For Spinoza, these drives are moved by the "power to think" and the "body's power to act"[12]; passion is thus channeled by action. For him a mutual relation between mind and body presupposes the dynamic of affects as the mind is moved by the body and the body is moved by the mind.

Thus, as Brian Massumi notes, affects bear the "ability to affect and be affected."[13] In this regard, he differentiates between "affects" and "affection." For Massumi, "the passage from one experiential state of the body to another [. . .] implying an augmentation or diminution in that body's capacity to act," denotes the moment of affect, while affection represents an encounter between the "affected body" and the "affecting body."[14] Affection denotes the relational character of affects. Affects do not exist as sealed entities, they are energies and flows, impacting on people's bodies and shaping people's actions. Our power to affect or be affected increases or diminishes in regard to our affective life forces motivating our thinking and actions. As Teresa Brennan puts it, affects:

> enhance when they are projected outward, when one is relieved of them . . . affects deplete when they are introjected, when one carries the affective burden of another, either by a straightforward transfer or because the other's anger becomes your depression. But the other's feelings can enhance: affection does this, hence the expression of warmth. Simply you become energized when you are with some loves or some friends. With others you are bored or drained, tired or depressed. (Brennan, *The Transmission of Affect*, 6)

Affect emerges when it is transmitted to or oriented towards others. Though affect might seem detached from any societal context, it holds reactions and memories[15] emerging from the encounter with others, leaving an "impression,"[16] an imprint or trace on our bodies. As we have seen in the case of Elena, the energy she encounters in her employer's apartment impacts on her, it leaves the sensation of "madness," while her activity of arranging the space is infusing this "lifeless" apartment with vitality. Both moments of "madness" and "vitality" circulate as affects in this apartment, transmitting feelings, emotions, desires and yearning. Elena's labor in the household is thus infused by these affects, determining her reaction to the household and her own feelings towards herself and her environment. Thus, through the transmission of affect, as Spinoza argues, our ability to create is enhanced or diminished, promoted or hindered, depending on the feelings that are evoked and transmitted.[17] Bodies can be moved or kept in stillness through affection, thereby altering our bodies. Accordingly, the stillness or movement of a body depends on the other body's stillness or movement. It is the dynamic of movement and rest that ensures that affects are in constant motion. They are "becomings."[18] In this relationality an individual is composed, decomposed or modified through the intensities of affects, projected externally or internally, "augmenting or diminishing [her/his] power to act."[19] Affect is therefore to be understood as the extension of bodies.[20]

All human beings are governed by affects—they are excited by the "power to affect the world around us and our power to be affected by it."[21] Hence, while affects might express the immediacy of internal sensations, these sensations are produced within a specific historical, geographical and political context. Affect is sensation as it is context at the same time. Thus, the body has its own experience of sensation and intensity that is not always reflected in language as it "doesn't just absorb pulses or discrete stimulations; it unfolds contexts."[22] Considering these observations, affect and affection are driven and expressed through sensations embedded in a societal context. The exchange of affects, hence, operates in the matrix of social inequalities. Feelings are not accidentally addressed to a random person. The address occurs within a historical and geopolitical context of global and local power dynamics. As such affect is not just an individually interiorized sensation but the sensorial incorporation of the social. It binds the singularity of feelings with its socioemotional corporeality, shaped in particular by relations of labor, as I will discuss in the following in regard to affective labor.

AFFECTIVE LABOR—A RELATIONALITY OF THE MOMENT

> But these things to unpack them all and clean them—that was it for me. For me it was actually closeness to a person who I actually do not

know and who can actually do it himself. And I couldn't understand how somebody—so close, yeah, allows someone to come, without knowing the person and without actually needing it. I find that totally *absurd*, that is this activity that is part of it. (Elena, domestic worker, Hamburg)

Continuing her account, Elena discloses how cleaning the apartment produces a feeling of "closeness," although her relationship to her employer is marked by absence, by distance. "Closeness" is a sensation arising from her activities, unpacking and cleaning things that are intimate personal possessions. A relationship is established without a personal encounter. The cleaning of the apartment is not directly linked to the taking care of a person as this person is largely absent. Why is she cleaning this apartment if no one inhabits it? This is a question that Elena raises as there is no evident need for her services. Employing a domestic worker or a cleaner could indicate more than just the need for support to arrange the household. Nor is it just an attempt to mark social distinction. Maybe it is the activity of infusing the household with vitality, touching personal things and rearranging them, that is in demand here. Elena's cleaning and arranging infuses the household with vitality, the negligence and solitude embedded in this apartment due to its emptiness is removed through Elena's activities. Elena's labor is determined through the affects produced in and through the relations in this space. She herself is involved in this relationality and transforms it through her activities. The touching of objects, the arranging of the space, inevitably leave the presence of another person, connecting the household with another social space brought in by the domestic worker.

Although largely ignored by the employer, Elena's presence contributes to the recreation of the apartment as a space of potential conviviality. Interestingly, this is not perceived as such by the employer. Instead the employer detaches the affective and sensual forces from a person, objectifying and reducing her domestic work to the mere realization of physical tasks. However, when a domestic worker enters a household, she immediately becomes part of a network of energetic and affective relations. Her presence bears social suffering as well as individual yearnings, hopes and joy. She enters the space of the private household and encounters the affective traces of the people inhabiting it. She works through these energies, expressed sometimes in emotions, when she sees, for example, her employer crying silently in the kitchen, or when she encounters feelings of insecurity or ignorance.

It is this dimension of affective labor that interests us here; this should not be conflated with the more cognitive approach to emotional labor in private households. Feminist literature has focused on women's specific abilities (as discussed in Chapter 4 of this volume) emanating from female socialization, such as "caring for others," empathy and friendliness, as characteristics of emotional labor; affective labor is not to be confused with emotional labor. As previously discussed, feminist work on emotional labor has highlighted care work. Emotions are perceived here in regard to the intention of the subject to be empathetic and attentive to others. Faculties are deployed in orientation to the well-being of somebody else. However, affects have a less rational and cognitive side to them. They emerge in the coming together of bodily reactions and transmission of feelings, leaving an imprint on a subject's body or environment and at the same time reflecting these sensations to other bodies. Though affects shape our thinking and drive us to act, their expression is not always intentional and clearly goal driven. Rather, they are spontaneous corporeal reactions to our environment and encounters. As Massumi notes, affect is a pre-personal intensity and affection a relational moment, through which the capacity to act is decreased or increased through the encounters between bodies, affected and/or affecting each other. Nonetheless, as they are expressions of our affective quality as human beings, they channel our lives. Affects in this regard play a significant role in the production process.

This has led some post-Marxist scholars to identify affective labor as one of the axes of production in the knowledge, media, information and creative industries.[23] Besides integrating creative, cognitive and communicative skills, the labor-power realized in "technological processes of cybernetics and communication, as well as the investment of immaterial and scientific labour,"[24] also demands affective skills. In particular, Michael Hardt has insisted on the affective dimension of productive labor, indicating the "immaterial" character of this labor as its products cannot be easily measured in quantitative terms.[25] Well-being, comfort and warmth, on the one hand, and anxiety, fear and disgust on the other, are feelings that cannot be materially conceived. Nonetheless, their circulation shapes the ways in which we work, our productive energies and the context of our labor.

On the other hand, affects are not free-floating energies. They emerge in a space delimited by a concrete historical and geopolitical context, structured by inequalities. Our affects act and react in this context, bearing traces of the materiality that they transcend through their energy, but in which they remain embedded through their context of emergence. The expression and transmission of affects, thus, occur in a space marked by historically produced, socially configured and culturally located power relations. The affective potential of feelings transpire in spaces, tied to histories of oppression, haunted by memories of feelings of subjugation and exclusion, invoked and repeated in moments of encounters and disencounters. Happiness and disgust, for example, can be differently addressed and received in regard to the social status of their agents. Further, as Sianne Ngai notes, these feelings are desires depleting different corporeal and emotional reactions to an object.[26] They stand in a certain asymmetry to each other. While "happiness" has an animating affect, "disgust" is, for Ngai, "the ugliest of the 'ugly feelings'"[27]; its effect attempts to deanimate its object of projection, to dehumanize it. Referring to Nietzsche's *Genealogy of Morals* and his distinction between the "happy and self-secure 'noble man'" and the morality of the slave, marked by contempt coupled with a simulated tolerance for the abhorrent or dislikable, Ngai stresses the historical legacies embedded in the consistency and effectiveness of affects.[28] In the private household this relationship is less configured by "the noble man" and "the slave" than by the asymmetry between officially recognized citizens and disregarded or negated other citizens ("undocumented migrants"). However, this is only one part of the story because, as feminized subjects, both women, "citizen" and "noncitizen," are objects of the social revulsion projected onto domestic work. Both women need to deal with the repugnance socially attributed to this labor. Nonetheless, the employment of another woman to do the work releases the female employers from negative affect so they have the opportunity to feel happy within their own four walls.

Between Well-being and Happiness

Social boundaries are expressed in the transmission of affect. Karin, a manager living in Hamburg with her husband and two children, tells us how her need to relax is attached to the possibility of delegating household work:

> There is simply a point in time when one asks oneself do I still feel like cleaning the toilet on a Sunday evening at around eleven and to make the bed, which I *can* naturally do but I don't feel like it anymore and I gave it up.

Karin relates to domestic work as something that she doesn't "feel like anymore" and therefore, she "gave it up." Her negative feelings for household work are taken care of by a domestic worker that she has employed. This enables her to detach herself from her responsibilities, reiterated in the gendered division of work that persists in her household. Though she describes the approach of her household to domestic work as an egalitarian one she still needs to organize it. In the course of the conversation, however, she reveals that the feelings attached to domestic work "stick"[29] to her. Ultimately, she removes herself from the interpellation of "housewife" by employing another woman, which simultaneously enables her to pursue her vision of an egalitarian household. As she says:

> Each one must decide for himself how he places the balance. And what I find very important is that *domestic* work, whether it is work done by housewives or *domestic* work done by professional women is completely irrelevant or whether by domestic workers, I say all the time—in inverted commas—it is irrelevant. Because it is very important work that must be done, so, there—we decided at some point in time because

[*takes a deep breath*] it is important sometimes for one's *own* battery to say, okay, I drink a cup of tea for a half an hour and don't do these things. (Karin, employer, Hamburg)

Karin presents us with a solution in which "each one must decide for himself how he places the balance." The use of the masculine pronoun is not insignificant. Though she uses the masculine pronoun as a way to generalize the choices that each of the household members can make, factually those making these choices are the male members in the household. She also makes domestic work the preserve of women when she lists housewives, professional women and domestic workers as those doing this work. Interestingly, although Karin does not mention directly that she has employed a domestic worker so that she can "drink a cup of tea for a half an hour," the new quality of her time with the possibility of drinking a cup of tea is connected to this fact. In Karin's extract we encounter one of the reasons why professional households opt for employing a domestic worker. The reason is mentioned straightaway as being "for one's *own* battery." The "things"—"cleaning," "making the bed" or "domestic work"—become tasks that are postponed until late at night or the weekend. Karin's argument that she cannot do this work as she needs to recharge her batteries is understandable. While doing these tasks might be subsumed under the reproductive character of domestic work, it implies more than this. The domestic worker doing this work is immediately connected to Karin's well-being, to her affective (re)production and concretely, to her ability to relax. Other employers expressed these feelings of well-being and relaxation by emphasizing "happiness." For example, Antonia, a teacher who lives with her daughter in Vienna, refers to her domestic worker in flowery terms:

> Our fairy, she simply helps us—we both sense it quite strongly. This just makes us happy. She is like our fairy. I say it too. She is a fairy [*laughs*]—a real miracle. She lives and flourishes! And she works like one too. (Antonia, employer, Vienna)[30]

Antonia emphatically talks about her domestic worker as "our fairy." She is the person who gives "happiness," a "miracle" who brings vitality into the household, at the same time that she is a hard worker. Emphasizing her domestic worker's personal and working qualities, Antonia and her daughter both "sense strongly" her presence in the household. She brings "happiness" to the household, she "lives" and "flourishes."

Both Antonia's and Karin's accounts engage with the affective quality of time and life gained through the employment of a domestic worker. The management of work and leisure time is a constant topic in the interviews with the employers. This topic reemerges because the sphere of domestic work echoes with memories that some of the female employers would like to forget. For example, Stefanie, a teacher who lives with her two children in Linz, told the Austrian team about her experience of staying at home to take care of her children:

> I would get sick of the sight of these four walls. I mean, I stayed at home for four and a half years. I was basically the cleaning woman, the nursemaid. Ultimately, I am happy, that I have a job outside of the home, where I am not confronted with household or children—my own children. I still work with children and I have gained a certain distance. (Stefanie, employer, Linz)[31]

Stefanie states that she would get "sick" if she became a stay-at-home mother. She connects happiness with the ability to be a professional woman. It might be this sense of time and personal autonomy that the employers recuperate when they employ another woman to do the work of cleaning or caring. The unhappiness described here by Stefanie is thus displaced onto another woman's body, leaving Stefanie with a sense of happiness. Happiness enunciates the fulfillment of desires. It is connected to an affirmation of one's needs and wishes. In contrast, for the domestic workers personal autonomy and happiness are slightly differently connoted. They describe moments of happiness when they walk through the streets of Berlin, Madrid, Vienna or Leeds, when they navigate through the city unnoticed by the police, enjoying the sun and their glimpses of freedom from servitude.

Between Happiness and Servitude

In the interviews with the domestic workers, time is linked to their experiences of commodified labor. In all four countries the domestic workers usually work in "patchwork" arrangements.[32] This often means working in numerous households through the course of one day, as Myriam, an Ecuadorian domestic worker in Hamburg, told us:

> If you really want to survive, you don't only, you don't only have to work for one, you can work in three households in one day. You start from eight, maybe there are three hours for one house at nine, ten, eleven, you finish, and you have to rush to another. (Myriam, domestic worker, Hamburg)

Flexible time management is one of the skills reported by the domestic workers. Carmela, a Peruvian domestic worker in Madrid, stated:

> My entire morning until twelve noon is spent being stressed and looking at the clock, looking at the clock. Time. Time passes so quickly. You don't realise at all and eh there's no time to eat anything! (Carmela, domestic worker, Madrid)[33]

The pressure of time and the pace at which the work needs to be done produces the feeling of "stress" in the domestic workers. Though they skillfully navigate time through the city, combining different jobs and locations, little time is left for their own recreation. No time for a "cup of tea," not even time for a meal, as Carmela tells us, is left. The feeling of well-being or relaxation, of gaining time through delegation of domestic work to another person that the employers reported, is almost nonexistent in the domestic workers' accounts. This does not mean that the domestic workers do not experience instances of well-being and happiness. For example, Julieta, from Ecuador, told me how living in Berlin "cheers" her up:

> I like Berlin a lot. I didn't know that it was so pretty.
> You can walk around with a Cherokee and the people say ah! Great, you can walk around with a hole in your clothes and no one notices it. It has its disadvantages, but I like it a lot, because you are free as long as they [the police] do not notice you. I very often ride around with my bike, it cheers me up. I love it. You can meet at one corner a Turkish person, on the other a Swiss, in front of you somebody else from a different country—I like it a lot. (Julieta, domestic worker, Berlin)

Julieta's account tells us about how the vibrancy of Berlin infuses her with positive energy. She loves the city and she tells us about her different everyday encounters. She feels "free" as long the police do not notice her. Traveling through Berlin gives her a sense of personal autonomy, of being part of a vibrant cosmopolitan and unconventional space. Other research participants report similar stories about Berlin. Isabel from Peru, for example, told me:

> I didn't know that Berlin was so green and had so much water, because I only knew Berlin from Holocaust movies, which always were placed in winter, grey, trees without leaves, when I arrived, what a surprise! (Isabel, domestic worker, Berlin)

Pleasantly surprised by the beauty of the city, Isabel enjoys living in Berlin. Like the other research participants, she also needs to hide from the police. Nonetheless, she enjoys everyday glimpses of freedom. Happiness is thus signified by the intensity of life, as Bibiana (from Chile and working in Leeds) puts it, "I live all my days intensively." Moments of happiness and well-being are experienced, although they may dissipate when domestic workers need to run from the risk of detention or from one household to the other, or when they are overwhelmed by worries about their children or families. It is outside the workplace where positive sensations resurge; the household being worked in itself bears feelings of exhaustion and exploitation.

There is no end to household work for the domestic workers, as they repeatedly state, because they often continue the day cleaning in their own homes. Feminist migration research has foregrounded changes in gender relations in migrant households, as very often women take the role of the sole breadwinner.[34] In the case of the domestic workers in our research, similar household patterns were revealed. In general, migration is undertaken individually due to the restrictions on family reunification imposed by migration policies, but also because "undocumented migrants" cannot undertake the migration journey as a family. All the women we interviewed migrated alone. While some of them arranged for the migration of one child, very few could afford legally and financially to have all their children and family members with them.[35] This goal is pursued on the basis that the migration project is conceived as being for a limited time in order to provide financial support for the extended family or to supply a financial base for the establishment of a small business. During this time family ties are transnationally organized through phone calls, letters and visits, but also new partnerships are forged, resulting, in some cases, in patchwork families with children of each partner and new children held in common. Nonetheless, in these various household arrangements, the domestic work journey continues for the majority of domestic workers in their own households. Paula, a Chilean and mother of two working in Hamburg, sums it up as follows, "I always say I have been a paid servant and I am a servant at home."

The condition of "servitude" leaves affective traces on domestic workers' bodies. It is the sensation of "servility" that is constantly projected towards them, even though this is not always explicitly expressed; it leaves an impression on their bodies. It does this through the symbolic and actual violence they experience in their everyday lives. The affective transmission of this violence is manifested through the household tasks assigned to them and the living conditions that they are exposed to as "undocumented migrants." "Servility" is affectively addressed and impressed on these women's bodies through a variety of feelings, expressed on occasion by the projection of disgust and contempt onto them.

Between Disgust and Contempt

> The worst for me, we could say are the toilets! So, you, you see people who are really spick-and-span, but you can forget it. Really! I therefore wear gloves everywhere. You know rubber gloves?! [...] Because I don't know?! It could be, they are people who may be superclean, but to the outside world! But you, you know the people in the kitchen and in the toilets! So, really! Brushes are available everywhere! Thank God we drink only tea now! [*smiles*] Brushes, these toilet brushes are available everywhere! At least, what can you do? What you can do is make it a little bit cleaner. But it is sprayed all over! Pee all over! The men cannot pee properly at all! (Carmen, domestic worker, Hamburg)

"Cleaning the toilet" is linked to feelings of disgust and being despised. It is a task that within a professional scale denotes the bottom of the social ladder. At the same time, the toilet is the ultimate sphere of privacy. The domestic worker in charge of cleaning the toilet is confronted with both sides. On the one hand, she is obliged to clean the "pee" and, on the other, she gets to know a new, less agreeable side of her employers. Leaving the toilet dirty, ignoring the brushes, transmits an explicit message that affectively expresses contempt. Contempt for William Miller transmits the message to an object or subject of being "not noticeworthy."[36] Thus, the subjects addressing this feeling to somebody else might "condescend" to treat this person "decently," to even feel "pity" for them, but it is through this attitude that the person treated this way remains "invisible or utterly and safely disattendable."[37] As such, the object of contempt is addressed as "inferior" by dismissing and ignoring it.

Not cleaning the toilet, nonuse of the brushes, demonstrates the maybe "unintentional" but actual lack of care and respect of the employer towards his/her domestic worker. It expresses ignorance of the domestic worker's labor, feelings and values. Through contempt Carmen is made "invisible" in the household, and as such her presence is "tolerated" as it does not disturb the household's routines. Rather, she enables the flow of the expected "normality." Paradoxically, while her presence is denied, she shares the most intimate moments of the household's members, an intimacy that she has not chosen but that she needs to face. Thus, she is affected by the energies involuntarily, and in some cases intentionally, transmitted by her employers. This dismissal affects her and she reacts to this with repulsion and disgust. The transmission of disgust has two sides, as is the case with other affects. It can affect others and it is affected by others. In the household the transmission of contempt is received by the domestic workers as an expression of disgust. At the same time, while not explicitly intended, the contempt demonstrated turns to disgust when repulsion becomes evident. In comparison to contempt, disgust is a strong feeling, one that Ngai suggests is "a structured and agonistic emotion carrying a strong and unmistakable signal."[38] Disgust, for Ngai, is not ambivalent about its objects. The behavior of Carmen's employer in the toilet, while it is embedded in contempt, has a clear signal and message. This message is received by Carmen as disgust.

If we compare Carmen's extract with Karin's, we note how differently energies and affects can be experienced in the household. While the employment of a domestic worker means that Karin is able to have some quality time, for Carmen and the other domestic workers the household is the workplace. It is the place where the domestic worker is impressed with sensations of stress, servility, contempt and disgust. None of our research participants, employers or domestic workers alike, share positive sensations with regard to full-time household work. The employers, as we have seen, start to enjoy the household in the moment they can delegate some of the work to a domestic worker. Then domestic work is sensed as "quality time" and the household becomes a place of joy. For the domestic worker, in the meantime, domestic work continues to be the space of servility and disgust. Through the exchange and circulation of these feelings, the corporeal sensation of "dirty work" or "enjoyable work" is transmitted and projected on bodies and spaces. The ordinariness of cleaning the toilet or arranging the living room become more than simple household tasks. Rather, in the delivery of these tasks a social meaning emerges, played out affectively in the interpersonal interaction between domestic workers and their employers. Considering the role of affect and affection in domestic work thus brings us back to the question of value.

AFFECTIVE VALUE

Negri and Hardt identify affective labor as one of the crucial aspects of the new quality of labor. No longer stopping at the gates of the factory, capital expands into the social sphere, into private interpersonal networks, absorbing the labor-power created outside the commands of organized production. This labor-power emanates from the vital forces of human beings, their subjective faculties, their abilities to be creative, relational and affective. Production, from this perspective, is no longer set within a clear chronometric timescale, nor is the space of production just defined by the assembly line. Through the compression scales of time and space, productivity is acquired from the flexible flows of production emerging from the cooperative, creative and affective character of *living labor*. New technologies enable this unlimited expansion of capital by connecting the home to the office or factory. Projects can be brought home, e-mails can be answered from everywhere, online conferences facilitate working beyond the restrictions of time zones and geographical distances. This indefinite expansion of capital accumulation sets the center of value production on the pulses of "life," its biopolitical forces. Its target is the labor-power produced by a whole social network of affective, creative and communicative relations.[39] It is within these new modes of production relying on the relational and dispersed character of affects that Negri argues that "the theory of value loses its reference to the subject."[40] Instead, as Sandro Mezzadra notes, affect becomes the new cipher for capital accumulation as labor increasingly "resides in affect, that is, in living labor that is made autonomous in the capital relation."[41] Drawing on Marx's concept of "living labor,"[42] Mezzadra conceives *living labor* as the primary resource of capital accumulation, bound to ongoing "*open processes* both from the point of view of capital and from the point of view of the subjectivities that make up living labor itself."[43]

While the exploitation of *living labor* and its affective dimension have been discussed as one of the fundamental aspects of the mode of production of the "new economy," if we turn our attention to domestic work this aspect seems not to be at all so new. As feminist scholars have pointed out (see Chapter 4 of this volume), domestic work is paradigmatic for the production of affective labor. Here labor becomes affect.[44] As the examples discussed have demonstrated, the affects transmitted by the energies and feelings in the household intersect with the regular tasks of cleaning, ironing or cooking, driving the "power to act" and to be affected by these energies. Affects do speak about the societal corporeality of our senses and feelings, in short our human existence. Thus, behind the emotional expression of caring for others and cleaning the household hides more than mere happiness or disgust. Happiness and disgust only become meaningful in their ability to affect and be affected by other sensations and intensities. In other words, affects are inscribed in a social fabric that is corporeally sensed and expressed. In these interactions productivity is realized based on the affective bonds established, dissipated and transformed in the household.

Thus, the question of value surfaces here in a new light by making us aware of the senses and sensations, "the optic nerves," as Marx notes in the preceding, which conceal the productive character of domestic work as affective labor. As the products surfacing from affective labor are immaterial because a smile or sweeping the floor, for example, cannot be quantified, affects remain unseen by the naked eye. But affects constitute the social and cultural fabric from which *living labor* and its productive power stems. The capital accumulated here does not draw on the equivalent value form, money, as the codification of this value form relates to a social text in which this labor is devalued. Rather, productivity relies on the fact that the value of this labor-power is masked. As Negri asserts, "the more the value of labor-power is extended and intervenes in a global terrain, a biopolitical terrain," the more "labor finds its value in affect."[45] Nonetheless, within the chain of value coding, this labor is marked by the absence of its affective productivity.

Coding Value

Affect does involve more than caring emotionally for others. It is also about the way we react to the feelings and energies of others. Consequently, the value extracted from affective labor is not straightforwardly translatable into categories of "use-value" or "exchange-value." It overcomes this dichotomy through the specific texture of its expression ("to affect") and dynamics of impression ("affecting"). Hence, the affective quality of labor refers to a new understanding of value production under conditions of flexible capital accumulation in which the extraction of surplus labor does not solely rely on the exploitation of physical labor but its societal, relational character expressed in affect.

The societal perception of value in domestic work, for example, is expressed through its equivalent value form, money. Domestic work, as we have discussed in the previous chapters, is unwaged or low-waged labor. The value attributed to it represents a "code"[46] of a more complex process of valuation, historically produced and geopolitically contextualized. What appears as the equivalent value form of domestic work, in other words, is a social hieroglyph. In this code, the concrete labor expended, its emotional, physical, social and affective power, remains unseen. Instead, in the translation of domestic work into an equivalent value form, concrete value is translated into an abstract idea of value, reflecting the value and norms of a particular society. As Marx makes clear in the earlier quote, products become commodities because they are social things "whose qualities are at the same time perceptible and imperceptible by the senses."[47]

Consequently, what we perceive as the social value of domestic work is not necessarily its value. It is, rather, an expression of the hegemonic cultural coding of this labor. This results in a chain of value coding that relates to the societal value attributed to its labor force. In Deleuze and Guattari's words:

> Let us remember once again one of Marx's caveats: we cannot tell from the mere taste of wheat who grew it; the product gives us no hint as to the system and the relations of production. The product appears to be all the more specific, incredibly specific and readily describable, the more closely the theoretician relates it to ideal forms of causation, comprehension, or expression, rather than to the real process of production on which it depends. (Deleuze and Guattari, *A Thousand Plateaus* 24)

The value attached to a product, but also to its labor and labor force, is thus less a result of its qualities than of its social and historical codification. Concretely, the domestic worker expends all her labor-power cleaning the household, taking care of her employers and involuntarily or voluntarily engaging with the circuits of affective social (re)production. However, while she will produce through this labor a remarkable amount of value, this value will not fully revert to her. It is this value that flows not only into the individual reproduction of the household but society as a whole, which is not reflected in the social and cultural codification of this labor reduced to physical reproductive tasks. The affective character and biopolitical quality of domestic work as affective labor are not reflected in this equation.

Nonetheless, while affective value stresses the relational character of *living labor* and the dispersed circuits of value production, its expression and transmission is bound to a concrete labor force and historical and geopolitical production context. It is informed by what Spivak calls "the materialist predication" of capital. Thus, it is not insignificant where domestic work is geopolitically located and who does it. The feminized and racialized codification of the corporeality of labor and its geopolitical location still predetermine the social assertion of its value. Thus, while affect invites us to rethink the fluid and evasive character of capital accumulation, the phenomenological character of value coding in the logic of capital, the inclusion of the materialist predication of the subject, alerts us to its ontological dimension.

The Materialist Predication of the Subject

> I have so far been arguing, among other things, that to set the labor
> theory of value aside is to forget the textual and axiological implica-
> tions of a materialist predication of the subject. (Spivak, "Scattered
> Speculations on the Question of Value," 89)

Contrary to Negri and Hardt's assertion that capital has become globalized, has flooded metropolitan territories[48] and lost its central point of command and control, dissipating fixed regional coordinates like North/South
and East/West, Spivak reminds us about the axiological and textual impli-
cation of the materialist predication of the subject. In contrast to Negri's
assertion that "the theory of value loses its reference to the subject"[49] in
the new modes of production, Spivak stresses that original forms of capital
accumulation have not been replaced by the new modes of production in
advanced capitalism. Rather, they work simultaneously, as the "primitive
notion of money must work complicitously with the contemporary subla-
tion of money where it seems to question the 'materialistic' predication of
the subject; that the post-modern, in spite of all the cant of modernization,
reproduces the 'pre-modern' on another scene."[50] Territorialized relationships of economic dependence between political centres and peripheries,
rooted in Europe's colonial divides and the hegemonic post-1945 Western
status quo, still delineate the vectors of capital exploitation. This is even
the case when we consider new global alliances like BRIC (Brazil, Russia,
India, China), which with their rapid economic growth have transformed
the coordinates of global governance signaled by the transformation of the
G8 to the G20. This development brings Negri, to erroneously conclude
(alluding implicitly to Wallerstein's model of the international division of
work) that this model has "lost [its] specificity (and thus the possibility of
reactivating the theory of value in concrete instances)."[51] As both Spivak's
and Ramón Grosfoguel's critiques demonstrate,[52] Hardt and Negri's analysis is sustained by a Eurocentric perspective. Grosfoguel, in particular,
perceives a Eurocentric paradigm in this analysis that seems to deliver an
apparently "universal" critique of capitalism, limited to the analysis of the
economies of the Western hemisphere. As Spivak and Grosfoguel argue,
capital is still operating in the trenches of coloniality. Thus, as Anibal Quijano notes, "the structure of power was and even continues to be organized
on and around the colonial axis."[53] This is reflected, as I argue here, in the
persistent racialization and feminization of the labor market, instantiated
by policies of differentiation, established by EU migration and asylum policies. Value, set in this context, has not lost the "materialist predication of
the subject," but precedes it.

The employment of "undocumented migrant" workers from Latin
America, Africa, Asia and Eastern Europe mirrors global relationships
of economic dependence, driven by the effects of structural adjustment

programs, the impact of the global economy on the national level and global political conflicts. These are the reasons why most of the domestic workers we interviewed were forced to migrate. As I commented in Chapters 2 and 3 of this volume, after their tourist visa runs out they lose their residency permit. Without a residency permit their access to the labor market is severely curtailed to a few jobs in the feminized, racialized, unsafe, precarious and exploitative labor sectors. Despite recent achievements in regard to "migrant" domestic workers' rights in some EU Member States, as discussed in Chapter 3 of this volume, to a large extent this labor is kept outside the framework of institutionalized workers' rights (as I will discuss in more detail in the next chapter). Nonetheless, the persistent colonial character of this labor complements the modernist ambitions of European nation-states striving for gender equality on the public and private levels. Thus, the career needs of professional households, but also advanced forms of capital accumulation related to the flow of finance and capital, can only be achieved through the "free" or cheap labor done by feminized, racialized subjects, supporting the material grounds for capital accumulation. It is within this context that the "textual and axiological implications" of the value of domestic work becomes evident. The question of value, as Spivak suggests, bears an ontophenomenological dimension, inscribed in the textuality of value.[54] Capital is discerned by clear territories and mobilized by concrete subjects. It is not accidental that it is the "gendered subaltern who shoulders the system,"[55] "a person at the ground level of society who is already a victim of patriarchal practices."[56] It is in this textuality that affective value is produced and accumulated.

The Textuality of Value

> The binary opposition between the economic and the cultural is so deeply entrenched that the full implications of the question of Value posed in terms of the "materialist" predication of the subject are difficult to conceptualize. (Spivak, "Scattered Speculations on the Question of Value," 83)

Reading value against a deterministic economist interpretation of value and a cultural relativist approach that disregards its materialist predication, obscuring the "irreducible rift of the International division of labor,"[57] Spivak asserts[58] that the value form needs to be explored beyond its economic presupposition by considering its "cognitive, cultural, political, or affective"[59] dimensions. In order to address these dimensions, we need to work with a perspective that explores the level of codification. This brings us back to the codification of value.

As Marx notes in regard to the fetish character of the commodity and the expanded form of value expressed in money, what attributes value to these two things—"commodity" and "money"—is not their substantial equivalence in value expressed in other commodities (expanded relative value form) nor is it their equivalence to a specific commodity that composes this commodity (particular equivalent value form). Rather, the exchange of commodities operates on the level of a twofold process in which commensurability is created through a cultural process of identification along the poles of sameness and difference. Products are exchanged based on the assumption that they are similar in value even within their difference. So, what makes them comparable and reducible to a common denominator?

Whilst the process of exchange appears as a clear equation between two quantifiable objects, each bearing a materialized value, value is created through a process of textualization. The comparability between elements, marked by substantial difference, is realized through the creation of a third abstract element, manifested in the monetary equivalent value form. The abstract form of value lies behind this value form. Value, as stated earlier, is an abstract category, the outcome of a complex social and cultural relational process of meaning production. Value as a sign is configured by social practices of production, exchange and circulation, in which objects become signifiers and comparable to each other through the presupposition of identity or difference. Textualization, as Spivak indicates, is, thus, "the work of differentiation (both plus and minus) that opens up identity-as-equation."[60] What objects appear as identical are only so because they are codified as such within a logic of resemblance and difference.

Going back to domestic work, domestic work is measured as unwaged or low-waged labor. This is not because it is equivalent to any other low-waged or unwaged labor (expanded relative value form), or because the labor-power and labor-time infused in this labor (particular equivalent value form) are less valuable. Domestic work is unwaged or low waged because within the codification of the value system, it is set in "chain[s] . . . [or] endless series . . . of disparate and unconnected expressions of value"[61] signified by gender and the coloniality of labor. Hence, the value character of domestic work springs from its historical and social codification.

Domestic work is concrete and abstract labor at the same time. As concrete labor, domestic work articulates feminized and racialized labor. As abstract labor, due to the "endless series . . . of disparate and unconnected expression of value" in which its codification takes place, domestic work is more than "use-value" and "exchange-value." Its value is not easily quantifiable in these categories due to the immaterial character of its products. In contrast to the production of bread, which can be measured by the labor-power, labor-time, the ingredients, the relative market price and customers' demand, the value of a smile, a made bed and cleaned toilet and the labor-power that has been expended are hardly measurable within the standardized grammar of market circulation and exchange. The value of domestic work becomes perceptible only when we unravel its affective value.

The perspective on affective value in domestic work uncovers the corporeal and emotional vital forces ingrained in the production of this labor. These elements are not represented in the official codification of domestic work as nonproductive labor. The devaluation of domestic work and its labor force as racialized and feminized labor takes place within this value coding. Thus, in the moment this labor is done by a White, male labor force, domestic work becomes differently codified. It becomes a moderately well-paid profession as the employment of White, national male cleaners in cleaning agencies demonstrates.[62] The material manifestation or, as Spivak names it, "predication" resulting from this socially unjust system reflected in the coding of value is personified and sensed by the gendered subaltern and the devaluation of her/his labor force, labor-power and labor-time.

It is this textuality of value that determines the social value of domestic work particularly when it is done by an "undocumented migrant" woman. Through the chain of value coding of "woman," "migrant" and "non-European," the labor-power of an "undocumented migrant" domestic worker is codified as "value-less," or just contributing to the "use-value" of its immediate consumers. This codification, resulting in the social devaluation of domestic work, omits the fundamental role of feminized and racialized labor for the production and accumulation of capital in advanced capitalism. Value is, thus, culturally predicated and its value form is prescribed by the "materialist predication of the subject" doing the labor. In the case of the "undocumented migrant" domestic worker, her presence signals the "the ontophenomenological" script of the value character of domestic work, its "value sign" [63] (*Wertzeichen*[64]), the *Dasein*—"the mere being"[65]—of devalued feminized and racialized labor. Set at the bottom of the scale of value, domestic work as affective labor precedes the whole system of value coding. Only through its predisposition as "unproductive labor" can notions of productivity be formulated, comprising the myth of women's labor and the coloniality of labor as "naturally given," "naturally extracted," forming the stepping-stone of "original (primitive) accumulation."

From this perspective arises the potential of putting the economic text or economic interpretation of value "under erasure." Following Spivak's interpretation of Marx, to put the economic text "under erasure" is to acknowledge the importance of its "materialist predication" as well as interrogating the logic from which it resurges as an organizing script of social existence, as a "textual chain of value production."[66] Giving domestic workers a concrete face and analyzing domestic work as affective labor represent an erasure of the dominant impersonal script in which value is produced as a "neutral" abstract code. Further, it suffuses abstract categories of value and labor with the corporeal and emotional fabric from which our lives and encounters are constructed. In this regard, the affective value extracted in domestic work needs to be set within Ortiz's framework of transculturation.

CONCLUSION: TRANSCULTURALIZING
AFFECTIVE VALUE

Driven by the dynamics of global inequalities, the transmission of affects in private households, expressed through domestic work, illustrates the ambivalences in the encounters between two groups of women. These encounters bear the traces of transculturation, where two worlds meet that are geopolitically, economically and culturally separate. Thus, relations of economic dependency and labor exploitation circumscribe this encounter. For the "undocumented migrant" domestic workers, for example, domestic work is associated with a survival strategy, with a pursuit of social mobility and personal autonomy. For the employer, the transference of work to a domestic worker releases the opportunity of escaping the imposed interpellation as housewife, gaining time for her career goals or even just realizing the opportunity to relax. Thus, the encounter between domestic workers and their employers is not driven by amicable feelings or by the fact that these two individuals share the same group of friends, live in the same neighborhood and bring their children to the same school. Rather, their encounter is textured by the fact that they live in compartmentalized spaces, marked by clear geographical distances, as the domestic workers' accounts about the amount of time they spent on public transportation on their way to their workplaces illustrate. Nonetheless, the necessity of making a living for the domestic workers and the need for support to pursue their individual and household goals of happiness for the female employer push these two women together. It is in this context that these two women encounter each other, finding themselves in a relationship of power asymmetries that is also crossed by moments of unprecedented intimacy. These situations are infused with a complex mixture of contrasting sensations of closeness and distance, demonstrating the affective character of domestic work.

Domestic work as affective labor is more than just reproductive labor or a field in which gendered and racialized boundaries are negotiated. It is a field suffused with affects and mediated through affection. What domestic workers do is more than just caring for others or emotional labor, their labor is inherently connected to the exchange and circulation of affects. Their presence in the households denotes the system of the coloniality of labor and its feminization that still pervades modern and "postmodern" economies and household arrangements. The affects attached to this schism are tinted by contradictory emotions, sensations and intensities, played out in the transcultural encounter between domestic workers and their female employers. There are no moments of happiness or joy related to domestic work in the accounts of the domestic workers. These sentiments are only felt by Stefanie, Antonia, Karin and the other female employers when they find time for themselves. In contrast, in the narratives of Veronica, Marta, Elena and the other domestic workers joy is related to glimpses of autonomy and freedom, when they can roam unnoticed by the police through the streets of Berlin, Vienna, Madrid or Leeds.

Leaving the individual encounter between domestic workers and their employers aside, the analysis of affective labor within a transcultural setting demonstrates that there is no such phenomenon as "impersonal productive forces" or dynamics of "labor-power" or free-floating "biopolitical productivity." All these phenomena are ontophenomenological expressions of the semantics of a modern/colonial world-system of capital accumulation. In this regard, domestic work in private households marks zones of contact; spaces of encounter structured by the cultural codification of commodified social relations. Affective labor informs these relations by working with the sensations, intensities and desires that drive our lives. Affective value is extracted from this intermeshing of needs, desires, yearnings and suffering, in which symbolic power is expressed and a social order negotiated.

However, affects are also the realms that interrupt the sedimentation of territorialized structures of domination by showing us the corporeal and energetic tissue of our being. The expression of yearnings, suffering, desires and joy reflect our faculties as human beings to be compassionate and sensitive to each other. Affects also make us aware that we are interconnected, related to each other, that we do not exist as singular sealed "monads." Our bodies, our skins, are porous and open to somebody else's feelings, to the energies of our environment haunted by our past and energized by our present. Wounds and pain are thus not individually felt, but affectively sensed as a social moment of collective suffering. It is this productive power of affects that drives us to engage with the politics and ethics of affect.

Social injustice and global inequalities, thus, cannot be hidden and/or escaped by living in gated communities, sending children to private schools, visiting an expensive gym and keeping oneself apart from the misery in our neighborhoods, cities and villages. The necessity to employ a domestic worker brings these inequalities into the midst of affluent households in Europe. In order to address this local face of the global inequalities that govern our planet, we need a language that engages not only with social justice, economic distribution, political autonomy and with an end to oppression, but one that departs from the biopolitical value of affects and its implications for a decolonial politics of liberation. This is the subject of the next and final chapter.

7 Decolonial Ethics and the Politics of Affects

Talking Rights

> Thus, one is not just a worker; one is a person with a lot of things to give. (Sania, domestic worker, Madrid)

Reminding us that a worker is not a machine, but a person, Sania brings us back to consider the vital forces in domestic work. As I have argued throughout this volume, domestic work involves more than just cleaning or arranging the household. It demands the investment of subjective faculties. Further, domestic work in private households is a site of affects. Social relations are negotiated here not only through the balancing of racialized and gendered boundaries, but also through the affective energies, sensations and intensities mediating this space of encounter. The social fabric of daily encounters is thus impacted on by the affective energies shaping the space we inhabit.

However, in the discussion on domestic workers' rights, very often this point dissipates behind claims for better working conditions and the recognition of this work as a profession. While these are important claims, we need to go a step further, by embedding migrant domestic workers' rights within a framework of creolizing human rights. Such a perspective requires what Nelson Maldonado-Torres conceptualizes as "decolonial humanisms," a foregrounding of the "interrelationality of ethical contact,"[1] through which an attempt is made to restore the prerequisites for a "human social life in contexts of systematic dehumanization."[2] Thus, this chapter proposes to embark on a debate on transnationalizing migrant workers' rights, particularly domestic workers' rights, by suggesting that we frame this debate within a decolonial perspective on human rights, drawing on Boaventura de Sousa Santos, Edouard Glissant and Enrique Dussel before concluding with Maldonado-Torres's thoughts on the decolonial ethics of responsibility and Eve Sedgwick's discussion on the politics of affects. But before this, let us take a look at the debate on transnationalizing domestic workers' rights.

TRANSNATIONALIZING DOMESTIC WORKERS' RIGHTS

While national State policies are engaging in the individual promotion of care work through the introduction of service vouchers and fiscal measures related to the hiring of home-helps, domestic work remains a "private matter" attached to the individual arrangements in private households. Despite the political rhetoric on gender equality and work–life balance, very little is proposed and implemented in regard to the equal sharing of domestic work, and less is envisioned in terms of the protection of domestic workers in private households. Since the establishment of the International Labour Organization (ILO) in 1919, approximately 200 conventions have been passed, none of which have focused on domestic workers. This is astonishing if we bear in mind that in 1948 the ILO stated that it would consider a convention on domestic workers. Since that time the political goal of domestic workers' organizations to attain fundamental workers' rights has been postponed from resolution to resolution. In 1965 the ILO passed a resolution concerning the conditions of employment of domestic workers. The resolution proposed the introduction of protective measures and workers' training programs in accordance with international standards for in-country as well as "foreign" domestic workers. Unfortunately, the resolution was not followed up by international or national political measures. It was not until 1996 that the ILO commissioned a new report that showed that domestic workers were excluded from social protection and labor legislation. This was the case because domestic workers' employment situation does not seem to "fit" into the general framework of existing employment laws; the workplace is in some cases private and employment contracts are arranged on an individual basis.

Though the European Parliament passed a resolution in 2000 regarding the regulation of domestic work in the formal economy, this recommendation has had little impact on the national level.[3] The employment of domestic workers in private households remains a private matter negotiated between the household and the domestic worker. However, in some countries, as I discussed in Chapter 3 of this volume, national employment regulations like the House-Keeper Collective Agreement in Germany (Employment Ordinance, § 21 Haushaltshilfen-Domestic Helpers) and Austria do exist. These agreements guarantee a 38.5 hour working week, two days off per week, two free weekends per month, 26 to 30 days holiday a year, a remuneration agreement concerning wages and Christmas bonuses.[4] Housekeepers have a right to a period of notice of termination of employment and social insurance is covered at a minimum level. Although the remuneration agreement only covers the parties to the agreement, the wage level set serves as a guideline for other workers. Any domestic worker, whether a union member or not, can go to court for the minimum wage or pension rights. This has been used by advocacy groups to claim minimum wages and regular salaries for "undocumented migrant" domestic workers. In Spain, where domestic work is regulated by the specific regime for domestic service, very low protection for domestic workers exists. A written contract is only obligatory when the job exceeds 80 hours a month. This leaves untouched the majority of employment arrangements that do not exceed these working hours and gives little protection along the lines of the right to social benefits, a contract or health and unemployment security. The domestic worker pays for her own social security, which is a factor that adds to the precarious conditions of her work. Though there is no collective agreement regarding domestic work, the regulations on caregivers, introduced by the Socialist government through the *Ley de Dependencia* (The Dependency Law) in 2007, mean that domestic work is indirectly regulated as generally the employment of a care worker is also tied to the delivery of domestic work. All these different measures are halfhearted as they do not follow trade union recommendations, nor do they provide any secure working conditions.

"Undeclared" work in household service is a widespread phenomenon in the EU. Some estimate that 70 to 80 percent of domestic workers employed are not officially declared.[5] Parallel to the lack of regulation of domestic work in private households, domestic work does not appear as a special area for labor recruitment in official labor policies. For example, within the EU there are no special migrant workers recruitment programs for the domestic work sector. Only very recently and as a part of migration amnesty programs has this area of work been taken into consideration, and "undocumented migrant" domestic workers employed in private households have been "regularized," for example, in Spain and Italy.[6] In the UK and Germany the employment of domestic workers in diplomat households has received attention in the last decade also, leading to the "Overseas Domestic Worker Visa"[7] in the UK and to specific policy measures regarding the employment of "personal servants in diplomat households" in Germany.[8]

Despite these different initiatives, domestic work in private households remains a highly unprotected area by the State. Due to the widely shared conviction that the household is primarily a private sphere and as such needs to be safeguarded from State intervention, the employment relationships entertained in these spheres are relegated to informal and personal agreements and arrangements that largely do not respect general trade union agreements. Paradoxically, the household, "governed by mutual dependence and affective relations, altruism, responsibility and duty,"[9] seems to be in stark contrast with the commodified character of formalized employment relationships within its own four walls. As such, employment relationships in private households are kept "private" and any attempt of regulation is met with suspicion and is highly contentious. For example, in most EU countries the control of private households by labor inspectors is not permitted.[10] No police raids or employment inspectors can interfere in this sphere, leaving the workers to the mercy of their employers. Physical, psychological and sexual abuses are not rare in this sector and the possibilities to tackle them legally are minimal.[11] This is a situation that has steered "undocumented migrant" workers and advocacy groups to work together on local, national and international levels in voicing the need for transnational workers' rights.

Challenging the Trade Union's National Paradigm

> So if, I mean, I'll just say to the employers out there, if they could just change that kind of attitude that the person who is coming here is suffering or the person who is coming here, she has to be a slave because we are paying her. (Marga, domestic worker, Hamburg)

Marga complicates the perception of domestic workers as "victims" or an exploitable labor force. She directly addresses the employers by demanding a change in their "colonial attitude," condensed in her treatment as exploited labor, not entitled to human and citizenship rights. She came to Germany with a plan and project. Her plan was to continue with her postgraduate studies, but after three months of struggling with the German university administration, which refused to recognize her Ecuadorian university degree, her tourist visa expired and she became "undocumented." Shortly afterwards, Marga was detained and ended up in prison awaiting deportation, which, thanks to the support of her political networks, she was able to prevent. Even though she experienced abusive situations in the private households, she refuses to reduce her life in Germany to just the experience of suffering. As an active member in a migrant domestic workers group, *Mujeres Sin Rostro*, she sees herself as both challenging and revolting against the infrahuman life conditions she faces as an "undocumented migrant" worker.

Mujeres Sin Rostro, which worked together with the Berlin strand of the European advocacy group on migrant domestic workers in Europe, *RESPECT*, supported different initiatives regarding the legalization of "undocumented" workers. In 2003, *Mujeres Sin Rostro* and *RESPECT* established conversations with the service sector trade union, *ver.di*, insisting on trade union membership for non-nationals and persons without legal residency status and demanding the same entitlement to employment rights and benefits as is the case for service sector workers. This includes a written work contract, social benefits, unemployment and health insurance, 13 months' salary, a 38-hour week and the minimum wage. In one of the interventions in the national *ver.di* meeting in 2003, *RESPECT* addressed the audience with the following demand: "We are workers and therefore we have a right to have rights. We don't want to be abused sexually in our workplace, we want higher salaries and finally to work in dignity like every one of you."[12] Significantly, with this claim *RESPECT* pointed out the correlation between union membership and legal status. "Undocumented migrant" workers were until this moment officially excluded from trade union membership. While *RESPECT* and its support network succeeded in voicing "undocumented migrant" workers' rights, leading to the establishment of an office for migration and labor (MigrAr: Migration and Arbeit) in 2008 supported by the trade union *ver.di*, dealing in particular with the situation of "undocumented migrant workers," this initiative is singular if we consider that trade unions in Europe are mainly organized along national lines. This does not correspond with the development of transnational workers' mobility and local labor force demand, as Anita, a Peruvian domestic worker, told the Spanish research team:

> From the angle of the trade unions, when they look at the migrant worker, they are unable to explain who the migrant workers are. They lack an internationalist or universal vision. They have a complete national perspective. If they would work on universal consciousness of class with national and migrant workers alike, then the scope regarding the strength for demands and interventions, of assembly, will be a different thing. (Anita, domestic worker, Madrid)[13]

The equation "worker equals national citizen or resident migrant" no longer represents the entire labor force, as Anita makes clear. Anita, working "undocumented" in private households, discerns the need for an internationalist and universal trade union approach to workers' rights. As feminist activists like *Precarias a la Deriva* have argued, labor does not stop at the gates of the factory. Rather, it starts and continues in the household. It emerges and is sustained through the labor that does not appear in any trade union manifesto and is not thought of when we solely direct our view to the public spectrum of trade union organizing in Europe. Insisting on the interpenetration of global production and labor organization, union struggles are doomed to fail if they solely perpetuate national ethnocentric and androcentric analyses of labor. Thus the trade unions' focus on the traditional White male factory worker in Western Europe, what has been described as the "Fordist Subject," needs urgent revision. Precarious residency status coupled with precarious working conditions are widely represented in the "low-paid," feminized and racialized labor sectors. The lack of regulation of employment conditions, in particular in the construction, hospitality, agricultural, gastronomy, personal service, cleaning and sweatshop industries, characterized by fixed-term contracts or hourly paid arrangements, terminable at any instant, means that migrant workers move jobs frequently, or even go back and forth between their country of origin and their immigration destination. This circular migration, enforced by the current economic crisis, displays the transnational character of migration, affected by precarious legal and working conditions.

As the *Sans Papiers* Movement in Europe makes us recall, trade unions need to react to these new working conditions, in which working status is not always accompanied by residency.[14] For example, in the European Social Forum in Paris in November 2003, the *Sans Papiers* Movement addressed the audience with the words, "We need your support, but the struggle is primarily ours."[15] Here the *Sans Papiers* Movement highlighted the need for self-organization and representation, which they also stated on

their banner "distribution of wealth, abolition of borders, papers for all."
As this movement shows, the question of migrant workers' rights entails the
question of human rights. What is at stake is not just the achievement of
some long overdue rights, but the right to a dignified life. Thus, campaigning in this field is often accompanied by a doubling of strategies.

Doubling Strategies

Seeking equal treatment regardless of legal residency status are claims that,
as Nicole Piper notes, are supported by a wide range of migrant, refugee
and *Sans Papiers* groups.[16] Though migrants, and in particular "undocumented migrants," are officially excluded from the right of assembly and
the formation of political organizations, since the late 1990s their engagement in civic and political organization has steadily grown. On a local level
this is articulated in regard to the organization of migrant domestic workers by groups like Kalayaan in the UK, *RESPECT* in Germany,[17] MAIZ in
Austria[18] and SEDOAC in Spain.[19] SEDOAC, for example, is fighting for
the abolition of the "special social security domestic worker's regime" of
1985. If we remember from Chapter 3 of this volume, through this special
regime domestic workers are partially entitled to employment rights and
benefits, but not equally treated under the "general social security regime."
The "general regime" respects and incorporates trade union agreements
regarding the minimum wage, termination of employment, social benefits,
health, accident and unemployment insurance.

This cooperation with trade unions is timely and driven by the prereq-
uisite of the right to residency and free movement for migrant and "undocumented migrant" workers. As the example of *RESPECT* and Kalayaan
demonstrates, some branches of the trade unions commit to supporting the
infrastructure of these groups by offering meeting rooms and union membership cards. In cooperation with the trade unions and other advocacy
organizations, international domestic workers' organizations have raised
the following demands:[20]

- recognition of domestic work as real work, and not simply an extension of unpaid household and care work
- recognition of domestic workers as workers
- recognition and valuing of domestic work and the skills involved
- equal workers' rights, including the right to organize and join trade
  unions and the right to representation
- decent conditions of work, including limitations on working hours,
  rest periods, overtime pay, paid holidays, sick leave, maternity leave
  and a living wage
- social security and protection; health care (including for those with
  HIV/AIDS) and pensions
- access and right to training

- freedom: of movement, to change employer, from harassment, from physical and psychological abuse and sexual exploitation
- decent living conditions, including housing and facilities
- favorable immigration laws
- regulation of recruitment and placement agencies

These demands are an outcome of a compromise between different domestic workers' organizations. They represent agreed-upon goals, debated between different political actors (social movements, traditional political bodies and the trade unions), working along the lines of transnational workers' rights. It is in this regard that the domestic worker international platform has campaigned for an ILO Convention on Domestic Work.

Noticing that a series of ILO Conventions that can be applied to domestic workers do exist,[21] but that none address domestic work explicitly, the international domestic workers' network is demanding an ILO Convention on Domestic Work. National migrant domestic workers' organizations working with international domestic workers' organizations, cooperating with the international network of trade unions International Union of Food, Agricultural, Hotel, Restaurant, Catering, Tobacco and Allied Workers (IUF) and the ILO lobbying organization Women in the Informal Economy, Globalizing and Organizing (WIEGO) are campaigning for the ILO Convention on Domestic Work.[22] Due to their lobbying, on Women's Day 2008 the governing body of the ILO agreed to put "Decent Work for Domestic Workers" on the agenda of the 2010 International Labour Conference (ILC) with a view to adopting an ILO instrument (convention and/or recommendation) in 2011. The ILO Convention shall secure that domestic work does not remain excluded from international law or from national labor legislation and that a right to freedom of association and collective bargaining is guaranteed. Further, it will promote a public platform to fight against exploitative and discriminatory practices in domestic work. However, while the lobbying on migrant rights has resulted in an inclusion of a "rights-based" approach in the ILO Plan of Action on migrant workers in 2004,[23] as Norbert Cyrus notes, the ILO's intervention into the field of migrant rights is not always accompanied by a liberalization of migration policies.[24] In 2005 the ILO initiated a strategy on migration that combines human rights discourses on trafficking in women and migrant workers' exploitation with an enforcement of migration control and crime prevention, as well as the support and legal protection for "undocumented migrant" workers.[25]

Despite these political, in some instances controversial, initiatives, the situation of "undocumented migrants" needs to be tackled. ILO Conventions, while they may represent an official legal strategy, do not challenge the profound imposed divide of migration policies between "citizens" and "migrant," through which different legal statuses in regard to citizens' and workers' rights are produced. In order to dismantle this logic, a political strategy addressing the symptom as well as the origins of the problem is required. This twofold strategy reacts on the one side to immediate working rights claims and, on the other, it challenges the logic ingrained in a legal system bearing colonial legacies of exclusion, reactivated within the new vocabulary of control, regulation and management of migration. Thus, concrete initiatives to protect the human rights and working right of "undocumented migrants" and domestic workers, in particular, need to be embedded within a decolonial project of liberation, departing from the recognition of fundamental human, civil and workers' rights.[26] Thus, while the claims for State regulation of domestic work might envision protection, fair wages and dignified working conditions, it does not represent a fundamental questioning of the gendered and racialized segregation of the labor market. This approach does not tackle the logic of coloniality preconditioning not only the access to the labor market, but also the racialization and gendering of subaltern groups.

On the contrary, if regulations are in place that only address the interest of the national economy by coupling a residency permit to a work contract, threatening the "migrant" with deportation the moment the contract ends, the goal of being treated equally to other citizens is undermined. As the Spanish case of labor migration regulation shows, dependency relations with the employers can deepen if the residency permit is issued on the basis of a work contract.[27] The utilitarian and opportunistic logic of these measures, solely addressing the interests of the government and national economy, were made explicit in November 2008 when the Spanish minister of labor, Celestino Corbacho, reacted to the global economic crisis by proposing a "voluntary return program" for non-EU citizens. As Sami Naïr argues, this program had little impact as only 4,000 of the 80,000 targeted workers opted for it.[28] Producing an incentive that holds the message that one is no longer needed disregards the fact that these migrants have settled in Spain. Claims directed to national and international governmental bodies need to be carefully and thoroughly examined. A canny approach demands awareness of the strategies of appropriation and incorporation of human rights rhetoric by these actors. Nonetheless, the cooperation between trade unions and domestic workers' political organizations has produced some achievements in regard to pushing domestic work into the forefront of the transnationalization of workers' rights, conveyed in Piper's proposal of "portable rights."[29]

PORTABLE RIGHTS AND INTERSECTIONALITY

Why should a "migrant" not be entitled to claim her salary back if it has been withheld or denounce an employer for abusive treatment when she has left the country of immigration? For example, in the case of migrants returning home after deportation, the State in the immigration country should be held accountable for her or his rights. Entitlement to social security, fair wages and fair treatment cannot stop at national borders. Supporting claims for simultaneous rights, Piper approaches the entitlement of migrants to rights on two levels, in regard to the migrants living in the country of migration and those that were forced to leave it. Suggesting a portability of rights and portable trade union memberships, Piper sets workers' rights in relation to "unions without borders" and within a transnational context. Entitlement to rights, as she argues, should depart from the mobile character of workers today, fostered particularly by the increasing implementation of international schemes promoting temporary and seasonal migrant work in Europe, North America and Oceania.

This perspective on the transnationalization of workers' rights has been brought into the debate by the campaigning of refugee, migrant and *Sans Papiers* organizations. These groups have challenged the national paradigm of trade union organizing and uncovered the existence of precarious mobile non-national workers. Observing this development on the international tableau of negotiations between labor movements, international and national trade unions, NGOs and alter-globalization movements, Piper suggests that we abandon a national methodology.[30] This refers to Peter Waterman's proposal of understanding labor organizing today as a citizenship movement, operating beyond national boundaries.[31] Labor organizing, therefore, represents more than just a movement for working rights. It addresses fundamental citizenship issues arising from the global character of capital and the increasing mobility of the labor force. This perspective initiates thinking of citizenship rights through the angle of transnational migrant rights as a form of citizens' and workers' rights in motion.[32]

The transnational perspective on workers' rights raises questions in general in regard to human rights. Not only does this perspective shift away from a national framework, but it also unravels a more complex picture of social relations. As Margaret Satterthwaite argues, the overlapping of social relations and their interpenetration demand a new analytical framework to discuss discrimination beyond identity claims.[33] This is an aspect that she explores through an intersectional approach to human rights. Departing from the complexity of subjectivities and overlapping social relations, she addresses the need to formulate claims against discrimination based not solely on identities, but on the process of discrimination itself. Thus, a perspective on intersectionality "allows analysts to move beyond debates over the ontological "essence" of the myriad identity categories used by individuals, communities, and states."[34] While not explicitly mentioned in Satterthwaite, the intersectional approach in legal studies, emanating from critical race studies, stresses the more fluid definitions of human rights and subjectivity.[35] Also, as Linda Fregoso stresses, the inersectional approach resonates with indigenous notions of identity and collective property deriving from the *Américas*, delineating a "planetary civil society."[36] It is in this regard that the framework of intersectionality in human rights law goes beyond liberal concepts of the "social detached subject" and emphasizes, instead, its connection to other beings, the world and the universe.

This cosmology, intertwining each human being in the world to its cosmos, provides the matrix for an intersectional perspective in human rights not just emphasizing Satterthwaite's interest in discussing the intricacies of structural violence, but also embracing Linda Fregoso and Celina Romany's[37] aim to fundamentally include "socioeconomic rights" addressing "basic needs such as food, health care, a living wage, environmental safety, and shelter" in the human rights debate.[38] This perspective not only complicates the configuration of subjectivities in a mobile world, where working conditions are increasingly deregularized and precarity is becoming a main denominator, but it also addresses the specific geopolitical and historical context in which identities are formed. As Satterthwaite stresses, the perspective on intersectionality in human rights becomes especially important in regard to identities that cross borders, since the conditions that construct and impact on those identities are shaped by their specific context of emergence.[39] This leads us to think about decolonizing the feminization of labor.

DECOLONIZING THE FEMINIZATION OF LABOR

While theorizing on domestic work needs to address the new modes of production through the angle of the feminization of labor, it has to go beyond it by noting the racializing and persistent colonizing effects of the contemporary logic of capital accumulation. From a Marxist perspective, domestic work has been related to "use-value," and as such it has not been considered an integral part in the exchange and circulation of capital. Its products have been related to immediate consumption, serving immediate reproductive needs. Marxist feminists in the 1970s and 1980s questioned this interpretation and demonstrated that domestic work is a socially necessary labor and a main supplier of "surplus-value." Domestic work precedes the labor force. It is the origin of value production; the fundamental site of what Marx has coined "original (primitive) accumulation." Marx defines the exploitation of resources and labor-power by the European powers in their colonies as the fundamental step in capital accumulation. However, as Quijano, Mignolo, Grosfoguel and Dussel note, colonial exploitation is not limited to a single historical event. Rather, it constitutes the premises of capital accumulation up until today.[40] The modern logic of capital accumulation operates on the basis of the colonial condition of power, knowledge and being, reiterating a gendered and racialized system of classification structuring the labor market, the logic of governing and intimate relationships in private households. As Maldonado-Torres, in reference to Frantz Fanon, observes, "in the colonial context what happens at the level of the private and the intimate is fundamentally linked to social structures and to colonial cultural formations and forms of value."[41]

Migrant domestic workers in Europe articulate this correlation between colonial logic and capital accumulation. Paradoxically, domestic work signifies the social devaluation of feminized, racialized labor, while it produces a fundamental societal value. This is not only the case when we consider the reproductive and emotional value intrinsic to this labor, but in particular when we look at its affective value. This value is linked to affective labor, engaging with the immediate impulses of "life," its corporealities, sensibilities and energies, played out in intimate encounters, where social relations are shaped and transformed. When we bring global inequalities into the midst of the household, considered in liberal societies as the haven of privacy, the household becomes the location in which racialized and gendered boundaries are enacted. Social antagonisms are thus sensed bodily, expressed and exchanged in the immediacy of transcultural encounters between two parties that usually do not meet outside their employment relationship.

The household becomes a specific transcultural "contact zone." This process of transculturation is not determined by an equal sharing of power in which each group can influence and shape the space of conviviality on equal terms. The encounter between domestic workers and their employers is clearly determined by an employment relationship that can be terminated by the employer at any time. Friendship on equal terms can only emerge when the power coordinates demarcating the encounter are reversed. As *Precarias a la Deriva* remarks, this raises questions in regard to the identitarian angle of political organizing, and feminist politics in particular.[42] Acknowledging different social and economic positionalities among women and also relations of power between women, *Precarias a la Deriva* opts for a form of organization, a common shared principle shaped by specific life and working conditions. This organization is motivated by the aim for social justice emanating out of the heterogeneity of political practices, subjectiveness and languages striving for societal transformation. Collecting women's accounts about how they organize their everyday lives, they trace the experience of feminized precarity as the common, the incarnation and expression of a social being. Portraying the tightrope women walk, struggling and juggling with the effects imposed by a precarious, feminized labor market and their constant interpellation into a normative framework of "femininity," concealed in images of young, slim and fit bodies, *Precarias* proposes a new form of political organizing. Here, while a common situation of oppression and exploitation is asserted, differences are acknowledged. As they write:

> our situations are so diverse, so partial, that it is very hard for us to find common denominators from which to build alliances or the irreducible differences from which we gain mutual enrichment. It is hard for us to express ourselves, to define ourselves from the common ground of precarity; precarity capable of dispensing with a clear collective identity

which simplifies and defends, but which demands that we share and combine our thoughts and ideas. [...] Above all, however, we want to make it possible to collectively construct other possibilities of life by means of a united and creative fight. Insistence in singularity comes from the desire to develop a politics which does not, once again, reproduce false homogeneities. (Precarias a la Deriva, *A la Deriva*, 25)[43]

Not reproducing "false homogeneities" but understanding precarity as a commonly sensed situation is the point of departure for *Precarias*'s political organizing. As Angela Mitropoulos argues, precarity is not a new phenomenon and "has been the standard experience of work in capitalism."[44] Thus, the "experience of regular, full-time long-term employment" has been the exception in the majority of Southern European societies, not to mention that precarity is a constitutive and persistent feature of colonized and post- and neocolonial societies. While precarity seems to be a common feature in women's lives, its impacts differ in regard to citizenship status, economic position and the racializing effects of asylum and migration policies. Thus, precarity might have different implications for a single Spanish mother than for a female "undocumented migrant worker" from Ecuador. While both women might struggle against similar effects of precarity, its consequences vary in regard to their citizen or migrant status. The Spanish woman does not risk being deported on this basis, while the Ecuadorian woman's right to stay depends on a work contract, as we have seen in Chapter 3 of this volume. The Spanish woman is affected by the dismantling of a semifunctional Mediterranean Welfare State, whilst the precarious condition of the Latin American woman is a result of the enduring colonial logic perpetuated in EU migration policies and the racial segregation of the European labor market. These reduce her merely to exploited labor, to "sub-alternity,"[45] marked by the lack of rights, social recognition and respect. The precarity of the "undocumented migrant" domestic worker is textured by an attempt at complete dehumanization.

Though these two women might share the effects of structural violence against women, the exploitative effects of the logic of capital accumulation and heteronormativity, these moments are crossed by the logic of the coloniality of power. Thus, while these women might, for example, share the same nasty feeling of "disgust" attached to the social devaluation of domestic work, this feeling is connoted by different moments of domination. While the employer is able to divert the social imposition of devalued feminized labor to an "undocumented migrant" woman, the latter is doomed to do this work because she lives in a legal limbo, stripped of any citizen's, worker's or human rights. Domestic work is fatally linked to the coloniality of labor, reflected in the position of the "undocumented migrant" woman. Political organizing around the question of feminization of labor, thus, demands more than a retrieval of identity politics as the fabric of the feminization of labor is embedded in the coloniality of labor.

Political organizing, therefore, calls not only for a decentralization of an androcentric view on the question of labor and labor organizing, but also for a decolonial one.

It is in this regard that political organizing between the employer and the domestic worker needs to operate on the basis of transversal translation. A translation acknowledging the imbalance of power that preformed transcultural encounters. This attempt of translation is based on the assumption of the parallel existence of (un)translatability in translation. How far can we translate universal claims that are rooted and situated in one part of the world to other parts of the world? What makes a claim universal and translatable? Of course, related to domestic work, the claim to collectivized domestic work, to socially recognize the societal value generated through this labor, represents a universal claim. Nonetheless, this claim is only partly addressed if we depart from an analysis of the feminization of labor, disregarding the enduring effects of coloniality. Translating these views into the field of domestic workers' rights requires that we acknowledge the conditions underlying the translation.

Translation here is marked by "lived existence."[46] Maldonado-Torres discusses the concept of "lived existence" in Frantz Fanon's critique of Hegelian ontology. Reversing Hegel's dialectic of master/slave, Fanon insists on the "lived experience" resulting from the relationship between the presupposed "authentic Being" (the master) and the abjected Other, the "non-Being" (the enslaved subject). As Maldonado-Torres notes, it "is for this reason that, for Fanon, beyond a 'science of being' we must engage in a science of the relations between being and non-being, describing how the exclusion from being is performed and how non-beingness is lived or experienced."[47] It is in this dynamic of the "institutional authorization of Being" and its negation that a translation of affective labor as an expression of living labor enables us to approach a decolonial ethical framework of human rights in regard to domestic work.

TRANSLATING AFFECTIVE LABOR AND CREOLIZING HUMAN RIGHTS

> Please, employers, when you are employing somebody, just know that this person has also got a background. Maybe theirs is better than yours. I mean, being here in Europe, it's not really that I'm, I'm suffering, or like I'm so desperate, or I am *pobre*—I mean I am poor—or anything. I'm not rich or poor but I'm a human being as you are. And, we all need to live a normal life, and I mean of *all* the people in the world—people have to respect people who are cleaning for them, because you couldn't do it. Ask yourself why? (Teresa, domestic worker, Berlin)

Teresa, from Ecuador and living in Berlin for four years, addresses the question of critical humanism. She is a human being as are *"all* the people in the world." The claim of universal equality is profoundly represented in this extract. Teresa refuses to occupy the place of the victim. She is not the one that is just "suffering," "desperate" and "pobre." She is a human being who is working, doing the "cleaning" so that others can prosper. Her observation leads us to rethinking human rights from a decolonial perspective, as suggested by Boaventura de Sousa Santos.

Stating that the official discourse on human rights is based on a Eurocentric normative framework that disregards the intrinsic connection of European Enlightenment to European colonialism,[48] Santos suggests developing a decolonial perspective. This perspective acknowledges the historical ambivalence in which human rights were proclaimed. When human rights were announced in France in 1789, colonialism and the slave trade were flourishing. While the European White male bourgeoisie was celebrating its autonomy as sovereign subjects, women, the peasantry, the emerging working class and the colonized and enslaved population were excluded from this right. Today we still find different degrees of exclusion from human rights articulated by the gradual recognition or negation of citizenship rights within European nation-states in regard, for example, to migrants, refugees and *Sans Papiers.* A colonial logic is still in place in terms of who is considered a full citizen and who stands at the margins or is completely excluded from citizenship. On a global scale, the inherent fallacy in the European proclamation of human rights resonates with an international human rights discourse, which solely allocates perpetrations of human rights abuses outside their own territorial borders.

Since 9/11, the liberal human rights discourse has served to legitimize imperial and bellicose ambitions, manifested in the occupations of Iraq and Afghanistan by Western allied forces.[49] It is a difficult task to decenter the imperial political implications of this discourse. Nonetheless, this should not stop us in our attempt to unfold the counterhegemonic potential inherent in the universal proclamation of human rights. Instead of giving up a universal conviction that departs from the principles of human dignity and structural equality, following Santos we need to infuse them with a radical democratic content. Normative predications need to be accompanied by structural material changes, setting the grounds for a dignified life and equal economic distribution, accompanied by the decolonization of the epistemological premises sustaining the Western discourse on human rights, ultimately linked to a project of liberation.[50] This project pursues interconnected but different struggles of decolonization addressing, on the one hand, economic decolonization and, on the other, epistemological decolonization.[51]

It is along these lines that anticolonial, decolonial, feminist, LGBTIQ and post-Marxist movements have developed counterdiscourses, emphasizing workers', civil and social rights. Further, these movements have introduced new conceptualizations of personhood, departing from critical border epistemology and decolonial queer theory, in which subjecthood is no longer defined by national boundaries or heterosexual gender frontiers, but as transborder, transgender and transsexual ontologies. An emancipatory human rights project needs to combine these claims with questions of wealth distribution, the entitlement of human beings to a dignified life, access to health, housing, education and knowledge production as well as the right to active democratic representation and participation.[52] Seen from a decolonial perspective, the human rights discourse represents a counter-hegemonic project in which radical concepts of democracy and economic distribution are related to a constituency that embraces creolization.

Creolizing Human Rights

> And, they just have to consider that they don't just have to look down upon people that are cleaning for them, or that I was meant for it or something, no. It's only that I'm from a different country, which has different laws. I go back to my country, I'll be managing other people or anything. But, you know, there is one funny thing, which really surprised me. All these people, if they come to our countries, they are given the respect which, I mean, nobody else is getting in this country, nobody else. They are given the respect which makes them feel worthwhile, we never asked you people, these people to come into our country and start cleaning, no. They migrate when they want, when they wish, but nobody sends them away. But I wonder why do they treat us like this? Really, I wonder. (Elvira, domestic worker, Hamburg)

Elvira came from Quito, Ecuador, to learn German and enroll in a postgraduate program. Now, two years later, she cleans houses in Hamburg. Before coming to Germany she lived for a couple of years in Boston, where she practiced her English. After returning and working as an administrator in a US oil company in Ecuador, she decided to travel to Germany. She told me that she has some German friends in Quito who supported her in her aim to live in Germany for a while. When Elvira mentions the differences between her treatment in Germany and the treatment of Germans in Ecuador, she has her friends in mind. As I have argued here, the experience of deskilling is commonly shared by the women that participated in this study. The process of deskilling is closely linked to Quijano's coloniality of power, the "global cultural order revolving around European or Western hegemony" in the global organization and production of knowledge. In order to decenter this perspective, we need to shift the "geography of reason" in which human rights are treated as a European invention. Such a shift occurs through a creolization of human rights.

The French Caribbean debate on creolization offers us an epistemological framework to reverse the Eurocentric heteronormative racialized foundation of human rights. Focusing on the relational character of conviviality brought about under conditions of coloniality, Edouard Glissant departs from the observation that the whole world is becoming creolized.[53] This is an observation also shared by the three Martiniquan intellectuals, Jean Bernabé, Patrick Chamoiseau and Raphaël Confiant. In their *Éloge de la Créolité* (translated in 1990 as *In Praise of Creoleness*), a founding text of creoleness, they introduce *créolité* as an ethical framework.[54] Drawing from the works of Aimé Césaire and Glissant, Bernabé, Confiant and Chamoiseau sought to elaborate an ethics of vigilance, "a sort of mental envelope in the middle of which our world will be built in full consciousness of the outer world."[55] Further, they conceived the principles of interconnectedness and interdependency as the basis for the conviviality of *créolité*. While *créolité* defined a Caribbean specificity, which they described in their declaration as "[n]either Europeans, nor Africans, nor Asians, we proclaim ourselves Creoles,"[56] it proposes a vision of diversity based on the Negritude movement. However, it goes beyond it by creating a space for what they described as "kaleidoscopic totality," the "nontotalitarian consciousness of a preserved diversity."[57] To the cultural critics of the French Antilles, *créolité* and creolization are two distinct notions.

Glissant favors creolization over *créolité* because, he argues, creolization refers to an ongoing process. Drawing on the genealogy of Black antislavery and anticolonial resistance in the French Caribbean, creolization indicates a being and becoming in the world characterized by Du Boisian "double consciousness."[58] Thus, creolization encompasses what Jane Anna Gordon and Neil Roberts define as a "New World View, a political epistemological and ontological global realignment of the normative subject and the heretical condemned of the earth—Fanon's *Damné*."[59] Glissant emphasizes the rhizomatic mobile character of a process of identification, which trespasses fixed lines of identity formation; for him creolization is characterized by its relational nature. As Gordon and Roberts argue, for Glissant identification is linked to "multiple, rather than singular, roots and foundations that, when taken as a whole, aim at the dual objectives of liberation and of setting foundations for freedom beyond the trappings of dialectics of asymmetrical recognition."[60] This perspective introduces us methodologically to what Glissant calls an ethnographic "poetics of relation" and an analytics of "transversality."[61]

Considering the historical semantics and regional differences embedded in the concept of creolization, caution is required when we translate localized and historically situated notions of *creolization* into a framework of universal human rights. So, how do we translate this to the European context of migrant workers and domestic workers' rights? In the European context, *creolization* not only signals "the underside of European modernity,"[62] but it also brings to mind the transformation of European societies through the impact of movements of postcolonial migration and diaspora. It frames a space in which national rhetoric about identity and community is contested and challenged.

In this sense, Glissant describes Europe as inevitably inscribed in the project of creolization. Creolization, thus, might delineate a different understanding of human rights that focuses on the relational dimension of convivial transversality, embracing the principles of interconnectedness and interdependence. Creolizing human rights, hence, evokes a cosmological perception of rights, one that attaches rights not to a single individual or subject, but to the relationship of this individual or subject to others and his/her environment. From this angle, human rights cannot depart from the separation between the Self and the Other or the Human and the Environment. Rather, it engages with an ethics of relationality and transversality. An example of this can be found in the Quechua Aymara concept of *pacha mama* that Enrique Dussel discusses in regard to his eco-political postulate of "perpetual life."[63] The term *pacha mama*, or what Dussel names *terra mater*, stands for the interconnectedness between environment and human beings. It makes us aware that we cannot exploit the world's resources endlessly as what we are dealing with is our "perpetual life" in the generations that will follow. In Dussel's words, "We must behave such that our actions and institutions allow for the existence of human life on planet Earth forever, perpetually!"[64]

Thus, framing domestic workers' rights from the perspective of *creolizing* human rights entails more than just fighting for fair working conditions or professionalization of domestic work. Rather, it interconnects domestic work as affective labor to a cosmological perspective, uncovering it as the main source for the production and maintenance of human vitality, the sustenance of "perpetual life." Further, it urges us to locate this labor within a collective framework of sustainability and transversal conviviality, departing from a decolonial ethics of affects. On a concrete level, this has implications for the debate on the professionalization of domestic work.

Domestic Work beyond Professionalization

> I don't know how, how other women feel, if they also experience the same or how they deal with it. Besides, there is a reevaluation in the entire society as to what cleaning is and so it is simply a job for the lost. So . . . it's for the invisible. So . . . and I believe that to change the term *cleaning* to another term, this won't make the job better. I find that the conditions are the worst and not at all the name. (Elvira, domestic worker, Hamburg)

Elvira, from Ecuador and working in a private household in Hamburg, reminds us here that the change of the term *cleaner* to *housekeeper* will not necessarily change the working conditions and social dismissal attached to this labor. As Bridget Anderson asserts, claims for paying for and/or professionalizing domestic work are based on the conviction that what is at stake here is labor and that it produces value.[65] What if we start to conceive and treat domestic work as another profession, leading us to a "satisfactory and mutually beneficial solution"[66] for both women, the domestic worker and her employer? As Anderson asks, what if the employer is a single mother struggling with the fact that she is alone with childcare and household work? Shouldn't we find strategies for supporting this woman and what better than to socially recognize and remunerate this labor accordingly when done by another woman? Wouldn't this solution give the migrant domestic worker secure employment with fair wages, health insurance and social benefits? Of course, what is at stake here is a labor attributed to feminized subjects that need to find a way out of a situation for which they have been made socially responsible. Hiring another woman to do the work represents an immediate solution, considering this person a worker with rights and entitlements to a fair salary, social benefits, health insurance and social recognition like other workers should be indisputable.

Domestic work, as I have discussed, is the neuralgic point of affective labor. The value inherent in domestic work is affective value and affective value cannot be just translated into an equivalent monetary form. Affective value transcends the logic of capital. It resonates with the eco-political postulate of "perpetual life." It addresses the value resulting from transversal conviviality, from the ontological character of a creolized society based on power asymmetries, interdependencies and interconnectedness. Its translation into the monetary equivalent value form or the claims for professionalization of domestic work might represent a short-term strategy. Clearly, a long-term strategy needs to expand this pragmatic discourse by focusing on the epistemological premises of human rights. Such a perspective is interested in a decolonial ethics of responsibility, as proposed by Maldonado-Torres, which I would like to connect to the ethics of a politics of affects. Initiatives like the one proposed by *Precarias a la Deriva* for *laboratorio de trabajadoras* (female workers' laboratories), while not explicitly subscribing to this framework, work along these lines of solidarity and reciprocity. As one of the members, Marta explains in regard to the organization of care work:

> Just at a moment, we thought about how to intervene in this terrain. We thought of something like contestation, like the "escraches,"[67] to denounce ungrateful employers, but also agencies, though we were not thinking so much about NGOs, which seems to me to be ungrateful, but yes, we mean these informal agencies which are owned by people making money. Then we also thought of other types of initiatives to recreate a visibility of care work. But we thought that this needed to be laid down in a kind of aggregation, able to build alliances between migrant women and non-migrant women. It should be a physical space. It should be a space where an exchange of information of women taking part in it happens. A space, where resources can be mixed, ways of getting jobs attached to rights. Yes, because of course as Sania often tells us, when you

arrive alone, without legal documentation, without resources, with the aim to send money back to your country, and then on top you are being told that you need to claim for rights. On the other side, autochthonous people, who are precarious, who can be critical in regard to migration laws, if they don't have a direct and lively contact with migrants, they might see it as a question not related to them. Thus, the aim is to create a vital bond, which allows us to create political claims as at the same time resources and work for those that need it.[68]

Situating the *laboratorio de trabajadoras* beyond a state framework of labor regulation and professionalization, *Precarias a la Deriva* delineates a space engaging with a decolonial ethics of responsibility. Refusing to take an entrepreneurial route by cooperating with intermediary agencies exploiting these women's work, they opt for a different model of agency, one resurfacing from the "alliances between migrant women and non-migrant women," constituting a node of support and exchange of information based on women's resources. In this space, political connections between different levels of domination, like those brought about through migration regimes and precarity, can be explored. Solidarity is practiced here on the mutual recognition of support and sharing of resources and knowledge, as well as through the creation of affective bonds. The social and cultural value extracted from *trabajo de cuidados* as affective labor is thus brought back to the community, recreating a common awareness of global inequalities sustaining local intimacies. The *laboratorio de trabajadoras*, while structured by social antagonism as their members hold different degrees of citizenship rights and access to material and symbolic resources, represents a micro-attempt to create and apply new approaches to equal distribution and support. The question raised by Maldonado-Torres in regard to who does the recognizing and who is recognized as subject is set here on a communal basis as everyone is responsible for everyone. The Hegelian relationship of recognition, in which the subject reconstitutes himself through the negation of another subject by reducing him to his object, is dissolved here by replacing it by a decolonial ethics of responsibility, placing attention on the interconnected and interdependent character of the politics of affects.

DECOLONIAL ETHICS OF RESPONSIBILITY
AND THE POLITICS OF AFFECTS

I know that it is difficult, but you can make changes. You know there are a lot of things to talk about, a lot of things to speak about. The same government tells you that you can't go further. It forbids you a lot of things. I know that I have a lot of things against me. I do not have a legal status in this country, but if I would have one, this would be better then. I could speak about a lot more things. I would say more about things that are happening. For example, that there are still political prisoners in Latin America, that in Argentina and Chile the discrimination against indigenous people is terrible. That there is terrible racism in Latin America. That everything is getting globalized. That the gap in salaries is getting immense. That in Guatemala there are people that are hungry. That the governments are not changing anything. That in Mexico women are disappearing and the government is doing little. This is happening in our continent. Therefore, I like Berlin. Here I can say a lot of things, but we need to release this fear. Life is risky, when you are out on the street you can be run over by a car. If we remain silent, we won't change anything. Five hundred years we have been exploited and we will continue to be exploited, if we don't speak up. Therefore, it is good that people come to this country; young people come to this country as they know what is going on. (Carla, domestic worker, Berlin)

In the recognition of the ontological condition of oppression lies the moment of radical responsibility. Consequently, the decolonial ethics of responsibility "highlights the *epistemic priority* of the problem of the color line,"[69] giving a preference to the voices of "the peoples on the periphery," their proposals on "truth, justice, love, critique, community life,"[70] conviviality and reciprocity. It is from this vantage point that I would like to conclude by embedding claims for domestic workers' rights within a decolonial ethics of responsibility deriving from the politics of affects. Such a proposal is suggested here by Carla, who is an "undocumented migrant" in Berlin. While Carla asserts her own situation of dehumanization, as she is officially left without a "voice" due to the lack of recognition of her presence by the German State, she immediately links her personal situation to a broader global societal framework. Carla sets decolonial ethics in relation to the interconnectedness and interdependency of our being. Knowledge and social transformation emanate from the linkage between different situations of oppression and subjugation. The structural moments binding these diverse situations create the universal basis on which claims for a critical humanism are formulated. This is a humanism that departs from the universal recognition of all human beings, fundamental respect and the right to a dignified life. This is only possible if the logic of exploitation and the epistemological premises of an autonomous subject, detached from its environment, its social and affective being, are dismantled. Humanity does not have its end in the individual recognition of the subject; humanity is realized when we embrace a decolonial vision of cosmology, involving not individual property rights, but the recognition of the interconnectedness and interdependency of the whole of humanity.

Carla's vision is clearly embedded in a political proposal of radical responsibility. She reminds us that colonial legacies reframe the present attempts of dehumanization channeled by migration and asylum policies and the dynamics of inequalities incessantly produced in a modern/colonial world-system. Her labor force, while demanded and exploited, is officially negated, leaving her outside of the legal framework of worker's and citizen's rights. Further, as I have discussed throughout this volume, her affective labor not only contributes to the "regeneration" of the individual household she is employed by, but to society as a whole. Her labor generates affective value, a value that is not recognized in society because her subjective contributions as an "undocumented migrant" woman are constantly ignored, undermined and erased.

Domestic work set within the context of "undocumented" migration reveals more than just the reproductive and emotional reproduction of society; it leads us to the neuralgic point of our lives, our affects. What Carla and the other women interviewed in this study do is not just cleaning the house, looking after the children of other women or entertaining the elderly, they are immersed in the affective relations of the household, being affected by them and, more importantly, affecting them. Without the domestic workers some apartments would be left without "life," some households would be reminded that communal life—and life as such—demands care and love for each other and our environment. This brings us to consider what Eve Sedgwick defines as the politics of affects, a visionary political project emphasizing caring for ourselves as communal beings, embracing solidarity, responsibility, generosity and reciprocity.[71] Affect, while exploited as affective labor and extracted as affective value within the logic of capital accumulation, holds the potential of creating an alternative to this same logic.

Relating domestic workers' rights to what Gibson-Graham calls an "ethical subject of a post-capitalist order," means claiming that dignified working conditions, portable workers' rights and social recognition need to be readdressed in regard to a subject that represents a new cosmological vision of transversal conviviality, based on the acknowledgment of interconnectedness and interdependency. Further, this framework needs to be contrasted with the social and cultural order emanating from the coloniality of power, in which a global order is still reinstated, dividing zones of production and zones of exploitation. The migration from the "global South" to the "global North" indicates the overlapping of these segregated zones, recreating instances of "exteriority," "the outside created by the rhetoric of modernity,"[72] within the borders of European nation-states. In order to destabilize this project of dehumanization, based on the exploitation and sedimentation of precarious living and working conditions for gendered and racialized subjects projected as the "Other" of Europe, I aim here to reinforce political strategies focusing on the politics of affects and embracing a decolonial ethics of responsibility. To some extent both parties, domestic workers and female employers, both feminized subjects, experience a devaluation and exploitation of their feminized socialized faculties of empathy, care and attention for others. On the other hand, the organization of their feminized labor within a framework of coloniality places them in a diametrical opposition to each other by elevating one to the owner of the other's labor. In the meantime, the gendered order in affluent private household remains untouched; keeping men out of this sphere and relegating to their female partners the organization of this labor. This is an expression of a broader devaluation of affective labor and ethical sensibility in society, expressed through the societal misrecognition of feelings, the dedicated attention towards others and the principle of care. As feminist theories engaging with the ethics of care[73] have argued, a society based on solidarity needs to share the common understanding that care and love are fundamental for conviviality. This assertion represents the foundation of a decolonial ethics of responsibility based on the politics of affects, departing from "new ethical practices of thinking economy and becoming different kinds of economic beings."[74] As the Argentinean Colectivo Situaciones states, "there is no other form of attacking capital without seeing, at the same time, that its power is that of sadness, powerlessness, individualism, separation, the commodity. Hence, there is no combat against capitalism other than that which consists of producing other forms of sociability, other images of happiness, another politics that no longer separates itself from life."[76]

Notes

NOTES TO THE INTRODUCTION

1. See Alt, *Illegalität im Städtevergleich: Leipzig-München-Berlin.*
2. For the discussion on the simultaneity of flexibilization and perpetuation of gender roles, see Pühl and Schultz, "Gouvernementalität und Geschlecht— Über das Paradox der Festschreibung und Flexibilisierung der Geschlechterverhältnisse."
3. This book draws on a comparative ethnographic study conducted with colleagues in Spain (see Vega Solís and Monteros, *Servicio doméstico y de cuidados*); Germany (see Gutiérrez Rodríguez, "Das postkoloniale Europa dekonstruieren"; "The 'Hidden' Side of the New Economy"; Gutiérrez Rodríguez et al., *Housework and Care Work in Germany*); Austria (see MAIZ, *Housework and Care Work in Austria*); and the UK (see Tate, *Housework and Caretaking in the UK*).
4. See Romero, *Maid in the U.S.A.*, 3. For the discussion on how "race" is configured in the relationship between domestic workers and their employers, see Rollins, *Between Women.* Also the negotiation of class and "race" between employers and domestic workers has represented a main topic in research engaging with global inequalities. See discussion in Hondagneu-Sotelo, *Doméstica*; Constable, *Maid to Order in Hong Kong: Stories of Filipina Workers*; Anderson, *Doing the Dirty Work*; Lan, *Global Cinderellas*; Parreñas, *Servants of Globalization*; Momsen, *Gender, Migration and Domestic Service.*
5. See further discussion in Hondagneu-Sotelo, *Doméstica.*
6. For further discussion, see Escriva and Skinner, "Domestic Work and Trannational Care Chains in Spain"; Williams and Gavanas, "The Intersection of Childcare Regimes and Migration Regimes: A Three-Country Study"; Anderson, "A Very Private Business: Exploring the Demand for Migrant Domestic Workers".
7. For further discussion, see Lutz, *Migration and Domestic Work*; Wills et al., *Global Cities at Work. New Migrant Division of Labour*; *European Journal of Women's Studies* 14(3).
8. Anderson, "A Very Private Business: Migration and Domestic Work," 5.
9. International Restructuring Education Network and International Food, Agriculture, Hotel, Restaurant, Catering, Tobacco and Allied Workers' Association, *Respect and Rights*; Sedoac, *Briefing on Domestic Workers Rights in Spain*; European Trade Union Conference, *Out of the Shadow*; RESPECT and Kalayaan, *Taking Liberties.*

10. See Anderson, *Doing the Dirty Work* and "A Very Private Business: Exploring the Demand for Migrant Domestic Workers"; European Trade Union Conference, *Out of the Shadow*.
11. This program provides care users with a state allowance to make arrangements for their individual care needs.
12. In the UK the role of private agencies providing the supply for care work has been fostered by the privatization of many care services, contracted out by the state. See Anderson, "A Very Private Business: Exploring the Demand for Migrant Domestic Workers."
13. Numerous studies have shown that this division is untenable. See, for example, Escriva, *Securing Care and Welfare of Dependants Transnationally*; Williams and Gavanas, "The Intersection of Childcare Regimes and Migration Regimes: A Three-Country Study"; Vega Solís, *Culturas del Cuidado en Transición*.
14. The coloniality of labor refers here to Anibal Quijano's observations, discussed in "Coloniality of Power, Eurocentrism, and Social Classification."
15. Williams, "The Analysis of Culture," 36.
16. Stewart, *Odinary Affect*.
17. Williams, "The Analysis of Culture," 36.
18. For further discussion on affects and language, see Riley, *Impersonal Passion*.
19. Ibid.
20. Massumi, Parables for the Virtual, 30.
21. Stewart, *Ordinary Affects*, 3.
22. Hochschild, *The Commercialization of Intimate Life* and *The Time Bind*; Carrington, *No Place like Home*; Rollins, *Between Women*; Romero, *Maid in the U.S.A.*; Hondagneu-Sotelo, *Doméstica*; Lan, *Global Cinderellas*.
23. Spinoza, *The Ethics*.
24. Hardt, "Foreword: What Affects Are Good For," x.
25. For Spinoza, "passion" is affect produced by external causes; see *The Ethics*, 154.
26. Ibid., 160ff.
27. See discussion in Ngai, *Ugly Feelings*.
28. Discussions on the "multilayered texture" of oppression can be found in Combahee River Collective, "The Combahee River Collective Statement." For discussion on "interlocking systems of oppression," see Patricia Hill Collins, "Learning from the Outsider Within" and "The Social Construction of Black Feminist Thought."
29. See, for example, Gordon, *Fanon and the Crisis of European Man*; Maldonado-Torres, *Against War*; Davis, *Women, Race & Class*; Lorde, *Sister Outsider*; Anzaldúa, *Borderlands/La Frontera*; Sandoval, *Methodology of the Oppressed*.
30. Spinoza, *The Ethics*, 125.
31. Brennan, *The Transmission of Affect*, 6.
32. Ibid.
33. For further discussion, see Massumi, Parables for the Virtual.
34. Jasbir Puar discusses how through "information and surveillance technologies of control" bodies are produced as "body-as-information," and through their impact on "organic" bodies (Puar, *Terrorist Assemblages*, 175).
35. Ngai, *Ugly Feelings*, 32.
36. Ibid.
37. We conducted in-depth interviews with domestic workers from Eastern Europe, West Africa and Latin America, and with middle-aged, professional, national White women who employed a domestic worker. Further, we held

focus groups with domestic workers about their migration, working conditions and political organizations. The excerpts presented in this book form part of the interviews and conversations conducted in this project. All the research participants gave their consent for this research and authorized the use of the material within the agreed ethical parameters. In each country we conducted 25 interviews and held 10 focus groups. See also Caixeta et al., *Homes, Care, and Borders—Hogares, Cuidados y Fronteras* and "Politiken der Vereinbarkeit verqueren oder" . . . aber hier putzen und pflegen wir alle."

38. Domestic work as a site of contact zones is also discussed in Yeah and Huang, "Singapore Women and Foreign Domestic Workers," p. 274 ff.
39. Pratt, *Imperial Eyes*, 4.
40. Published in Spanish in 1940 as *Contrapunteo Cubano del Tabaco y el Azúcar*, English publication in 1947.
41. Ortiz, Cuban Counterpoints, 103.
42. Through transculturation Ortiz challenges the notions of "cultural contact" and "acculturation" that were being debated in Britain and the United States in the 1930s because for him they disregarded the effects of European colonization and slavery. For further discussion, see Malinowski, "Introduction"; Coronil, "Introduction."
43. See discussion in Quijano, "Coloniality of Power, Eurocentrism, and Social Classification."
44. Gibson-Graham, *The End Of Capitalism (As We Know It). A Feminist Critique of Political Economy*, 68.
45. Coronil, "Introduction," xiv.
46. Enrique Dussel (*1492: El encubrimiento del Otro* and *The Invention of the Americas*) defines the "exteriority" to Europe in regard to the European colonial project, in which an "Other" outside of European modernity and civilization is projected and practically translated into technologies of extermination, exclusion and control. An aspect that Maldonado-Torres (*Against War: Views from the Underside of Modernity*) explores in his analysis of "war" as the underside of modernity and that we can find in discussion in regard to Mbembe's ("Necropolitics") concept of "necropolitics," the continuation of war with other means.
47. For a further discussion on migrant female domestic workers in Europe, see Anderson, *Doing the Dirty Work*; Colectivo Ioé, *Mujer, inmigración y trabajo*; Caixeta et al., *Homes, Care, and Borders—Hogares, Cuidados y Fronteras*; Precarias a la Deriva, *A la Deriva. Por los circuitos de la precariedad femenina*; Hess, *Globalisierte Hausarbeit: Au Pair als Migrationsstrategie von Frauen aus Osteuropa*; Herrera et al., *La migración ecuatoriana: Transnacionalismo, redes e identidades*; Lutz, *Vom Weltmarkt in den Privathaushalt*.
48. For further discussion, see Glick Schiller and Wimmer, "Methodological Nationalism and Beyond."
49. In 2005, the Office of National Statistics Labour Force Survey counted 18,000 Colombians (an increase from 8,000 in 1997), 25,000 Brazilians (an increase from 4,000), 4,000 Argentineans (an increase from 3,000), 1,000 Chileans (a decline from 2,000) and 16,000 Guyanese (McIlwaine, *Living in Latin London*, 7).
50. In 2005, the Austrian Agency of Statistics counted Brazilians as the biggest Latin American group in Austria with 1,859 (in 2001 they were 1,368), followed by Dominicans with 1,409 (in 2001 they were 810), Peruvians with 566 (in 2001 they were 471), Columbians with 533 (in 2001 they were 401) and Chileans with 334. See Statistik Austria.

51. While in the 1970s and 1980s Chileans represented the biggest community in Germany, in the late 1990s, according to statistics from the National Statistics Agency, the Dominican, Columbian, Brazilian and Peruvian communities were the largest. The National Statistics Agency (*Statistisches Bundesamt*) counted 99,858 Latin Americans, 48.8 percent living an average of nine years in Germany. It is estimated that 65 percent are women (Cerda-Hegerl, *Feminisierung der Migration*, 141). In 1995 the Dominicans were 1,943 and in 2007, 5,980, living an average of seven years in Germany. From Ecuador in 1995 the number was 1,145, and in 2007, 8,947. Peru in 1995 was 3,655 and in 2007, 8,947. Chile in 1995 was 3,316 and in 2007, 5,959. These figures only reflect persons with legal residency, which in this case are student visas, work contract or/and married to a European. The number of "undocumented migrant workers" is much higher and mostly based in the urban areas with an extensive personal service and cleaning service demand.
52. For further discussion, see Dalla Costa and James, *The Power of Women and the Subversion of the Community.*
53. Hartmann, "The Unhappy Marriage of Marxism and Feminism"; Delphy, *Close to Home*; Kontos and Walser, "Überlegungen zu einer feministischen Theorie der Hausarbeit"; Kontos, "Zur Geschichte der Hausarbeit"; Werlhof, "Frauenarbeit: Der blinde Fleck in der Kritik der politischen Ökonomie" and "Der Proletarier ist tot. Es lebe die Hausfrau?"
54. See Hondagneu-Sotelo, *Doméstica.*
55. See discussion in Hochschild, "Global Care Chains and Emotional Surplus Value"; Hondagneu-Sotelo, *Doméstica*; Parreñas, *Servants of Globalization.*
56. See discussion in Himmelweit, "The Discovery of 'Unpaid Work'"; Merletti, *El trabajo de cuidados y las nuevas formas de depedencia centro-periferia*; Vega Solís, *Culturas del Cuidado en Transición.*
57. See Hochschild, *The Commercialization of Intimate Life.*
58. Massumi, Parables for the Virtual, 260.
59. Ibid., 28.
60. See discussion in Grossberg, *We Gotta Get Out of This Place.*
61. Negri discusses this aspect in "Value and Affect."
62. Ngai, *Ugly Feelings*, 22.
63. Spivak, "Scattered Speculations on the Question of Value," 74.
64. Gibson-Graham, *Postcapitalist Politics*, xxviii.
65. Spivak, "The Politics of Translation," 179.

NOTES TO CHAPTER 1

1. As my colleague Adrià Castells Ferrando pointed out to me, the process of political, cultural and linguistic unification undertaken by Castile eventuates for the first time in a conflictive manner in the seventeenth century. However, a more visible opposition to the political-administrative and linguistic diversity in the Peninsula is accentuated with Philip V in the eighteenth century, which led to the imposition of the Castilian and the suppression of the language variety in the Peninsula.
2. See further discussion in Puar, *Terrorist Assemblages.*
3. Different theorists have discussed the epistemic prerequisites of "embodied knowledge" and "situated knowledge." See Audre Lorde, *Sister Outsider*; bell hooks, *Feminist Theory*; Gloria Anzaldúa, *Borderlands/La Frontera*; Patricia Hill Collins, *Black Feminist Thought*; Donna Haraway, *Simians,*

Cyborgs and Women; Chandra T. Mohanty, "Under Western Eyes"; Ramón Grosfoguel, "Colonial Difference, Geopolitics of Knowledge and Global Coloniality in the Modern/Colonial Capitalist World-System."
4. Assad, "The Concept of Cultural Translation in British Social Anthropology."
5. Mignolo and Schiwy, "Double Translation: Transculturation and the Colonial Difference."
6. Ibid., 5.
7. Further discussed in Quijano, "Coloniality of Power and Eurocentrism in Latin America."
8. In *The Invention of the Americas*, Dussel discusses how the colonization of the *Américas* extended the violent expansive and oppressive character of the Spanish crown, enforcing a Catholic nation, predominated by the Castilian, demonstrated by the defeat of Boabdil, the last sultan of Granada, in January 6, 1492, the inauguration of the Spanish inquisition in 1481, expulsion of the Spanish Jews in March 31, 1492, and the forced conversion and cultural repression of Spanish Muslims in 1502, resulting in the Edict of Expulsion in 1609. This signaled the end of a rich intercultural intellectual encounter in the Peninsula, in which global knowledge circulated from Baghdad to Córdoba to Toledo. For further discussion see Menocal, "The Culture of Translation."
9. Hegel, "Die Phänomenologie des Geistes," 200ff.
10. For further discussion, see Spivak, *In Other Worlds*.
11. Dussel, *The Invention of the Americas*, 39.
12. Quijano, "Coloniality of Power, Eurocentrism, and Social Classification," 182.
13. See discussion in Mignolo and Schiwy, "Double Translation: Transculturation and the Colonial Difference."
14. Ibid., 11.
15. See discussion in Benjamin, "The Task of the Translator."
16. Benjamin writes: "There is a matter of showing that in cognition there could be no objectivity, not even a claim to it, if it dealt with images of reality; here it can be demonstrated that no translation would be possible if in its ultimate essence it strove for likeness to the original" ("The Task of the Translator," 73).
17. See further discussion in Ricoeur, *On Translation*.
18. Ibid.
19. Ibid., 6.
20. Ibid.
21. Spivak, "The Politics of Translation," 179.
22. Spivak, "Translation as Culture," 22. I would also like to thank Lorraine Pannett for drawing my attention to this aspect.
23. Spivak, "The Politics of Translation," 179.
24. Ibid.
25. For further discussion, see, for example, Nirinjana, *Siting Translation*; Spivak, "The Politics of Translation"; Pratt, "The Traffic in Meaning. Translation, Contagion, Infiltration"; Scharlau, "Repensar la Colonia, las relaciones interculturales y la traducción."
26. Jaaware, "Of Demons and Angels and Historical Humans: Some Events and Questions in Translation and Post-Colonial Theory," 736.
27. Ibid.
28. Mignolo and Schiwy, "Double Translation: Transculturation and the Colonial Difference," 4.
29. Historically, translation also has enabled the transference of Greek philosophy into Arabic and subsequently into Latin between the seventh and ninth

centuries. As Maria Rosa Menocal notes, between the seventh and ninth centuries the Abbasids in Baghdad translated major parts of Greek philosophy and the scientific canon into Arabic. This was enthusiastically received by the intellectual circles of the Ummayads in Córdoba. See Menocal, "The Culture of Translation."

30. Published in 1947 in English as *Cuban Counterpoint: Tobacco and Sugar.*
31. With transculturation Ortiz intervenes in a salient debate in 1940s anthropology on cultural contact by introducing a sociohistorical and ethnocentric critical perspective. This debate was marked by two poles, on the one hand by the British anthropologist Bronislaw Malinowski and his notion of "cultural contact," and on the other by the US-American scholar Melville J. Herskovits and his concept of "acculturation" (Santi, "Introduction," 69; Coronil, "Introduction," xxx). Malinowski interprets "acculturation" to be nothing more than an instantiation of assimilation. In his introduction to *Cuban Counterpoints* he states, "It is an ethnocentric word with a moral connotation. The immigrant has to *acculturate* himself; so do the natives [. . .] who enjoy the benefits of being under the sway of our great Western culture. The word *acculturation* implies, because of the preposition *ad* with which it starts, the idea of a *terminus ad quem*. The 'uncultured' is to receive the benefits of 'our culture'; it is he who must change and become converted into 'one of us'" (Malinowski, "Introduction," lviii).
32. See Coronil, "Transcultural Anthropology in the Américas (with an Accent): The Use of Fernando Ortiz."
33. See discussion in Spivak, "Feminism and Deconstruction," 132.
34. See discussion in Spivak, "Position without Identity," 254.
35. Mignolo and Schiwy, "Double Translation: Transculturation and the Colonial Difference," 17.
36. Maria Ruido's documentary *Memoria Interior* (*Internal Memory*, 2002); Ainhoa Montoya Arteabaro's documentary *La generación olvidada* (*The Forgotten Generation*, 2005) and Marta Arribas and Ana Pérez's *El Tren de La Memoria* (*The Train of Memory*, 2005) depict the situation of this generation.
37. Spivak, "The Politics of Translation," 179.
38. Quijano, "Coloniality of Power and Eurocentrism in Latin America."
39. Mehrez, "Translating Gender," 109.
40. Mehrez shows that the transcription of *genus* "is transformed into an Arabic triliteral root and becomes *janasa*. It proceeds to accumulate a whole range of new significations that do not necessarily coincide with the 'original' word *genus* from which it is transcribed" (ibid.).
41. Ibid.
42. Ibid., 117.
43. For further discussion, see Iveković, "On Permanent Translation." See also Price, "Translating Social Science."
44. Derrida, *Positions*, 54.
45. Iveković, "On Permanent Translation," 121.
46. Spivak, "The Politics of Translation," 177.
47. Spivak, "Can the Subaltern Speak?"
48. Mignolo and Schiwy, "Double Translation: Transculturation and the Colonial Difference," 6.
49. Spivak, *A Critique of Postcolonial Reason*, 103.
50. In *Against War* Nelson Maldonado-Torres discusses decolonial ethics as politics of liberation. I am engaging with this perspective in my last chapter in this book.

51. See Dussel, *The Invention of the Americas: Eclipse of "the Other" and the Myth of Modernity* (Spanish version: *1492: El encrubrimiento del Otro: Hacia el origin del "mito de la modernidad"*); Mignolo, *Local Histories, Global Designs*; Grosfoguel, "Colonial Difference, Geopolitics of Knowledge and Global Coloniality in the Modern/Colonial Capitalist World-System;" Maldonado-Torres, *Against War: Views from the Underside of Modernity*; Escobar, "Mundos y conocimientos de otro modo"; Lugones, "Heterosexualism and the Colonial/Modern Gender System" and "The Inseparability of Race, Class, and Gender."
52. See Mignolo, "De-linking" and "Rousseau and Fanon on Inequality and the Human Sciences."
53. Mignolo, *The Idea of Latin America*, x.
54. Wallerstein, *Unthinking Social Science*.
55. Interestingly, through this perspective Europe's societies are represented as highly complex, individualized and differentiated, whilst the reference to non-European societies exposes little knowledge about the intricate civilizations of Mesopotamia, Persia, China, Mesoamerica (Aztecs and Mayan) and the Andes (Incas and Aymaras), to name just a few. For further discussion, see Gutiérrez Rodríguez et al., *Decolonizing European Sociology*.
56. Dussel discusses the "exteriority" of European modernity in regard to the *Américas*. I like to stress here the "exteriority" within Europe's borders. For further discussion, see Dussel, *The Invention of the Americas*.
57. Mignolo, "De-linking," 497.
58. Anzaldúa, *Borderlands/La Frontera*, 76.
59. Mignolo, "De-linking," 455.
60. Dussel, *The Invention of the Americas*.
61. Ibid., 60.
62. Sandoval notes that *la facultad* (a semiotic vector), the "outsider/within" (a deconstructive vector), "strategic essentialism" (a meta-ideologizing vector), *la conciencia de la mestiza*, "world traveling" or "loving cross-cultures" (differential vectors) and "womanism" (a democratizing, moral vector) represent the "differential technologies of oppositional consciousness, as utilized and theorized by a racially diverse U.S. coalition of women of color" (*Methodology of the Oppressed*, 180–181).
63. Anzaldúa, *Entrevista—Interviews*, 123.
64. For further discussion, see Collins, *Black Feminist Thought*.
65. Ibid., 257.
66. Mies, "Towards a Methodology for Feminist Research."
67. Ibid.
68. See further discussion in Gutiérrez Rodríguez, "'We Need Your Support, but the Struggle Is Primarily Ours': On Representation, Migration and the Sans Papiers Movement."
69. For further discussion, see Bourdieu, *Homo Academicus*.
70. For further discussion, see Gutiérrez Rodríguez, "Decolonizing Postcolonial Rhetorics"; Jones, "Falling between the Cracks: What Diversity Means for Black Women in Higher Education."
71. Elsewhere I have written about the promotion of scholars with a migration background in Germany; see Gutiérrez Rodríguez, "Akrobatik in der Marginalität" and "Akademisches Wissen und militante Forschung. Repräsentationen zwischen Krise und Transfer."
72. See Ortiz, "As ciêncías sociais e o inglês."
73. In Germany the research was conducted by a team composed of researchers, an assistant professor on fixed-term contracts and an associate professor in

a permanent position. The work contracts of the researchers were tied to research funding.

74. The term *precarity* has been translated from the Spanish *precariedad*. Besides referring to "precariousness," an ontological state, "precarity" also denotes a historical and political mode of production, shaping social relations, particularly those of labor. For further discussion, see Precarias a la Deriva, *A la Deriva. Por los circuitos de la precariedad femenina*; Neilson and Rossiter, "Precarity as a Political Concept, or, Fordism as Exception."
75. Mignolo, "De-linking," 498.
76. Anzaldúa, *Borderlands/La Frontera*, 79.
77. Gibson-Graham, *Postcapitalist Politics*, xxviii.
78. Ibid., x.
79. See, for further discussion, Adorno, *Der Positivismusstreit in der deutschen Soziologie*.
80. For further discussion, see Adorno, "Kulturkritik und Gesellschaft."
81. Spivak, "Position without Identity," 254.

NOTES TO CHAPTER 2

1. "Arpilleras" are hand-sewn three dimensional textile pictures, illustrating political issues and life scenes. "Arpilleras" are used as political art forms to contest and illustrate situations of social injustice. In particular, women in Chile and Peru engage with this art form.
2. I would like to thank Margaret Lorraine Pannett for her insights in regard to the cultural prescription and ethical implications of codifying refugees as "asylum seekers" in the UK. In my supervision of her PhD on *Making a Livable Life in Diaspora: Doing Justice to Refugees*, I had the opportunity to discuss this question.
3. See discussion in Puar, *Terrorist Assemblage*.
4. For further discussion, see Kofman and Raghuram, "Gender and skilled migrants."
5. See discussion in Dussel, *The Invention of the Americas*.
6. Castro-Gómez and Grosfoguel, "Prólogo. Giro decolonial, teoría crítica y pensamiento heterárquico," 13.
7. Mignolo, *Local Histories/Global Designs*, 16.
8. See further discussion in Mignolo, "De-linking," and Grosfoguel, "Del Imperialismo de Lenin al Imperio de Hardt y Negri."
9. Marx, *Capital*, paragraph 474, 1027.
10. Mezzadra, "Living in Transition."
11. Marx, *Capital*, 1022 and 1023.
12. See discussion in Mezzadra, "Living in Transition."
13. Ong, *Neoliberalism as Exception*.
14. Ibid., 121.
15. Ibid., 124.
16. Ibid., 125.
17. Ibid.
18. Mezzadra discussed this in regard to Jason Read's analysis of the micro-politics of capital. See Mezzadra, "Living in Transition," and Read, *The Micro-Politics of Capital*.
19. While at the time of writing this chapter the data on the impact of the economic crisis on women's employment is scarce, some surveys show that it is impacting on both genders. For example, in the UK the economic downturn has impacted less on women in employment than men. Some sources

assume that the difference is due to the fact that women are more likely to work in the public sector than men. For example, fewer women than men have been made redundant in the three months prior to December 2008. The redundancy rate for women was 6.6 per 1,000 employees, less than half for men, which was 13.6 per 1,000 employers. See Office for National Statistics, "Labour Force Survey and Returns from Public Sector Organisations." In comparison, in Spain the gap between men's and women's unemployment has not been significantly altered by the economic crisis, as women's unemployment rate (6.57 percent) in January 2009 was slightly higher than men's unemployment rate (6.14 percent). Both unemployment rates were extremely high, reaching 3.3 million unemployed at this time. See "El Gobierno admite que el paro puede llegar a los cuatro milliones traz el alza récord de enero," *El Pais*. The unemployment rate in Spain in the month of March 2009 was 17.36, one of the highest in the EU. See Servicio Público de Empleo Estatal, "Employment Statistics."

20. For further discussion, see Quijano, "Coloniality of Power, Eurocentrism, and Social Classification," and Mignolo, "De-linking."
21. Dussel, *The Invention of the Americas*.
22. Mignolo, *Local Histories/Global Designs*.
23. Anderson, "A Very Private Business: Migration and Domestic Work."
24. Ibid., 11.
25. Anderson, *Motherhood, Apple Pie and Slavery: Reflections on Trafficking Debates*, 2.
26. Broeders and Engbersen, "The Fight against Illegal Migration," 1594.
27. Figures in this area are very difficult to estimate, but following regularization programs in the 1990s and 2000s in Belgium, France, Italy, Greece, Spain and Portugal, nearly three million migrants have been regularized. See Organisation for Economic Co-operation and Development, *Trends in International Migration*, 56.
28. This principle, rhetorically connecting to the idea of "bellum iustum" (the "just war"), "combines two elements: the legitimacy of the military apparatus as ethically grounded—think of the human rights discourse against rogue states—and the legitimacy (*qua* its effectiveness) of the military action to establish the desired Other and the so-called peace" (Atzert and Müller, "The Continuation of War: Polizeywissenschaft, Extended Version").
29. See also discussion in Maldonado-Torres, *Against War*.
30. Ibid.
31. Ibid.
32. This pact is based on a previous communication on "A Common Immigration Policy to Europe: Principles, Actions and Tools" (European Commission, Memo/08/402) and the policy plan "Asylum—An Integrated Approach to Protection across the EU" (European Commission, "Communication from the Commission").
33. See COM (2007, 512).
34. See COM (2006, 402).
35. See COM (2005, 390).
36. See discussion in Kimball, *The Transit State*, on the role of Mexico in regard to migration to the United States, and Morocco in regard to the EU as states that have transformed from "transit states" to states of immigration. This phenomenon is also depicted in the documentary *Wetback*.
37. See article from Bárbulo, "El fiasco de 'Guantanamito,'" in *El País*.
38. The connection between migration and "human trafficking" gravitates around the principle of "security," defining migrants as victims and silencing the dehumanizing effects of migration control policies. This perspective negates migrants' need to escape from poverty, war and persecution.

Through the diagnosis of "human trafficking" the responsibility of the EU Member States for killing thousands of people who attempt to cross European borders seeking a "good life" is avoided by blaming "mafia rings" for these conditions. Discursively, the EU recreates itself as impotent in face of these uncontrollable global networks of "human trafficking," a side effect of border regimes.

39. See discussion in Schumacher and Peyrl, *Fremdenrecht (f. Öster.)*.
40. In summer 2008 the Home Office published a proposal controlling the recruitment of students in universities and colleges. Non-European students will be only able to come if they are sponsored by a UK Border Agency–licensed educational institution and prove that they have the means to support themselves and their families. They need to supply fingerprints, which already marks them as potential suspects. Further, higher education institutions are asked to report to the UK Border Agency about failures in enrollment.
41. This has been debated in Germany along the idea of *Leitkultur*—core culture. The question as to what the fundamentals of German culture are composed of remains fluid. Is the Bavarian Weisswurst (white sausage) more German than the Berlin kebab?
42. Home Office. UKBA, http://www.ukba.homeoffice.gov.uk/managingborders/ borderscitizenshipbill/ (accessed May 5, 2009).
43. In March 2009 the Labour government announced the imposition of a £50 levy on non-European migrants and students to contribute to the costs of the public services. A migration impact fund will be created to cover the costs produced on local public services including councils, schools, the NHS and police. See *Guardian*, "Ministers Impose £50 Levy on Economic Migrants to Pay for Public Services," www.guardian.co.uk/uk/2009/mar/19/immigrants-50 (accessed August 8, 2009).
44. See discussion in Sommerville, *Immigration under New Labour*.
45. Gil Araújo, Las argucias de la integración. Políticas migratorias, construcción nacional y cuestión social.
46. Ibid.
47. Edouard Glissant's claim is that there is an "irreversible creolization of the world." He speaks of the languages of the "creolized streets" of Rio de Janeiro, Mexico or the Parisian suburbs. For him these spaces show the speed of innovation and creativity in culture. He notes that not all of these cultures and subcultures last, but they leave traces of sensibility in their communities. For Glissant, the moment of creolization is not fixed by geographical locations. See Glissant, *Poetics of Relation*.
48. See Gutiérrez Rodríguez, "Transculturation in German and Spanish Migrant and Diasporic Cinema," and Göktürk, "Turkish Women on German Streets."
49. See Gutiérrez Rodríguez et al., *Decolonizing European Sociology*.
50. As Shirley Anne Tate discusses in reference to Frantz Fanon; see Tate, *Black Beauty*.
51. See discussion in Balibar, *Race, Nation, Class*.
52. Jean Charles de Menezes was misidentified by the London Metropolitan Police and shot dead at Stockwell metro station on July 22, 2005.
53. See discussion in Actis, "Inmigrantes Latinoamericanos en España," and CEPAL, *Migración internacional, derechos humanos y desarrollo*.
54. See Actis, "Inmigrantes Latinoamericanos en España."
55. See Pellegrino, *Trends in International Migration in Latin America and the Caribbean*; Padilla and Peixoto, "Latin American Immigration to Southern Europe."
56. See discussion in Herrera et al., *La migración ecuatoriana*.
57. Ibid.

58. See discussion in Actis and Esteban, "Argentina en España: inmigrantes, a pesar de todo."
59. For example, in 2006 Mexico estimated that 30 percent of its citizens were born in other Latin American and Caribbean countries. See CEPAL, *Migración internacional, derechos humanos y desarrollo.*
60. See discussion in Herrera et al., *La migración ecuatoriana.*
61. See Gil Araújo, "Las migraciones en las políticas de la fortaleza. Sobre las múltiples fronteras de la Europa comunitaria."
62. For further discussion on this topic, see Izquierdo, "Cuatro razones para pensar la inmigración irregular"; Martinez Buján and Golías Pérez, "La latinoamericanización de la inmigración a España"; Arango, "Europa y la integración, una relación difícil."
63. In 1996, 4,000 Ecuadorians were officially registered, while in 2001 33,000 were counted; also the figures of officially registered Colombians rose in the same period from 12,500 to 20,200. See Arango, "La población inmigrada en España."
64. See Pedone, "Tú, siempre jalas a los tuyos"; Pagnotta, "Ni aquí, ni allá. L'immigrazione feminile dell'Ecuador."
65. See García-Calvo Rosell, *Las relaciones bilaterales España-Ecuador*; Actis, "Inmigrantes Latinoamericanos en España."
66. Actis, "Inmigrantes Latinoamericanos en España."
67. See further discussion in Herrera, *Ecuador.*
68. Ibid.
69. Spain's labor market is regulated by three social security regimes: general security regime, agricultural regime and domestic work regime. See Actis, "Ecuatorianos y ecuatorianas en España."
70. Ibid.
71. Ibid.
72. Actis, "Inmigrantes Latinoamericanos en España."
73. Ibid.
74. See discussion in Bulmer-Thomas, *The Economic History of Latin America since Independence.*
75. See Peñaloza, "Appropriating the 'Unattainable': The British Travel Experience in Patagonia."
76. McIlwaine, *Living in Latin London*; Carlisle, "Marginalisation and Ideas of Community among Latin American Migrants to the UK"; Román-Velázquez, *The Making of Latin London*; Block, *Multilingual Identities in a Global City: London Stories.*
77. For further discussion, see Kyambi, *Beyond Black and White.*
78. Ibid., 8.
79. See Anderson, "A Very Private Business."
80. See further discussion in Anderson et al., *Migrants' Lives beyond the Workplace.*
81. Hsiao-Hung Pai, "An Ethnography of Global Labour Migration" and *Chinese Whispers.*
82. For further discussion, see Kalayaan and Oxfam, *The New Bonded Labour?*
83. McIlwaine, *Living in Latin London*, 3 and for further discussion, Wills et al., *Global Cities at Work.*
84. Kyambi, *Beyond Black and White*, 102.
85. McIlwaine, *Living in Latin London*, 7.
86. See Bermúdez Torres, "Colombian Migration to Europe: Gender, Political Transnationalism and Conflict"; Buchuck, *Crossing Borders.*
87. Però, "Migrants' Mobilization and Anthropology. Reflections from the Experience of Latin Americans in the United Kingdom."

88. See James, *Ecuadorian Identity, Community and Multicultural Integration*.
89. See Sveinsson, *Bolivians in London*.
90. Però, "Political Engagement of Latin Americans in the UK."
91. Germany's official colonial history in West (Cameroon, Nigeria, Ghana, Togo), South (Namibia, Botswana) and East Africa (Tanzania, Rwanda, Burundi, parts of Kenya and Mozambique) lasted from 1883 to 1919. See Friedrichsmeyer et al., *The Imperialist Imagination. German Colonialism and Its Legacy*; Oguntoye et al., *Farbe bekennen: Afro-deutsche Frauen auf den Spuren ihrer Geschichte.*
92. Kolinsky and van der Will, *The Cambridge Companion to Modern German Culture*; Bade, *Europa in Bewegung.*
93. See Hannah Arendt's critique on the fear of "Pan-Slavismus" in the German Empire in *The Origins of Totalitarianism* (original title: *Elemente und Ursprünge totaler Herrschaft*).
94. Kolinsky and van der Will, *The Cambridge Companion to Modern German Culture*, 112.
95. Ibid.
96. Ibid., 113.
97. For further discussion see Herbert, *Nationalsozialistische Vernichtungspolitik 1939–1945* and Schulte, *Zwangsarbeit und Vernichtung.*
98. Between 1959 and 1968, the Federal Employment Agency (*Bundesanstalt für Arbeit*) set up recruitment agencies and issued contracts with Spain, Greece, Turkey, Morocco, Portugal, Tunisia and Yugoslavia. In 1955, 1,000 Italian immigrants arrived, in 1960 280,000 migrants were living in West Germany (Kolinsky and van der Will, *The Cambridge Companion to Modern German Culture*, 117) Parallel to the development in the FRG, in the GDR a similar process of "foreign worker" recruitment took place between the 1960s and 1970s, based on workers' exchange programs with the so-called "socialist brother states," notably Vietnam, Mozambique, Angola, Poland, Hungary and Cuba.
99. See the films *La generación olvidada* (*The Forgotten Generation*), *La Memoria Interior* (*The Interior Memory*), *El Tren de La Memoria* (*The Train of Memory*).
100. In 1993, for example, the right to asylum based on individual evidences of political persecution was changed. From then on, asylum petitions could be made if the country of origin was one of the countries considered "politically unsafe" by the Agency of Foreign Affairs.
101. Paz de la Torre, "Lateinamerikanische Immigrantinnen und ihre Integration in den deutschen Dienstleistungssektor"; Hernandez and Kron, "Schatten im Paradies"; Cerda-Hegerl, "Wo gehst du hin?"; Gruner-Domić, *Latinas in Deutschland.*
102. Krämer, "Das verschmähte Erbe." Statistisches Bundesamt, *Lateinamerikaner in Deutschland*, 2007.
103. Ibid.
104. Cerda-Hegerl, "Feminisierung der Migration von Lateinamerika nach Deutschland," 141.
105. Ibid., 143.
106. Ibid.
107. Alt, *Illegalität im Städtevergleich.*
108. The limited number of persons in the Austrian workforce was primarily the result of the increase in compulsory education, improved pension plans, and the emigration of Austrian citizens (See MAIZ, *Housework and Care Work in Austria*).

109. See also the exhibition catalog *Gastarbajteri: 40 Years of Work Migration* by *Initiative Minderheiten* (the Austrian Platform for Minorities), Vienna Museum, 2004.
110. Bauböck, "'Nach Rasse und Sprache verschieden.'"
111. See MAIZ, *Housework and Caretaking in Austria.*
112. Receipt of a (temporary or permanent) residence permit is dependant upon the legally predefined and validated purpose (education, employment, *au pair* or family reunification). See MAIZ, *Housework and Caretaking in Austria*, 19.
113. Ibid.
114. Haidinger, "Contingencies among Households," 134.
115. LEFÖ, see www.lefoe.at; MAIZ, see www.maiz.at; Peregrina, see www.peregrina.at.
116. Up until about 20 years ago, women most commonly came to Austria with (or followed) their husbands (for family reunification). Since the 1990s, more and more women have migrated alone to Austria to join the labor force of care workers (in the formal and informal sectors) or for other jobs, such as sex work. Women have also come as refugees or because of marriage to an Austrian citizen. Up until 2001, the gender structure of the migrant population had changed, as there was a distinct shift toward an increase in women. This development is primarily due to family reunification. Secondly, the patterns and structures of migration to Austria in the last 10 to 15 years show a significant increase in female migrants from Central Europe. See discussion in MAIZ, *Housework and Caretaking in Austria.*
117. Sex work in Austria is regulated through the "artist visa." However, this visa entitles women just to work in a determined establishment and for a certain period of time. If the sex worker changes employment or her work contract has terminated, she slips into a situation of irregularity. See discussion in Caixeta, "Jenseits eines simplen Verelendungsdiskurses."
118. See MAIZ, *Housework and Caretaking in Austria*; Haidinger, "Contingencies among Households."
119. Düvell, *Illegal Immigration in Europe*, 239.

NOTES TO CHAPTER 3

1. EU Report, "Equality between Women and Men."
2. This is particularly significant in leading positions. For example, the proportion of company directors who are women is stagnating at 33 percent, and in politics, 23 percent of national Members of Parliament (MPs) and 33 percent of Members of the European Parliament (MEPs) are women. EU Report, "Equality between Women and Men."
3. Foucault et al., "La 'gouvernementalité.'"
4. Ibid.
5. Ibid.
6. For further discussion, see Rose, *Governing the Soul.*
7. Misra et al., "The Globalization of Care Work."
8. See discussion in Caixeta et al., *Homes, Cares and Borders.*
9. For a critique of this program in Spain, see Pietersen, "Framing Domestic Work(ers) in Gender Equality Policies in Spain."
10. In Spain the provision of maternity and paternity leave is relatively low in comparison to Scandinavian countries. In 1995 only 31.2 percent of women were benefiting from maternity leave, in 2002 the number was raised to 54 percent (Flaquer, "La articulación entre familia y el Estado de

bienestar en los países de la Europa del sur," 34). Maternity leave can be taken for 16 weeks and split between partners. However, only 1.4 percent of men took paternity leave in 2007 (Unión General de Trabojadores, *Press News: Avanza la Igualdad*). This is not just a result of a preexistent gender role model, but also of the fact that women earn on average 30 percent less than men (Unión General de Trabojadores, *Press News: Avanza la Igualdad*; EU Report, "Equality between Women and Men"). The option to go part-time to care for children or the elderly is taken by 98.6 percent of women.

11. In general, Austria and Spain guarantee sixteen weeks of full paid maternity leave, while Germany offers 14 weeks full paid maternity leave plus 12 months at 67 percent, which can be taken by each partner. The UK, instead, guarantees the first six weeks of paid maternity leave at 90 percent. In the UK 25 percent of the employed population works part-time, in Germany 21 percent, in Austria 19 percent and in Spain 8 percent.

12. In Spain, for example, a subsidy of 100 euros a month for working mothers with children under three was introduced in 2002 (Williams and Gavanas, "The Intersection of Childcare Regimes and Migration Regimes," 18).

13. In 2007, Germany introduced "parents' money" (*Elterngeld*) to give professional women or men an incentive to stay home from work for a year and look after their children. If a new mother does so, she will receive 67 percent of her net salary up to a maximum of 1,800 euros a month.

14. See discussion in Escriva and Skinner, "Domestic Work and Transnational Care Chains in Spain"; Williams and Gavanas, "The Intersection of Childcare Regimes and Migration Regimes"

15. For further discussion, see MAIZ, *Housework and Caretaking in Austria.*

16. The German example illustrates that care provision is a complex topic related to communal and country-specific conditions. In Germany, for example, the provision of childcare is a *Bundesland* (federal state) issue and varies in regard to the political agenda and individual budget of each *Bundesland*. A report of the journal Parents (*Eltern*) and the Initiative for a New Social Market Economy (*Initiative Neue Soziale Marktwirtschaft*) shows disparities between the regional North and South as well as East and West. For example, in one of the richest federal states in Germany, Baden-Württemberg, in the city of Tübingen, a family can pay up to 3,552 euros for two kindergarten places, while in Heilbronn, a city in the state of North-Rhine Westphalia, access to childcare is free for children between three and six.

17. In Spain, for example, studies on care work and first analysis of the "law of dependency," a law that introduces the right for public care for "dependant" persons, demonstrate that largely migrant women are employed in this sector. See Escriva, *Securing Care and Welfare of Dependants Transnationally*; Anderson, *Doing the Dirty Work*; Escriva and Skinner, "Domestic Work and Transnational Care Chains in Spain"; Williams and Gavanas, "The Intersection of Childcare Regimes and Migration Regimes."

18. In the year 2005 a total number of 1,667 women were placed as care workers for the elderly, in 2006 the number rose to 2,241. See http://www.arbeitsagentur.de (accessed February 2, 2008).

19. See Williams, "Race, Ethnicity, Gender and Class in Welfare States"; Williams and Gavanas, "The Intersection of Childcare Regimes and Migration Regimes"; Lutz, *Migration and Domestic Work*; Misra et al., "The Globalization of Care Work"; Hobson et al., *Contested Concepts in Gender and Social Politics.*

20. Williams and Gavanas, "The Intersection of Childcare Regimes and Migration Regimes," 15.
21. See Hondagneu-Sotelo, *Doméstica*; Parreñas, *Servants of Globalization*.
22. Hondagneu-Sotelo, *Doméstica*, 13.
23. Anderson, "A Very Private Business," 248.
24. Anderson and O'Connell Davison, *Is Trafficking in Human Beings Demand Driven?*
25. Misra et al., "The Globalization of Care Work," 320.
26. See discussion in Herrera et al., *La migración ecuatoriana*; Sassen, *Globalization and Its Discontents*; Ehrenreich and Hochschild, *Global Woman*.
27. See Herrera, *Ecuador*.
28. Lewis, "Welcome to the Margins," 554.
29. *RESPECT* and Kalayaan, European Network of Migrant Domestic Workers, Solidar and Kalayaan. *Taking Liberties*.
30. For further information, see, http://www.kalayaan.org.uk/.
31. Anderson, "The Devil Is in the Detail."
32. Ibid.
33. Home Office, *Domestic Workers*.
34. Anderson, "A Very Private Business"; Williams and Gavanas, "The Intersection of Childcare Regimes and Migration Regimes."
35. The debate on amnesty is surfacing slowly. In spring 2009 the media reported the London mayor Boris Johnson's proposal for an amnesty for "illegal workers." However, this proposal has not been pursued further. Instead, in June 2009, "undocumented migrant" cleaners at SOAS who had joined UNISON and organized to win the London Living Wage suffered a brutal immigration raid. This raid is indicative of the increasing persecution of "undocumented migrant" workers in the London area.
36. Anderson and Ruhs, *Semi-Compliance in the Migrant Labour Market*.
37. As Andersson discusses, according "to UK Household Satellite Accounts (The Office for National Statistics) the value of unpaid work ranges from 44 per cent to 104 per cent of GDP [. . .]. For those who are paying for child or elderly care, i.e. a full time worker, if they are using the formal economy, once they have paid tax and National Insurance out of their taxed income even low rates of pay can cost the middle class employer a lot relative to their income" ("A Very Private Business," 4).
38. Ibid.
39. Ibid., 12.
40. See discussion in Williams and Gavanas, "The Intersection of Childcare Regimes and Migration Regimes."
41. Ibid., 18.
42. Anderson, "A Very Private Business"; Wills et al., *Global Cities at Work*.
43. Tate, *Housework and Caretaking in the UK*.
44. Pla Julián and Sánchez, *Luces y Sombras de la Reconcialiación*.
45. In 1998, the average monthly social security contributions for domestic workers came to approximately 108.37 euros, compared with 493.49 euros for normal workers.
46. Women's employment has jumped from 31.5 percent in 1993 to 54.6 percent in 2007. See Unión General de Trabajadores, *Press News: Avanza la Igualdad*.
47. For further discussion, see Parella Rubio, *Mujer, inmigrante y trabajadora*; Monteros and Vega Solís, *Servicio doméstico y de cuidados*; Caixeta et al., *Homes, Care and Borders*.
48. Servicio Público de Empleo Estatal, "Employment Statistics."
49. Colectivo Ioé, *Mujer, inmigración y trabajo*.

50. Instituto de la Mujer and Center of Economic Studies Tomillo, *La presencia de las mujeres en el empleo irregular.* For further discussion, see also Galloti, *The Gender Dimension of Domestic Work in Western Europe.*
51. The dual character of professional formation in Germany consists of a practical and a theoretical part. During three years students work with an employer and attend vocational schools twice a week, where they receive a theoretical preparation into their profession.
52. Heubach, "Migrantinnen aus Mittel- und Osteuropa in ungeschützten Arbeitsverhältnisse."
53. "Mini-jobs" are jobs not exceeding more than 400 euros a month.
54. See Gather et al., *Weltmarkt Privathaushalt*; Hess, *Globalisierte Hausarbeit*; Schultz, "Domestic Slavery oder Green Card? Feministische Strategien zu bezahlter Arbeit"; Caixeta et al., "Politiken der Vereinbarkeit verqueren oder . . . aber hier putzen und pflegen wir alle"; Gutiérrez Rodríguez, "The 'Hidden Side' of the New Economy" and "Das postkoloniale Europa dekonstruieren"; Lutz, *Vom Weltmarkt in den Privathaushalt*; Odierna, *Die heimliche Rückkehr der Dienstmädchen.*
55. Baethge and Alda, *Berichterstattung zur sozioökonomischen Entwicklung in Deutschland*, 429.
56. Schupp, "Quantitative Verbreitung von Erwerbstätigkeit in privaten Haushalten Deutschlands," 65.
57. Baethge and Alda, *Berichterstattung zur sozioökonomischen Entwicklung in Deutschland*, 429.
58. Ibid., 430.
59. Under these circumstances work is organized based on different employers, configuring what Susanne Schultz denominates a "patchwork" employment. See Schultz, "Domestic Slavery oder Green Card? Feministische Strategien zu bezahlter Arbeit."
60. Gutiérrez Rodríguez et al., *Housework and Care Work in Germany.*
61. See also the discussions in Odierna, *Die heimliche Rückkehr der Dienstmädchen*, and Schultz, "Domestic Slavery oder Green Card? Feministische Strategien zu bezahlter Arbeit."
62. See http://www.minijobzentrale.de/3_Privathaushalte_als_Arbeitgeber/index.html (accessed February 23, 2008).
63. See http://www.bundesregierung.de/Themen-AZ/Arbeit-,9922/Minijobs.htm (accessed September 27, 2006).
64. MAIZ, *Housework and Caretaking in Austria.*
65. This law substituted the term "servant" (*Dienstbote*) with "domestic help" (*Hausgehilfe*).
66. MAIZ, *Housework and Caretaking in Austria*, 12.
67. Ibid., 16.
68. The share of migrant employees in the economic sector of private households was 16.4 percent in 2000, compared to the percentage of migrant employees in all sectors, which was only 10.3 percent. Only 0.2 percent (660 persons in 2000) of all foreign employees work in private households (MAIZ, *Housework and Care Work in Austria*, 15).
69. MAIZ, *Housework and Caretaking in Austria.*
70. Ibid.
71. Haidinger, "Contingencies among Households," 128.
72. Ibid.
73. MAIZ, *Housework and Caretaking in Austria*, 32.
74. Ibid.
75. Ibid., 18.
76. Anderson, *Doing the Dirty Work.*
77. Lan, *Global Cinderellas.*

NOTES TO CHAPTER 4

1. Fraad et al., *Bringing It All Back Home*; Gibson-Graham, *The End of Capitalism*, 65–66; Hochschild, *The Time Bind*.
2. For further discussion, see Lan, *Global Cinderellas*.
3. See Carrington, *No Place like Home*.
4. Hartmann, "The Unhappy Marriage of Marxism and Feminism"; Delphy, *Close to Home*; Dalla Costa and James, *The Power of Women and the Subversion of the Community*.
5. Dalla Costa and James, *The Power of Women and the Subversion of the Community*.
6. Marx, *Capital*, 45.
7. Ibid., 20.
8. Ibid., 138.
9. Ibid., 20.
10. The analysis of the production, exchange and circulation of commodities is crucial for Marx. Thus, the commodity congeals the complex dynamics in which labor-power and labor-time are transformed into value. "The purchase of labour-power for a fixed period is the prelude to the production process; and this prelude is constantly repeated when the period of time for which the labour-power has been sold comes to an end, when a definite period of production, such as a week or a month, has elapsed. But the worker is not paid until after he has expended his labour-power, and realized both the value of his labour-power and a certain quantity of surplus-value in the shape of commodities" (Marx, *Capital*, 712).
11. Ibid.
12. Ibid., 35.
13. The *ursprüngliche Akkumulation* (original accumulation) appears in Marx's work in regard to the primary exploitation of the raw resources in the European colonies of Africa, America, Asia and Oceania. The term *ursprüngliche Akkumulation* is translated as "primitive accumulation." I prefer to translate it as "original accumulation" as the idea that is conveyed in this term is the origins of capitalism. The Marxist concept of *ursprüngliche Akkumulation* suggests a "primitive stage" previous to European colonization and industrialization, negating, for example, the precolonial economies of these continents.
14. Ibid.
15. Ibid.
16. In the original German version: "Die Menschen beziehen also ihre Arbeitsprodukte nicht aufeinander als Werte, weil diese Sachen ihnen als bloß sachliche Hüllen gleichartig menschlicher Arbeit gelten. Umgekehrt. Indem sie ihre verschiedenartigen Produkte einander im Austausch als Werte gleichsetzen, setzen sie ihre verschiednen Arbeiten einander als menschliche Arbeit gleich. Sie wissen das nicht, aber sie tun es. Es steht daher dem Werte nicht auf der Stirn geschrieben, was es ist. Der Wert verwandelt vielmehr jedes Arbeitsprodukt in eine gesellschaftliche Hieroglyphe" (MEW, 88).
17. Rollins, *Between Women*.
18. Marx, *Capital*, 15.
19. Ibid., 45.
20. Ibid., 317.
21. Ibid., 329.
22. Ibid., 331.
23. Dalla Costa and James, *The Power of Women and the Subversion of the Community*.
24. Dalla Costa and James, *The Power of Women and the Subversion of the Community*; Delphy, *Close to Home*; Kontos, "Zur Geschichte der Hausarbeit."

25. Dalla Costa and James, *The Power of Women and the Subversion of the Community*, 40.
26. This extract was translated by me.
27. See discussion in Werlhof, "Der Proletarier ist tot."
28. See further discussion in Mohanty, "Under Western Eyes."
29. Combahee River Collective, "The Combahee River Collective Statement," 275.
30. Spivak, "The Woman as Theatre."
31. See further discussion in Werlhof, "Frauenarbeit: Der blinde Fleck in der Kritik der politischen Ökonomie," 19.
32. See discussion in Hardt and Negri, *Empire*.
33. For further discussion, see Lazzarato, "Immaterial Labour."
34. Ong, *Neoliberalism as Exception*.
35. Ibid., 124.
36. For further discussion, see Lazzarato, "Immaterial Labour" and "From Biopower to Biopolitics"; Hardt and Negri, *Empire*; Hardt, "Affective Labor."
37. Precarias a la Deriva, *A la Deriva*.
38. As Laura Fantone observes, political activists in Spain, Italy, France and Germany "reclaimed [the word *precario*] in an attempt to raise consciousness and dissent over increasing temporary work contracts" in the late 1990s (Fantone, "Precarious Changes," 7).
39. Following the principle of the Situationist International movement and Guy Debord psychogeographies, *Precarias* develops a feminist methodology of linking personal stories to social spaces by engaging with the everyday itineraries, drifts, of women.
40. Precarias a la Deriva, *A la Deriva*, 28.
41. For further discussion, see Revel, "Devenir-Femme de la politique," where she discusses "Becoming Woman" as an expression of subjugation and subjectivation at the same time. "Becoming Woman" evolves at the threshold of these two moments.
42. For further discussion, see Deleuze and Guattari, *A Thousand Plateaus*.
43. See Vega Solís, *Culturas del Cuidado en Transición*.
44. Hochschild, *The Managed Heart*, 7.
45. Carrington, *No Place like Home*, 33.
46. Rose, *Governing the Soul*, 126.
47. Rollins, *Between Women*; Romero, *Maid in the U.S.A.*; Hondagneu-Sotelo, *Doméstica*; Lan, *Global Cinderellas*.
48. See Hochschild, *The Time Bind* and *The Commercialization of Intimate Life*; Carrington, *No Place like Home*; Lan, *Global Cinderellas*.
49. Carrington, *No Place like Home*, 14.
50. Ibid., 51.
51. Ibid., 58.
52. Wrigley, *Other People's Children*, 142.
53. See discussion in Anderson, *Doing the Dirty Work*.
54. Gibson-Graham, *The End of Capitalism*, 65.
55. For further discussion, see Casarino and Negri, *Praise of the Common*.
56. Lan, *Global Cinderellas*,13.
57. Dussel, *Twenty Theses on Politics*, 60.
58. Ibid.
59. Ibid., 26.
60. Ibid., 60.
61. This is a topic discussed in Casarino and Negri, *Praise of the Common*.
62. For further discussion, see Mbembe, "Necropolitics."

NOTES TO CHAPTER 5

1. For further discussion, see Horkheimer et al., *Dialectic of Enlightenment.*
2. Hall discusses this aspect in "The Local and the Global."
3. Lan, *Global Cinderellas*, 11.
4. Ibid.
5. For further discussion, see Bourdieu, *Language and Symbolic Power.*
6. See Saussure, *Écrits de linguistique générale.*
7. Bourdieu, *Language and Symbolic Power*, 54.
8. Ibid., 46.
9. Bourdieu, *Distinction*, 474.
10. Bourdieu, *Language and Symbolic Power*, 86.
11. For further discussion, see Austin, *How to Do Things with Words.*
12. Myles, "From Habitus to Mouth," 890.
13. See MAIZ, *Housework and Caretaking in Austria*, 68.
14. Anderson, *Doing the Dirty Work*, 21.
15. Lan, *Global Cinderellas*, 18.
16. Monteros and Vega Solís, *Servicio doméstico y de cuidados*, 46.
17. See discussion in Bourdieu, *Language and Symbolic Power*, 139ff., and "Symbolic Power."
18. MAIZ, *Housework and Caretaking in Austria.*
19. Ibid., 53–54.
20. Rollins, *Between Women*; Romero, *Maid in the U.S.A.*; Hondagneu-Sotelo, *Doméstica.*
21. For further discussion, see Anderson, *Doing the Dirty Work*; Odierna, *Die heimliche Rückkehr der Dienstmädchen*; Kofman et al., *Gender and International Migration in Europe*; Lutz, *Vom Weltmarkt in den Privathaushalt.*
22. Cohen, "The Working Conditions of Immigrant Women, Live-in Domestics" and "Women of Color in White Households."
23. In Germany, NGOs such as the *Zentrale Integrierte Anlaufstelle für Pendler-Innen aus Osteuropa* (ZAPO) have denounced, for example, the fact that migration status has an impact on the hourly rate. See Heubach, "Migrantinnen aus Mittel- und Osteuropa in ungeschützten Arbeitsverhältnisse."
24. MAIZ, *Housework and Caretaking in Austria*, 58.
25. Quijano, "Coloniality of Power, Eurocentrism, and Social Classification," 187.
26. This is an aspect that Margaret Lorraine Pannett discusses in her PhD on "Making a Livable Life in Diaspora: Doing Justice to Refugees."
27. MAIZ, *Housework and Caretaking in Austria*, 72.
28. As Bridget Anderson notes, "while on the one hand the Other is constructed as a homogenous creature, well suited for domestic labour, on the other a nineteenth-century hierarchy operates in which one 'race' is very clearly differentiated from another 'race'" (*Doing the Dirty Work*, 152).
29. Bourdieu, *Language and Symbolic Power*, 209.
30. See discussion on the "feminine condition" in Beauvoir, *Le deuxième sexe.*
31. For further discussion, see Kofman, "Female 'Birds of Passage' a Decade Later: Gender and Immigration in the European Union."
32. Quijano, "Coloniality of Power, Eurocentrism, and Social Classification," 189.
33. Ibid.
34. My translation. See Castro-Gómez and Grosfoguel, "Prólogo. Giro decolonial, teoria crítica y pensamiento heterárquico," 13: "Asistimos más bien a una transición del colonialismo moderno a la colonialidad global, proceso

que ciertamente ha modificado las formas de dominación desplegadas por la modernidad, pero no la estructura de las relaciones centro-periferia a escala mundial."
35. Anzaldúa, *Borderlands/La Frontera*, 76.
36. Anzaldúa, *Interviews—Entrevistas*, 235.
37. Anzaldúa, "Within the Crossroad," 122.
38. Ibid.
39. Quijano, "Coloniality of Power, Eurocentrism, and Social Classification," 189.
40. For further discussion, see Phizacklea, "Transnationalism, Gender and Global Workers."
41. This is an aspect that Ninna Nyberg Sørensen's discusses in regard to domestic workers from the Dominican Republic working in Madrid and New York. See Nyberg Sørensen, "Mobile Lebensführung zwischen der Dominikanischen Republik, New York und Madrid," and Nyberg Sørensen and Guarnizo, "Transnational Family Life Across the Atlantic."

NOTES TO CHAPTER 6

1. In the original German version: "Das Geheimnisvolle der Warenform besteht also einfach darin, dass sie den Menschen die gesellschaftliche Charaktere der Arbeitsprodukte selbst, als gesellschaftliche Natureigenschaften dieser Dinge zurückspiegelt, daher auch das gesellschaftliche Verhältnis der Produzenten zur Gesamtarbeit als ein außer ihnen existierendes gesellschaftliches Verhältnis von Gegenständen. Durch dies Quidproquo werden die Arbeitsprodukte Waren, sinnlich übersinnliche oder gesellschaftliche Dinge. So stellt sich der Lichteindruck eines Dinges auf den Sehnerv nicht als subjektiver Reiz des Sehnervs selbst, sondern als gegenständliche Forme eines Dings außerhalb des Auges dar. Aber beim Sehen wird wirklich Licht von einem Ding, dem äußeren Gegenstand, auf ein andres Ding, das Auge, geworfen" (MEW, 23, 86).
2. Gibson-Graham et al, *Class and Its "Others,"* 7.
3. Ibid.
4. Here, Vega Solís shares Sarah Ahmed's notion of affect as orientation. See Ahmed, *The Cultural Politics of Emotion*; Vega Solís, *Culturas del Cuidado en Transición.*
5. Translated by author, Vega Solís, *Culturas del Cuidado en Transición*, 188.
6. Ibid., 187.
7. Ibid., 189.
8. For further discussion, see Terada, *Feeling in Theory.*
9. See for further discussion in Aristotle, *The Art of Rhetoric.*
10. Spinoza, "The Ethics."
11. Ibid., 161.
12. Hardt, "Foreword: What Affects Are Good For," ix.
13. Massumi, Parables for the Virtual, xvii.
14. Ibid.
15. Spinoza, "The Ethics," 96.
16. Ahmed, *The Cultural Politics of Emotion.*
17. Spinoza, "The Ethics," 113.
18. Deleuze and Guattari, *A Thousand Plateaus*, 283.
19. Ibid.
20. Spinoza, "The Ethics," 115.

21. Hardt, "Foreword: What Affects Are Good For," ix; Deleuze and Guattari, *A Thousand Plateaus*, 288.
22. Massumi, *Parables for the Virtual*, 30.
23. Negri, "Value and Affect," 78.
24. Ibid.
25. Hardt, "Affective Labor."
26. Ngai, *Ugly Feelings*.
27. Ibid., 335.
28. Ibid., 336.
29. Sarah Ahmed discusses the "stickiness" of feelings in order to understand how projections impregnate our bodies. See, *The Cultural Politics of Emotion* and "Affective Economies."
30. MAIZ, *Housework and Care Work in Austria*, 69.
31. Ibid., 63.
32. Susanne Schultz, "Domestic Slavery oder Green Card?"
33. Monteros and Vega Solís, *Servicio doméstico y de cuidados*, 37.
34. For further discussion, see Hondagneu-Sotelo, *Doméstica*; Nyberg Sørensen, "Transnational Family Life across the Atlantic"; Pribilsky, "Aprendemos a convivir"; Manalansan, "Queer Intersections."
35. Regarding women single migration and children, see Pedone, "Tú, siempre jalas a los tuyos. Cadenas y redes migratorias."
36. Miller, *The Anatomy of Disgust*, 215.
37. Ibid.
38. Ngai, *Ugly Feelings*, 335.
39. Negri, "Value and Affect," 78.
40. Ibid., 80.
41. Ibid.
42. Marx, *Capital*, 139ff.
43. Mezzadra, "Living in Transition," 8.
44. Negri, "Value and Affect," 79.
45. Ibid.
46. Mezzadra, "Living in Transition."
47. Marx, *Capital*, 45.
48. Hardt and Negri, *Empire*.
49. Negri, "Value and Affect," 80.
50. Spivak, "Scattered Speculations on the Question of Value," 86.
51. Negri, "Value and Affect," 78.
52. Grosfoguel, "Del imperialismo de Lenin al imperio de Hardt y Negri: «fases superiors» del eurocentrismo."
53. Quijano, "Coloniality of Power, Eurocentrism, and Social Classification," 216.
54. Spivak, "Scattered Speculations on the Question of Value."
55. Spivak, *A Critique of Postcolonial Reason*, 102.
56. Ibid.
57. Ibid.
58. Spivak, "Scattered Speculations on the Question of Value."
59. Spivak, *A Critique of Postcolonial Reason*, 103.
60. Ibid., 81.
61. Spivak, *A Critique of Postcolonial Reason*, 101.
62. In regard to the relationship between professionalization and gender, see Cockburn and Omrad, *Gender & Technology in the Making*.
63. Spivak, "Scattered Speculations on the Question of Value," 81.
64. Marx, *Das Kapital*, 217.
65. Spivak, "Scattered Speculations on the Question of Value," 81.
66. Ibid., 85.

NOTES TO CHAPTER 7

1. Maldonado-Torres, "Rousseau and Fanon on Inequality and the Human Sciences," 132.
2. Ibid., 131.
3. See European Parliament, "Resolution on Regulating Domestic Help in the Informal Sector."
4. In the German case, these are agreements negotiated with the DHB. In 1952 this association was formed as a partner for Collective Bargaining Agreements because the law on minimum working condition was not applied on domestic work at this time. An agreement was reached in 1955. Since then, the association has opened up to men and service agencies.
5. For further discussion, see Caixeta et al., *Homes, Care and Borders*; Anderson, "A Very Private Business."
6. See Scrinzi, "Migration and the Restructuring of the Welfare State in Italy"; Vega Solís, *Culturas del Cuidado en Transición*.
7. Cyrus, "Being Illegal in Europe: Strategies and Policies for Fairer Treatment of Migrant Domestic Workers," 188.
8. Ibid.
9. Anderson, "A Very Private Business: Migration and Domestic Work," 9.
10. Cyrus, "Being Illegal in Europe: Strategies and Policies for Fairer Treatment of Migrant Domestic Workers"; Caixeta et al., *Homes, Care and Borders*.
11. See European Trade Union Conference Report, *Out of the Shadow*.
12. Cited in Gutiérrez Rodríguez, "'We Need Your Support, but the Struggle Is Primarily Ours,'" 154.
13. Monteros and Vega Solís, *Servicio doméstico y de cuidados*, 43.
14. See further discussion in Suárez-Navaz et al., *Las luchas de los sin papeles y la extensión de la ciudadanía*.
15. Gutiérrez Rodríguez, "'We Need Your Support, but the Struggle Is Primarily Ours,'" 153.
16. Piper, *New Perspectives on Gender and Migration*.
17. For further information on *RESPECT*, see http://solidarische-welt.de/sw170/respect.shtml.
18. For further information on MAIZ, see http://www.maiz.at/.
19. For further information on SEDOAC, see "Trabajadoras de hogar y su lucha."
20. Women in Informal Employment: Globalizing and Organizing (WIEGO).
21. These are, for example, ILO Conventions on migrant labor: Migration for Employment (Revised) Convention No. 97 (1949); Equality of Treatment (Social Security) Convention No. 118 (1962); Migrant Workers (Supplementary Provisions) Convention No. 143 (1975); Maintenance of Social Security Rights Convention No. 157 (1982); Private Employment Agencies Convention No. 181 (1997); as well as the ILO Conventions on occupational safety and health, equality and conditions of work. For further discussion see Piper, *New Perspectives on Gender and Migration*.
22. For further information on IRENE and IUF initiatives, see IRENE/IUF, *Respect and Rights*.
23. Piper, "Political Participation and Empowerment of Foreign Workers."
24. Cyrus, "Being Illegal in Europe: Strategies and Policies for Fairer Treatment of Migrant Domestic Workers."
25. For further discussion, see Cyrus, "Being Illegal in Europe: Strategies and Policies for Fairer Treatment of Migrant Domestic Workers"; Anderson and O'Connell Davidson, *Is Trafficking in Human Beings Demand Driven?*
26. For a further discussion on the concept of liberation, see Mignolo, "De-linking."

27. The Spanish labor migrant regulation from 2005 prescribes a previous approval by the employer before the work contract can be issued. The residency permit is issued on the basis of an existing work contract.
28. The voluntary return program offers migrants their entire contributions to social security in two parts. They receive 40 percent in Spain and 60 percent when they arrive in their country of origin. This is coupled with their renouncement of their residency and working permit for three years. See Naïr, "El fracaso del retorno voluntario de inmigrantes."
29. For further discussion, see Piper, "Political Participation and Empowerment of Foreign Workers."
30. Ibid.
31. For further discussion, see Waterman and Wills, *Place, Space and the New Labor Internationalisms*; Waterman, "Labor at the 2009 Belem World Social Forum: Between an Ambiguous Past and an Uncertain Future."
32. See discussion in Piper, "Political Participation and Empowerment of Foreign Workers."
33. See discussion in Satterthwaite, "Crossing Borders, Claiming Rights."
34. Satterthwaite, "Women Migrants' Rights under International Law," 168.
35. See discussion in Crenshaw, "Mapping the Margins."
36. Fregoso, *MeXicana Encounters*.
37. For further discussion, see Romany, "Themes for a Conversation on Race and Gender in International Human Rights Law."
38. Fregoso, *MeXicana Encounters*, 37.
39. For further discussion, see Satterthwaite, "Crossing Borders, Claiming Rights."
40. Dussel, *The Invention of the Americas*; Quijano, "Coloniality of Power and Eurocentrism in Latin America"; Mignolo, "De-linking."
41. Maldonado-Torres, *Against War*, 137.
42. Precarias a la Deriva, *A la Deriva*.
43. Translated from Spanish by Lauren Graham.
44. Mitropoulos, "Precari-Us?" 3.
45. See discussion in Maldonado-Torres, *Against War*, 127.
46. Ibid., 105.
47. Ibid.
48. Santos and Rodríguez Garavito, *El derecho y la globalización desde abajo*.
49. I have discussed this in regard to the incorporation of women's rights in an imperial discourse on human rights in "Jenseits einer binären Anerkennungslogik."
50. For further discussion, see Dussel, *Philosophy of Liberation*.
51. For further discussion, see Mignolo, "De-linking," 454ff.
52. Santos, "Beyond Abyssal Thinking."
53. Glissant, *Introduction à une poétique du divers*.
54. Bernabé et al., *Éloge de la Créolité*.
55. Ibid., 10 (my translation).
56. Ibid. (my translation).
57. Ibid., 28 (my translation).
58. Du Bois, *The Souls of Black Folk*.
59. Gordon and Roberts, "Introduction: The Project of Creolizing Rousseau," 6.
60. Ibid.
61. See further discussion in Glissant, *Introduction à une poétique du divers* and *Poetics of Relation*.
62. Dussel, *The Invention of the Americas*.
63. Dussel, *Twenty Theses on Politics*, 114–115.
64. Ibid., 114.

65. Anderson, "A Very Private Business: Migration and Domestic Work," 8.
66. Ibid.
67. A practice of denunciation promoted by the activist group Colectivo Situaciones to publically "out" members of the military regime. See Colectivo Situaciones, *Conocimiento inútil* and "Algo más sobre la Militancia de Investigación."
68. Monteros and Vega Solís, *Servicio doméstico y de cuidados*, 42.
69. Maldonado-Torres, *Against War*, 246.
70. Ibid.
71. Sedgwick, *Touching Feeling.*
72. Mignolo, "De-linking," 462.
73. For further discussion, see McDowell, "Work, Workfare, Work/Life Balance and an Ethic of Care."
74. Gibson-Graham, *Postcapitalist Politics*, xxviii.
75. Colectivo Situaciones, *Causes and Happenstance*. For further discussion, see also "Politicizing Sadness."

Bibliography

Actis, Walter. 2005. "Ecuatorianos y ecuatorianas en España. Inserción(es) en un mercado de trabajo fuertemente precarizado." In *La migración ecuatoriana. Transnacionalismo, redes e identidades*, edited by Gioconda Herrera, María Cristina Carillo Espinosa and Alicia Torres, 169–201. Quito: FLACSO.

———. 2009. "Inmigrantes Latinoamericanos en España: una visión en conjunto." *Migraçoes* 4:11–24.

Actis, Walter, and Fernando Esteban. 2008. "Argentina en España: inmigrantes, a pesar de todo." *Migraciones* 23:79–115.

Adorno, Theodor W. 1972. *Der Positivismusstreit in der deutschen Soziologie.* Frankfurt am Main: Luchterhand.

———. 2003. "Kulturkritik und Gesellschaft." In *Kulturkritik und Gesellschaft I*, 11–30, edited by Theodor W. Adorno. Frankfurt am Main: Suhrkamp.

Ahmed, Sara. 2004a. "Affective Economies." *Social Text* 22 (2): 121–139.

———. 2004b. *The Cultural Politics of Emotion.* Edinburgh: Edinburgh University Press.

Alt, Jörg. 2005. *Illegalität im Städtevergleich: Leipzig-München-Belin.* Osnabrück: IMIS Beiträge 27.

Anderson, Bridget. 2000. *Doing the Dirty Work? The Global Politics of Domestic Labour.* London: Zed Publishers.

———. 2004. "The Devil Is in the Detail: Lessons to be Drawn from the UK's Recent Exercise in Regularising Undocumented Workers in Europe." In *Platform for International Cooperation on Undocumented Migrants*, edited by Platform for International Cooperation on Undocumented Migrants, 89–101. Brussels/Leuven: Katholikeke Universiteit.

———. 2006. "A Very Private Business: Migration and Domestic Work." WP-06-28, COMPAS Working Paper no. 28, Oxford. http://www.compas.ox.ac.uk/fileadmin/files/pdfs/Bridget%20Anderson%20WPO628.pdf (accessed January 16, 2007).

———. 2007a. *Motherhood, Apple Pie and Slavery: Reflections on Trafficking Debates.* WP 07-48, COMPAS Working Paper no. 48, Oxford. http://www.compas.ox.ac.uk/publications/Working%20papers/Bridget%20Anderson%20WP0748.pdf (accessed January 20, 2008).

———. 2007b. "A Very Private Business: Exploring the Demand for Migrant Domestic Workers." *European Journal of Women's Studies*, 14(3): 247–264

Anderson, Bridget, and Julia O'Connell Davison. 2003. *Is Trafficking in Human Beings Demand Driven? A Multi-Country Pilot Study.* IOM Migration Series, no. 15, Geneva.

Anderson, Bridget, Ben Rogaly, Martin Ruhs and Sarah Spencer. 2007. *Migrants' Lives beyond the Workplace. The Experiences of Central and East Europeans in the UK.* York: Joseph Rowntree Foundation. http://www.jrf.org.uk/bookshop/eBooks/2045-migrants-experience.UK.pdf (accessed October 23, 2007).

Anderson, Bridget, and Martin Ruhs. 2006. *Semi-Compliance in the Migrant Labour Market*. WP-06–30, COMPAS Working Paper no. 30, Oxford. http://www.compas.ox.ac.uk/publications/Working%20papers/Ruhs%20Anderson%20WP0630.pdf (accessed January 22, 2007).

Antwort der Bundesregierung auf die kleine Anfrage der Abgeordneten Irmingard Schewe-Gerigk, Marieluise Beck (Bremen), Volker Beck (Köln) zu "Schutz der Personen im Diplomatenhaushalten," Drucksache 16/8288. Deutscher Bundestag, Wahlperiode 16 (February 20, 2008). http://dip21.bundestag.de/dip21/btd/16/082/1608288.pdf (accessed March 21, 2008).

Anzaldúa, Gloria. 1987. *Borderlands/La Frontera*. San Francisco: Aunt Lute Books.

———. 2000. "Within the Crossroads." *Interviews—Entrevistas*. Edited by Annalousie Keaton, 71–128. New York and London: Routledge.

Arango, Joaquín. 2004. "La población inmigrada en España." *Economistas, ENE* XXII (99): 6–14.

———. 2006. "Europa y la integración, una relación difícil." In *Migraciones. Nuevas movilidades en un mundo en movimiento*, edited by Cristina Blanco, 91–111. Barcelona: Anthropos.

Arendt, Hannah. 1986. *Elemente und Ursprünge totaler Herrschaft*. Munich: Piper.

———. 2002. *Vita activa*. Munich: Piper.

———. 2003. *The Origins of Totalitarianism*. Orlando: Harvest Books.

Aristotle. 1991. *The Art of Rhetoric*. Translated by H.C. Lawson-Trancred. Harmondsworth: Penguin.

Assad, Talal. 1986. "The Concept of Cultural Translation in British Social Anthropology." In *Writing Culture*, edited by James Clifford and George E. Marcus, 141–164. Santa Fe, NM: University of California.

Atzert, Thomas, and Jost Müller. 2004. "The Continuation of War: Polizeywissenschaft, Extended Version." make worlds 4. http://makeworlds.org/node/106 (accessed June 16, 2006).

Austin, John L. 1962. *How to Do Things with Words*. Cambridge, MA: Harvard University Press.

Bade, Klaus. 2000. *Europa in Bewegung. Migration vom späten 18. Jahrhundert bis zur Gegenwart*. Munich: Verlag C.H. Beck.

Baethge, Martin, and Holger Alda. 2005. *Berichterstattung zur sozioökonomischen Entwicklung in Deutschland*. Hamburg: VS Verlag.

Balibar, Etienne. 1992. *Race, Nation, Class*. London: Verso.

Bárbulo, Tomás. 2008. "El fiasco de 'Guantanamito.'" *El País*, July 10. http://elpais.com/articulo/espana/fiasco/Guantanamito/elpepunac/20080710elpepinac_17/Tes (accessed July 10, 2008).

Bauböck, Rainer. 1996. "'Nach Rasse und Sprache verschieden' Migrationspolitik in Österreich von der Monarchie bis heute." In *Reihe Politikwissenschaft/Political Science Series, no. 31*. Vienna: Institut für Höhere Studien/Institute for Advance Studies.

Beauvoir, Simone de. 1986. *Le deuxième sexe*. Paris: Gallimard.

Benjamin, Walter. 1996. "The Task of the Translator." In *Selected Writings Volume 1: 1913–1926*, translation by Michael W. Jennings. Cambridge and London: Belknap-Harvard University Press.

Bennholdt-Thomsen, Veronika, Maria Mies and Claudia von Werlhof. 1983. *Frauen, die letzte Kolonie*. Hamburg: Rowohlt.

Berlant, Lauren. 2000. *Intimacy*. Chicago: University of Chicago Press.

Bermúdez Torres, Anastasia. 2006. *Colombian Migration to Europe. Political Transnationalisms in the Middle of Conflict*. Working Paper Series no. 39, Compas-Centre on Migration Policy and Society, University of Oxford.

Bernabé, Jean, Patrick Chamoiseau and Raphaël Confiant. 1993. *Éloge de la Créolité. In Praise of Creoleness.* Paris: Gallimard.

Block, David. 2008. *Multilingual Identities in a Global City: London Stories.* Basingstoke: Palgrave Macmillan.

Bourdieu, Pierre. 1977. *Outline of a Theory of Practice.* Cambridge: Cambridge University Press.

———. 1979. "Symbolic Power." *Critique of Anthropology* 4:77–85.

———. 1984. *Distinction: A Social Critique of the Judgement of Taste.* Cambridge, MA: Harvard University Press.

———. 1988. *Homo Academicus.* Stanford: Stanford University Press.

———. 1991. *Language and Symbolic Power.* Cambridge, MA: Harvard University Press.

Brennan, Teresa. 2004. *The Transmission of Affect.* Ithaca, NY, and London: Cornell University Press.

Broeders, Dennis, and Godfried Engbersen. 2007. "The Fight against Illegal Migration." *American Behavioral Scientist* 50 (2): 1592–1609.

Buchuk, Sofia. 2007. *Crossing Borders: Latin American Exiles in London.* http://www.untoldlondon.org.uk/news/ART404/60.html (accessed March 11, 2008).

Bulmer-Thomas, Victor. 2003. *The Economic History of Latin America since Independence.* Cambridge: Cambridge University Press.

Butler, Judith. 1994. "Feminism by any Other Name. (Interview with Rosi Braidotti)." *Differences. A Journal of Feminist Cultural Studies* 6 (2–3): 27–35.

Caixeta, Luzenir. 2006. "Jenseits eines simplen Verelendungsdiskurses—Prekäre Arbeitsverhältnisse von Migratninnen." *Kulturrisse* 4:3–8.

Caixeta, Luzenir, Encarnación Gutiérrez Rodríguez, Shirley Tate and Cristina Vega Solís. 2004. *Homes, Care and Borders—Hogares, Cuidados y Fronteras.* Madrid: Traficantes de Sueños.

———. 2007. "Politiken der Vereinbarkeit verqueren oder ' . . . aber hier putzen und pflegen wir alle.' Heteronormativität, Einwanderung und alte Spannungen der Reproduktion." *Kurswechsel. Zeitschrift für gesellschafts-, wirtschafts- und umweltpolitische Alternativen* 2:21–32.

Carlisle, Frances. 2006. "Marginalization and Ideas of Community among Latin American Migrants to the UK." *Gender and Development* 14 (2): 235–245.

Carrington, Christopher. 1999. *No Place like Home. Relationships and Family Life among Lesbians and Gay Men.* Chicago and London: University of Chicago Press.

Casarino, Cesare, and Antonio Negri. 2008. *Praise of the Common: A Conversation on Philosophy and Politics.* Minneapolis: University of Minnesota Press.

Castro-Gómez, Santiago, and Ramón Grosfoguel. 2007. "Prólogo. Giro decolonial, teoría crítica y pensamiento heterárquico." In *El giro decolonial*, edited by Santiago Castro-Gómez and Ramón Grosfoguel, 9–24. Bogotá: Siglo de Hombres.

CEPAL. 2006. *Migración internacional, derechos humanos y desarrollo.* Santiago de Chile: CEPAL.

Cerda-Hegerl, Patricia. 2002. "'Wo gehtst du hin?' Motivation und Strategien in der Migration von Lateinamerikannerinnen in Deutschland." *Lateinamerika Analysen* 14:37–63.

———. 2007. "Feminisierung der Migration von Lateinamerika nach Deutschland." In *Sin Fronteras? Chancen und Probleme lateinamerikanischer Migration*, edited by Lena Berger, Irene Kögl, Julia Reiter, Frauke Schmidt and Michael Vogler, 137–160. Schriftenreihe zu den Passauer Lateinamerikagespräche Band 3. Munich: Martin Meidenbauer.

Cockburn, Cynthia, and Susan Omrad. 1993. *Gender & Technology in the Making.* London: Sage.

Cohen, Rina. 1987. "The Working Conditions of Immigrant Women, Live-in Domestics: Racisms, Sexual Abuse and Invisibility." *Resources for Feminist Research* 16 (1): 36–38.
———. 1991. "Women of Color in White Households: Coping Strategies of Live-In Domestic Workers." *Qualitative Sociology* 14:197–215.
Colectivo Ioé. 2001. *Mujer, inmigración y trabajo.* Madrid: Ministerio de Trabajo y Asuntos Sociales.
Colectivo Situaciones. 2001. *Conocimiento inútil.* Borradores de investigación 2. http://194.109.222/colectivosituaciones/borradores_02.htm (accessed May 7, 2004).
———. 2004a. "Algo más sobre la Militancia de Investigación." http://194.109.209.222/colectivosituaciones/articulos_15.htm (accessed April 3, 2005).
———. 2004b. *Causes and Happenstance: Dilemmas of Argentina's New Social Protagonism. The Commoner,* 8. http://www.commoner.org.uk/08situaciones. pdf (accessed March 4, 2005).
———. 2007. "Politicizing Sadness."http://194.109.209.222/colectivosituaciones/ articulos_29.htm (accessed February 7, 2008).
COM (2005) 390. 2005. *Communication from the Commission to the Council, the European Parliament, the European Economic and Social Committee and the Committee of the Regions: Migration and Development: Some Concrete Orientations.* Brussels: Commission of the European Union.
———. (2006) 402. 2006. *Communication from the Commission to the Council, the European Parliament, the European Economic and Social Committee and the Committee of the Regions: Policy Prescriptives in the Fight against Illegal Immigration of Third-Country Nationals.* Brussels: Commission of the European Union.
———. (2007) 512. 2007. *Communication from the Commission to the Council, the European Parliament, the European Economic and Social Committee and the Committee of the Regions: Third Annual Report on Migration and Integration.* Brussels: Commission of the European Union.
Combahee River Collective. 1983. "The Combahee River Collective Statement." In *Home Girls. A Black Feminist Anthology,* edited by Barbara Smith, 272–282. New York: Kitchen Table/Women of Color Press.
Constable, Nicole. 1997. *Maid to Order in Hong Kong: Stories of Filipina Workers.* Ithaca, NY: Cornell University Press.
Coronil, Fernando. 1995. "Introduction." In *Cuban Counterpoint. Tobacco and Sugar,* ix–lvi. Durham, NC: Duke University Press.
———. 2005. "Transcultural Anthropology in the Américas (with an Accent): The Use of Fernando Ortiz." In *Cuban Counterpoints. The Legacy of Fernando Ortiz,* edited by Mauricio A. Font and Alfonso W. Quiroz, 139–56. New York: Lexington Books.
Crenshaw, Kimberley W. 1995. "Mapping the Margins: Intersectionality, Identity, Politics, and Violence against Women of Color." In *Critical Race Theory. The Key Writings that Formed the Movement,* edited by Kimberley Crenshaw, N. Gotanda, G. Peller and K. Thomas, 357–384. New York: The New Press.
Cyrus, Norbert. 2008. "Being Illegal in Europe: Strategies and Policies for Fairer Treatment of Migrant Domestic Workers." In *Migration and Domestic Work. A European Perspective on a Global Theme,* edited by Helma Lutz, 177–194. Aldershot: Ashgate.
Dalla Costa, Mariarosa, and Selma James. 1972. *The Power of Women and the Subversion of the Community.* London: Butler and Tanner Ltd.
Davis, Angela Y. 1981. *Women, Race & Class.* New York: Vintage Books.

Deleuze, Gilles, and Felix Guattari. 2004. *A Thousand Plateaus. Capitalism and Schizophrenia.* London and New York: Continuum.

Delphy, Cristina. 1984. *Close to Home: A Materialist Analysis of Women's Oppression.* Translated by D. Leonard. London: Hutchinson.

Derrida, Jacques. 1972. *Positions.* Paris: Éditions de Minuit.

Donato, Katharine, Donna Gabaccia, Jennifer Holdaway, Martin Manalansan IV and Patricia R. Pessar. 2006. "A Glass Half Full? Gender in Migration Studies." *International Migration Review* 40 (1): 3–26.

Du Bois, W.E.B. 1999. *The Souls of Black Folk.* Edited by Henry Louis Gate Jr. and Terri Hume Oliver. New York: W.W. Norton.

Dussel, Enrique. 1994. 1492: *El encubrimiento del Otro: Hacia el origin de "mito de la modernidad."* La Paz, Bolivia: Plural Editores.

———. 1995. *The Invention of the Americas: Eclipse of "the Other" and the Myth of Modernity.* Translated by Michael D. Barber. New York: Continuum.

———. 2003. *Philosophy of Liberation.* Translated by Aquilina Martinez. Eugene: Wipf and Stock.

———. 2008. *Twenty Theses on Politics.* Durham, NC: Duke University Press.

Düvell, Franck. 2005. *Illegal Immigration in Europe. Beyond Control.* Houndsmills: Palgrave/MacMillan.

Ehrenreich, Barbara, and Arlie R. Hochschild. 2002. *Global Woman.* London: Penguin.

"El Gobierno admite que el paro puede llegar a los cuatro milliones tras el alza récord de enero." 2009. *El Pais,* February 3. http://www.elpais.com/articulo/economia/Gobierno/admite/paro/puede/llegar/millones/alza/record/enero/elpepueco/20090203elpepueco_2/Tes (accessed February 3, 2009).

Engels, Friedrich. 1972. *The Origin of the Family, Private Property and the State.* Translated by Alec West. New York: International Publishers.

Escobar, Arturo. 2003. "Mundos y conocimientos de otro modo." *Tabula Rasa* 1:51–86.

Escriva, Angeles. 2004. *Securing Care and Welfare of Dependants Transnationally.* Working paper, WP 404, Oxford Institute of Aging.

Escriva, Angeles, and Emmeline Skinner. 2008. "Domestic Work and Transnational Care Chains in Spain." In *Migration and Domestic Work. A European Perspective on a Global Theme,* edited by Helma Lutz, 113–126. Aldershot: Ashgate.

EU Report. 2008. "Equality between Women and Men." Brussels. http://europa.eu/scadplus/leg/en/cha/c10167.htm (accessed September 22, 2008).

European Commission. 2007. *Communication from the Commission to the European Parliament, the Council, the European Economic and Social Committee and the Committee of Regions, Policy Plan on Asylum—An Integrated Approach to Protection across the EU.* Brussels. http://europa.eu/scadplus/leg/en/cha/c10167.htm (accessed September 9, 2008).

———. 2008. *Memo/08/402: A Common Immigration Policy for Europe.* Brussels, June 17. http://europa.eu/rapid/pressReleaseAction.do?reference=MEMIO/08/402&format=HTML&aged=0&language=EN&guiLanguage=en (accessed July 13, 2008).

European Journal of Women's Studies, 2007, 14(3).

European Parliament. 2008. "Resolution on Regulating Domestic Help in the Informal Sector (200/2021 (INI))." http://www.europarl.europa.eu/sides/getDoc.do?pubRef=-//EP//TEXT+TA+P5-TA-2000-0542+0+DOC+XML+V0//EN (accessed June 2, 2008).

European Trade Union Conference Report. 2005. *Out of the Shadow: Organising Domestic Workers. Towards a Protective Regulatory Framework for Domestic Work.* Brussels: WIEGO.

Fantone, Laura. 2007. "Precarious Changes: Gender and Generational Politics in Contemporary Italy." *Feminist Review* 87:5–20.

Flaquer, Lluís. 2004. "La articulación entre familia y el Estado de bienestar en los países de la Europa del sur." *Universitat Autónoma de Barcelona, Papers* 53:27–58. http://ddd.ncb.es/pub/papers/0210286n73p27.pdf (accessed September 23, 2008).

Folbre. Nancy. 1994. *Who Pays for the Kids? Gender the Structure of Constraint.* New York: Routledge.

———. 2004. *Family Time: The Social Organization of Care.* New York: Routledge.

Foucault, Michel, Danile Defert and François Ewald. 1994. "La 'gouvernementalité.'" *Dits et Écrits* III:635–657.

Fraad, Harriet, Stephen Resnick and Richard Wolff. 1999. *Bringing It All Back Home.* London: Pluto.

Fregoso, Rosa Linda. 2003. *MeXicana encounters. The Making of Social Identities on the Borderlands.* Berkeley and Los Angeles: University of California Press.

Friedrichsmeyer, Sara, Sara Lennox and Susanne Zantop. 1999. *The Imperialist Imagination. German Colonialism and Its Legacy.* Ann Arbor: University of Michigan Press.

Gallotti, Maria. 2009. *The Gender Dimension of Domestic Work in Western Europe.* International Migration Papers, No. 96. ILO: Geneva.

García-Calvo Rosell, Carola. 2006. *Las relaciones bilaterales España-Ecuador: situación actual y perspectivas de futuro.* Análisis del Real Instituto Elcano (ARI), no.13.

Gather, Claudia, Birgit Geissler and Maria S. Rerrich. 2002. *Weltmarkt Privathaushalt. Bezahlte Hausarbeit im globalen Wandel.* Münster: Westfälisches Dampfboot.

Genova, Nicholas De. 2005. *Working the Boundaries. Race, Space, and "Illegality" in Mexican Chicago.* Durham, NC: Duke University Press.

Gibson-Graham, J.K. 1996. *The End of Capitalism (As We Know It). A Feminist Critique of Political Economy.* Minneapolis: University of Minnesota Press.

———. 2006. *Postcapitalist Politics.* Minneapolis: University of Minnesota Press.

Gibson-Graham, J.K., Stephen Resnick and Richard D. Wolff. 2000. *Class and Its "Others."* Minneapolis: University of Minnesota Press.

Gil Araújo, Sandra. 2003. "Las migraciones en las políticas de la Fortaleza. Sobre las multiples Fronteras de la Europa Comunitaria." ¿Un fenómeno o un problema?, edited by Sandra Gil Araújo and Mohammed Dahiri: Córdoba: Ayuntamiento de Córdoba/IECAH/INET.

———. Forthcoming. Las argucias de la integración. Políticas migratorias, construcción nacional y cuestión social. Madrid: IEPALA.

Glick Schiller, Nina, and Andreas Wimmer. 2002. "Methodological Nationalism and Beyond: Nation-State Building, Migration, and the Social Sciences." *Global Network* 2 (4): 301–334.

Glissant, Edouard. 1996. *Introduction à une poétique du divers.* Paris: Gallimard.

———. 1997. *Poetics of Relation.* Translated by Betsy Wing. Ann Arbor: University of Michigan Press.

Göktürk, Deniz. 2000. "Turkish Women on German Streets. Closure and Exposure in Transnational Cinema." In Spaces in European Cinema, edited by Myrto Konstantarakos, 64–76. Exeter and Portland: Intellect.

Gordon, Jane Anna, and Neil Roberts. 2009. "Introduction: The Project of Creolizing Rousseau." *CLR James Journal: Special Issue: Creolizing Rousseau* 15 (1): 1–16.

Gordon, Lewis R. 1995. *Fanon and the Crisis of European Man.* New York: Routledge.

Grosfoguel, Ramón. 2002. "Colonial Difference, Geopolitics of Knowledge and Global Coloniality in the Modern/Colonial Capitalist World-System." *Review* 25 (3): 203–224.

———. 2006. "La descolonización de la economía política y los estudios post-coloniales: Transmodernidad, pensamiento fronterizo y colonialidad global." *Tabula Rasa* 4:17–48.

———. 2008. "Del Imperialismo de Lenin al Imperio de Hardt y Negri: «fases superiores» del eurocentrismo." *universitas humanisticas* 65:15–26.

Grossberg, Lawrence. 1992. *We Gotta Get Out of This Place. Popular Conservatism and Postmodern Culture*. New York: Routledge.

Gruner-Domić, Sandra. 2005. *Latinas in Deutschland. Eine ethnologische Studie zu Migration, Fremdheit und Identität*. Munich: Waxmann.

Gutiérrez Rodríguez, Encarnación. 1999. *Intellektuelle Migrantinnen. Subjektivitäten im Zeitalter von Globalisierung*. Opladen: Leske and Budrich.

———. 2000. "Akrobatik in der Marginalität. Zu Produktionsbedingungen intellektueller Migrantinnen im Kontext der Arbeitsmigration." In *Auf Brüche*, edited by Cathy Gelbin, Kader Konuk and Peggy Piesche, 207–223. Taunustein am Main: Ulrike Helmer Verlag.

———. 2002. "Jenseits einer binären Anerkennungslogik: Eine radikal-demokratische Antwort auf der Geschlechterdemokratie." *Femina Politica. Journal of Women's Studies and Political Science* 2:62–71.

———. 2004. "'We Need Your Support, but the Struggle Is Primarily Ours': On Representation, Migration and the Sans Papiers Movement, ESF Paris, 12th–15th November 2003." *Feminist Review* 77:152–156.

———. 2005. "Das postkoloniale Europa dekonstruieren. Zu Prekarisierung, Migration und Arbeit in der EU." *Widerspruch* 48:71–83.

———. 2006. "Translating Positionality. On Post-Colonial Conjunctures and Transversal Understanding." *Translate. On-Line Journal for Cultural Theory and Cultural Studies*. http://translate.eipcp.net/transversal/0606/gutierrez-rodriguez/en (accessed February 2, 2007).

———. 2007a. "The 'Hidden Side' of the New Economy—On Transnational Migration, Domestic Work and Unprecedented Intimacy." *Frontiers: Journal of Women Studies* 28 (3): 60–83.

———. 2007b. "Reading Affect—On the Heterotopian Spaces of Care and Domestic Work in Private Households." *Forum: Qualitative Social Research* 8(1): art. 11. http://www.qualitative-research.ney/index.php/fqs/article/view/240/531 (accessed October 22, 2007).

———. 2008a. "Akademisches Wissen und militante Forschung. Repräsentationen zwischen Krise und Transfer." In Im Zeichen des Geschlechts. Repräsentationen, Konstruktionen, Interventionen, edited by Celine Camus et al., 80–95. Frankfurt am Main: Helmer Verlag.

———. 2008b. "Lost in Translation—Transcultural Translation and Decolonialization of Knowledge." *Translate. On-Line Journal for Cultural Theory and Cultural Studies*. http://translate.eipcp.net/transversal/0608/gutierrez-rodriguez/en (accessed October 15, 2008).

———. 2010: "Decolonizing Postcolonial Rhetoric." In *Decolonizing European Sociology*, edited by Encarnación Gutiérrez Rodríguez, Manuela Boatcă and Sérgio Costa. Farnham: Ashgate.

———. Forthcoming. "Transculturation in German and Spanish Migrant and Diasporic Cinema: On Constrained Spaces and Minor Intimacies in Princesses and A Little Bit of Freedom." In *Migrant and Diasporic Cinema in Europe*, edited by Daniela Berghahn and Claudia Sternberg. London: Palgrave Macmillan.

Gutiérrez Rodríguez, Encarnación, Manuela Boatcă and Sérgio Costa. Forthcoming. *Decolonizing European Sociology*. Farnham: Ashgate.

Gutiérrez Rodríguez, Encarnación, Macarena Gonzalez Ulloa, Efthimia Panagiotidis and Nina Schulz. 2004. *Housework and Care Work in Germany*. Unpublished report.
Habermas, Jürgen. 1981. *Theorie des kommunikativen Handelns*, vol. 2. Frankfurt: Suhrkamp.
Haidinger, Bettina. 2008. "Contingencies among Households: Gendered Division
of Labour and Transnational Household Organization—The Case of Ukraini-
ans in Austria." In *Migration and Domestic Work. A European Perspective
on a Global Theme*, edited by Helma Lutz, Helma, 127–142. Hampshire and
Aldershot: Ashgate.
Hall, Stuart. 1990. "The Local and the Global: Globalization and Ethnicity." In
Culture, Globalization and the World System, edited by Anthony King, 19–39.
London: MacMillan.
Haraway, Donna J. 1996. *Simians, Cyborgs and Women: The Reinvention of
Nature*. New York and London: Routledge.
Hardt, Michael. 1999. "Affective Labor." *boundary2* 26 (2): 89–100.
———. 2007. "Foreword: What Affects Are Good For." In *The Affective Turn.
Theorizing the Social*, edited by Patricia Ticineto Clough and Jean Halley, ix-
xiii. Durham, NC: Duke University Press.
Hardt, Michael and Antonio Negri. 2001. *Empire*. Cambridge and London: Har-
vard University Press.
Hartmann, Heidi. 1981. "The Unhappy Marriage of Marxism and Feminism:
Towards a More Progressive Union." *Capital and Class* 8:1–33.
Hegel, Georg Wilhelm Friedrich. 1983. "Die Phänomenologie des Geistes." In
*Enzyklopädie der philosophischen Wissenschaften im Grundrisse (1830). Dritter
Teil: Die Philosophie des Geistes*. Frankfurt am Main: Suhrkamp, 199–228.
Herbert, Ulrich. 2001. *Nationalsozialistische Vernichtungspolitik 1939–1945*.
Frankfurt am Main.
Hernandez, Berenice, and Stefanie Kron. 2000. "Schatten im Paradies." *Arranca!*
20:3–9.
Herrera, Gioconda. 2008. *Ecuador: la migración internacional en cifras*. Quito:
FLACSO.
Herrera, Giocanda, Maria Cristina Carillo and Alicia Torres. 2005. *La migración
ecuatoriana: Transnacionalismo, redes e identidades*. Quito: FLACSO.
Hess, Sabine. 2005. *Globalisierte Hausarbeit: Au Pair als Migrationsstrategie von
Frauen aus Osteuropa*. Wiesbaden: Verlag für Sozialwissenschaften.
Hess, Sabine, and Annete Puckhaber. 2004. "'Big Sisters Are Better Domestic Servants!?'
Comments on the Booming Au Pair Business." *Feminist Review* 77 (1): 65–78.
Heubach, Renate. 2001. "Migrantinnen aus Mittel- und Osteuropa in ungeschützten Arbeitsverhältnisse." Berlin: Rosa Luxemburg Stiftung. http://www.rosa-
lux.de/cms/index.php?id=3953&0 (accessed December 20, 2006).
Hill Collins, Patricia. 1986. "Learning from the Outsider Within: The Sociological
Significance of Black Feminist Thought." *Social Problems* 33 (6): 14–32.
———. 1989. "The Social Construction of Black Feminist Thought." *Signs* 14 (6):
745–773.
———. 2000. *Black Feminist Thought: Knowledge, Consciousness, and the Politics of Empowerment*. New York and London: Routledge.
Himmelweit, Susan. 1995. "The Discovery of 'Unpaid Work.' The Social Conse-
quences of the Expansion of 'Work.'" *Feminist Economics* 1 (2): 1–19.
Hobson, B., J. Lewis and Birte Siim. 2002. *Contested Concepts in Gender and
Social Politics*. Cheltenham and Camberley: Edward Elgar Publishing.
Hochschild, Arlie Russel. 1983. *The Managed Heart: Commercialization of
Human Feelings*. Berkeley: University of California Press.
———. 2000. *The Time Bind: When Work Becomes Home and Home Becomes
Work*. New York: Holt.

————. 2001. "Global Care Chains and Emotional Surplus Value." In *On the Edge: Living with Global Capitalism*, edited by W. Hutton and Anthony Giddens, 130–146. New York: Oxford University Press.

————. 2003. *The Commercialization of Intimate Life. Notes from Home and Work*. Berkeley, Los Angeles and London: University of California Press.

Home Office. 2008. *Domestic Workers*. http://www.bia.homeoffice.gov.uk/workingintheuk/othercategories/domesticworkers/ (accessed September 24, 2008).

Hondagneu-Sotelo, Pierrete. 2001. *Doméstica: Immigrant Workers Cleaning and Caring in the Shadows of Affluence*. Berkeley: University of California Press.

hooks, bell. 1984. *Feminist Theory. From Margin to Center*. Boston: South End Press.

Horkheimer, Max, and Theodor W. Adorno. 1988. *Dialektik der Aufklärung*. Frankfurt am Main: Fischer.

Horkheimer, Max, Theodor W. Adorno and John Cumming. 1997. *Dialectic of Enlightenment*. London and New York: Verso.

Hsiao-Hung Pai. 2004. "An Ethnography of Global Labour Migration." *Feminist Review* 77:129–131.

————. 2008. *Chinese Whispers: The True Story Behind Britain's Hidden Army of Labour*. London: Penguin.

Hull, Gloria T., Patricia B. Scott and Barbara Smith. 1982. *All the Women Are White, All the Blacks Are Men, But Some of Us Are Brave*. New York: The Feminist Press.

Initiative Minderheiten (Austrian Platform for Minorities). 2004. *Gastarbajteri: 40 Years of Work Migration*. Vienna: Vienna Museum.

Instituto de la Mujer and Centro de Estudios Económicos Tomillo. 2009. *La Presencia de las mujeres en el empleo irregular*. Observatorio 4. Madrid: Instituto de la Mujer.

Instituto Nacional de Empleo. 2001. *Population Statistics*.

————. 2008. *Spanish Labor Market Statistics*.

International Restructuring Education Network and International Food, Agriculture, Hotel, Restaurant, Catering, Tobacco and Allied Workers' Association. 2008. *Respect and Rights. Protection for Domestic/Household Workers. Report of the International Conference Held in Amsterdam, 8–10 November 2006*. Brussels.

Iveković, Rada. 2002. "On Permanent Translation (We Are in Translation)." *Transeuropéennes* 22:121–145.

Izquierdo, Antonio. 2006. "Cuatro razones para pensar la inmigración irregular." In *Migraciones. Nuevas movilidades en un mundo en movimiento*, edited by Cristina Blanco, 139–163. Barcelona: Anthropos.

Jaaware, Aniket. 2002. "Of Demons and Angels and Historical Humans: Some Events and Questions in Translation and Post-Colonial Theory." *European Legacy* 7 (6): 735–745.

James, Malcolm. 2005. *Ecuadorian Identity, Community and Multicultural Integration*. London: The Runnymede Trust. http://www.runnymedetrust.org/uploads/projects/EcuadorianIdentityCommunity.pdf (accessed July 7, 2007).

Jones, Cecily. 2006. "Falling between the Cracks: What Diversity Means for Black Women in Higher Education." *Policy Futures in Education* 4 (2): 145–159.

Kalayaan and Oxfam. 2008a. *The New Bonded Labour?* London: Oxfam.

————. 2008b. *Parliamentary Briefing: Proposed Changes to the Domestic Worker Visa*. London: Oxfam.

Kimball, Ann. 2007. *The Transit State: A Comparative Analysis of Mexican and Moroccan Immigration Policies*. Working Paper 150, The Center for Comparative Immigration Studies, University of California.

Kofman, Eleonore. 1999. "Female 'Birds of Passage' a Decade Later: Gender and Immigration in the European Union." *International Migration Review* 33 (2): 269–299.

Kofman, Eleonore and Parvati Raghuram. 2005. "Gender and skilled migrants: into and beyond the work place." *Geoforum* 36(2): 149–154.

Kofman, Eleonore, Annie Phizacklea, Parvathi Raghuram and R. Sales. 2000. *Gender and International Migration in Europe: Employment, Welfare & Politics.* London: Routledge.

Kolinsky, Eva, and Wilfried van der Will. 1998. *The Cambridge Companion to Modern German Culture.* Cambridge: Cambridge University Press.

Kontos, Silvia. 1985. "Zur Geschichte der Hausarbeit." In *Geschichte entdecken. Erfahrungen und Projekte der neuen Geschichtsbewegung,* edited by Hannes Heer, 174–181. Hamburg: Ullrich Volker.

Kontos, Silvia, and Karin Walser. 1978. "Überlegungen zu einer feministischen Theorie der Hausarbeit." *alternative. Zeitschrift für Literatur und Diskussion* 21:152–158.

Krämer, Raimund. 1999. "Das verschmähte Erbe." *Kulturaustausch* 2. http://www.ifa.de/pub/kulturaustausch/archiv/zfk-1999/lateinamerika/kraemer0/ (accessed January 11, 2007).

Kyambi, Sarah. 2005. *Beyond Black and White: Mapping New Immigrant Communities.* London: Institute for Public Policy Research.

Lan, Pei-Chia. 2006. *Global Cinderellas: Migrant Domestics and Newly Rich Employers in Taiwan.* Durham, NC: Duke University Press.

Lazzarato, Maurizio. 1996. "Immaterial Labour." In *Radical Thought in Italy,* edited by Paolo Virno and Michael Hardt, 132–146. Minneapolis: University of Minnesota Press.

———. 2002. "From Biopower to Biopolitics." Translated by Ivan A. Ramirez. *Pli: The Warwick Journal of Philosophy* 13:112–125.

Lewis, Gayle. 2005. "Welcome to the Margins: Diversity, Tolerance, and Politics of Exclusion." *Ethnic and Racial Studies* 28 (3): 536–558.

Lorde, Audre. 1984. *Sister Outsider.* Freedom, CA: The Crossing Press.

Lugones, Maria. 2007. "Heterosexualism and the Colonial/Modern Gender System." *Hypathia* 22 (1): 186–209.

Lugones, Maria, and Joshua M. Price. 2003. "The Inseparability of Race, Class, and Gender." *Latino Studies Journal* 1 (2): 329–332.

Luhmann, Niklas. 2006. *Die Gesellschaft der Gesellschaft,* vol. 2. Frankfurt: Suhrkamp.

Lutz, Helma. 2008a. *Migration and Domestic Work. A European Perspective on a Global Theme.* Aldershot: Ashgate.

———. 2008b. *Vom Weltmarkt in den Privathaushalt.* Opladen and Farmington Hills: Verlag Barbara Budrich.

MAIZ (Sonja Rappold, Luzenir Caixeta, Barbara Haas, Bettina Haidinger, Daniela Rechling and Pamela Ripota). 2004. *Housework and Caretaking in Austria: Migrant Women in Private Households.* Unpublished report.

Maldonado-Torres, Nelson. 2008. *Against War: Views from the Underside of Modernity.* Durham, NC: Duke University Press.

———. 2009. "Rousseau and Fanon on Inequality and the Human Sciences." *CLR James Journal: Special Issue: Creolizing Rousseau* 15 (1): 113–134.

Malinowski, Bronislaw. 1995. "Introduction." In *Cuban Counterpoint. Tobacco and Sugar,* lvii–lxiv, edited by Fernando Ortiz. Durham, NC: Duke University Press.

Malo, Marta. 2004. *Nociones comunes. Experiencias y ensayos entre investigación y militancia.* Edited by Marta Malo. Madrid: Traficantes de Sueños.

Manalansan, Martin IV. 2006. "Queer Intersections: Sexuality and Gender in Migration Studies." *International Migration Review* 40 (1): 3–26.

Martinez Buján, Raquel, and Montse Golías Pérez. 2005. "La latinoamericanización de la inmigración a España." *Cuadernos Geográficos de la Universidad de Granada* 35:51–64.

Marx, Karl. 1998. *Das Kapital,* vol. 1. Berlin: Dietz.

————. 1999. *Capital, Volume I*. Translated by Ben Fowkes and Introduction by Ernest Mandel. New York: Penguin Books.

Massumi, Brian. 1987. "Notes on the Translation and Acknowledgements." In A Thousand Plateaus, edited by Gilles Deleuze and Felix Guattari, ix–xx. London: Continuum.

————. 2002. *Parables for the Virtual. Movement, Affect, Sensation*. Durham, NC: Duke University Press.

Mbembe, Achille. 2003. "Necropolitics." Translated by Libby Meintjes. *Public Culture* 15 (1): 11–40.

McDowell, Linda. 1991. "Life without Father and Ford: The New Gender Order of Post-Fordism." *Transaction of the Institute of British Geographers* 16:400–419.

————. 2004. "Work, Workfare, Work/Life Balance and an Ethic of Care." *Progress in Human Geography* 28 (2): 145–163.

McIlwaine, Cathy. 2007. *Living in Latin London: How Latin American Migrants Survive in the City*. London: Queens Mary University, The Leverhulme Trust. http://www.geog.qmul.ac.uk/docs/staff/4400.pdf (accessed November 11, 2007).

Mehrez, Samia. 2007. "Translating Gender." *Journal of Middle East Women's Studies* 3 (1): 106–127.

Memmi, Albert. 1992. *The Colonizer and the Colonized*. Boston: Beacon Press.

Menocal, Maria Rosa. 2007. "The Culture of Translation." *Words without Borders. Online Magazine for International Literature.*http://www.wordswithoutborders.org/article.php?lab=culture (accessed January 5, 2009).

Merletti, Marzia. 2005. *El trabajo de cuidados y las nuevas formas de dependencia centro-periferia*. Documentos de Trabajo no. 10. Instituto Universitario de Desarrollo y Cooperación. Universidad Complutense de Madrid.

Mezzadra, Sandro. 2007. "Living in Transition. Toward a Heterolingual Theory of the Multitude." *Transversal. Multilingual Webjournal* 6: 39 paragraphs. http://eipcp.net/transversal/1107/mezzadra/en (accessed July 25, 2007).

Mies, Maria. 1983. "Towards a Methodology for Feminist Research." In *Theories of Women's Studies*, edited by Gloria Bowles and Renate Duelli Klein, 117–139. Boston: Routledge and Kegan Paul.

Mignolo, Walter. 1985. *The Darker Side of the Renaissance: Literacy, Territoriality, and Colonization*. Ann Arbor: University of Michigan Press.

————. 2000. *Local Histories/Global Designs: Coloniality, Subaltern Knowledges, and Border Thinking*. Princeton, NJ: Princeton University Press.

————. 005. *The Idea of Latin America*. Oxford: Blackwell.

————. 2007. "De-linking." *Cultural Studies* 21 (2): 449–514.

Mignolo, Walter, and Freya Schiwy. 2003. "Double Translation: Transculturation and the Colonial Difference." In *Translation and Ethnography*, edited by Tullio Maranhão and Bernhard Streck, 3–29. Tucson: University of Arizona Press.

Miller, William Ian. 1998. *The Anatomy of Disgust*. Cambridge: Harvard University Press.

"Ministers Impose £50 Levy on Economic Migrants to Pay for Public Services." 2009. *Guardian*, March 19. www.guardian.co.uk/uk/2009/mar/19/immigrants-50 (accessed August 8, 2009).

Misra, Joya, Jonathan Woodring and Sabine Merz. 2006. "The Globalization of Care Work: Immigration, Economic Restructuring, and the World-System." *Globalization* 3 (3): 317–332.

Mitropoulos, Angela. 2005. "Precari-Us?" *republicart* 3. http://www.republicart.net/desc/precariat/mitropoulos01_en.htm#top (accessed February 2, 2006).

Mohanty, Chandra Talpade. 1991. "Under Western Eyes: Feminist Scholarship and Colonial Discourses." In *Third World Women and the Politics of Feminism*, edited by Chandra Talpade Mohanty, Anne Russo and Lourdes Torres, 51–80. Bloomington and Indianapolis: Indiana University Press.

Mohanty, Chandra Talpade, Anna Russo and Lourdes Torres. 1991. *Third World Women and the Politics of Feminism.* Bloomington and Indianapolis: Indiana University Press.
Momsen, Janet Henshall. 1999. *Gender, Migration and Domestic Service.* New York: Routledge.
Monteros, Silvina, and Cristina Vega Solís. 2004. *Servicio doméstico y de cuidados. La conciliación de la vida familiar y laboral y la participación de las mujeres inmigrantes.* Unpublished report.
Myles, John. 1999. "From Habitus to Mouth: Language and Class in Bourdieu's Sociology of Language." *Theory and Society* 28 (6): 879–901.
Naïr, Sami. 2009. "El fracaso del retorno voluntario de immigrantes." *El Pais,* 27.07.2009.
Negri, Antonio. 1999. "Value and Affect." *boundary2* 26 (2): 77–88.
———. 2003. *Negri on Negri. In Conversation with Anne Dufourmantelle.* New York: Routledge.
Neilson, Brett, and Ned Rossiter. 2008. "Precarity as a Political Concept, or, Fordism as Exception." *Theory, Culture & Society* 25 (78): 51–72.
Ngai, Sianne. 2007. *Ugly Feelings.* Cambridge, MA: Harvard University Press.
Niranjana, Tejaswini. 1992. *Siting Translation. History, Post-Structuralism, and the Colonial Context.* Berkeley, Los Angeles and Oxford: University of California Press.
Nyberg Sørensen, Ninna. 1999. "Mobile Lebensführung zwischen der Dominikanischen Republik, New York und Madrid." In *Migrationen: Lateinamerika, Analysen und Berichte 23,* 12–24, edited by Karin Gabbert et al. Bad Honnef: Bad Honnef Publication.
Nyberg Sørensen, Ninna and Luis E. Guarnizo. 2007. "Transnational Family across the Atlantic." In *Living Across Worlds,* edited by Nyberg Sørensen, 151–176. Geneva: IOM, International Organization for Migration.
Odierna, Simone. 2000. *Die heimliche Rückkehr der Dienstmädchen. Bezahlte Arbeit im privaten Haushalt.* Opladen: Leske and Budrich.
Office for National Statistics. 2008. "Labour Force Survey and Returns from Public Sector Organisations." http://www.statistics.gov.uk/CCInugget.asp?ID=2145&Pos=3&ColRank=2&Rank=224 (accessed May 25, 2009).
Oguntoye, Katharina, May Opitz, Dagmar Schultz and Audre Lorde. 1986. *Farbe bekennen: Afro-deutsche Frauen auf den Spuren ihrer Geschichte.* Berlin: Orlanda Frauenverlag.
Ong, Aihwa. 1987. *Spirit of Resistance and Capitalist Discipline: Factory Women in Malaysia.* New York: State University of New York Press.
———. 2006. *Neoliberalism as Exception. Mutations in Citizenship and Sovereignty.* Durham, NC: Duke University Press.
Ongaro, Sara. 2003. "De la reproduction productive à la production reproductive." *Multitudes* 12:145–154.
Organisation for Economic Co-operation and Development. 2001. *Trends in International Migration. Report 2001.* Paris: Organisation for Economic Co-operation and Development.
Ortiz, Fernando. 2002. *Contrapunteo Cubano del Tabaco y el Azúcar.* Madrid: Cátedra.
———. 2005. *Cuban Counterpoint. Tobacco and Sugar.* New York: A.A. Knopf, 1947. Revised version with foreword from Fernando Coronil. Durham, NC: Duke University Press.
Ortiz, Renato. 2004. "As ciências sociais e o inglês." *Revista Brasileira de Ciencias Sociais* 19 (54): 5–22.
Padilla, Beatriz, and João Peixoto. 2007. "Latin American Immigration to Southern Europe." *Migration Information Source.* Migration Policy Institute, Washington. http://www.migrationinformation.org/Feature/display.cfm?id=609 (accessed February 23, 2008).

Pagnotta, Chiara. 2005. "Ni aquí, ni allá. L'immigrazione feminile dell'Ecuador." *Alternativas: Cuadernos de Trabajo Social* 13:229–244.

Parella Rubio, Sonia. 2003. *Mujer, inmigrante y trabajadora. La triple discriminación.* Barcelona: Antropos.

Parreñas, Rhacel Salazar. 2001. *Servants of Globalization: Women, Migration and Domestic Work.* Stanford: Stanford University Press.

Paz de la Torre, Julia. 2005. "Lateinamerikanische Immigrantinnen und ihre Integration in den deutschen Dienstleistungssektor." In *Traumwelt, Migration und Arbeit*, edited by Aktionsgemeinschaft Solidarische Welt, 37–43. Berlin: Aktionsgesellschaft Solidarische Welt.

Pedone, Claudia. 2005. "Tú, siempre jalas a los tuyos. Cadenas y redes migratorias." In *La migración ecuatorian. Transnacionalismo, redes e identidades*, edited by Gioconda Herrera, María Cristina Carillo Espinosa and Alicia Torres, 105–143. Quito: FLACSO.

Pellegrino, Adela. 2004. *Trends in International Migration in Latin America and the Caribbean.* IOM Migration Research Series, no. 16.

Peñaloza, Fernanda. 2008. "Appropriating the 'Unattainable': The British Travel Experience in Patagonia." In Informal Empire in Latin America: Culture, Commerce and Capital, edited by Mathew Brown, 149–172. Oxford: Blackwell.

Però, Davide. 2008a. "Migrants' Mobilization and Anthropology. Reflections from the Experience of Latin Americans in the United Kingdom." In *Citizenship, Political Engagement, and Belonging*, edited by Deborah Reed-Damahay and Caroline Brettell, 103–123. New Brunswick, NJ: Rutgers University Press.

———. 2008b. "Political Engagement of Latin Americans in the UK." *Focaal— European Journal of Anthropology* 51:73–90.

Phizacklea, Annie. 2003. "Transnationalism, Gender and Global Workers." In *Crossing Borders and Shifting Boundaries*, edited by Umut Erel et al., 79–100. Opladen: Leske and Budrich.

Pietersen, Elin. 2007. "Framing Domestic Work(ers) in Gender Equality Policies in Spain." *European Journal of Women's Studies* 14 (3): 265–280.

Piper, Nicola. 2007a. *New Perspectives on Gender and Migration—Rights, Entitlements and Livelihoods.* London: Routledge.

Piper, Nicola. 2007b. "Political Participation and Empowerment of Foreign Workers—Gendered Advocacy and Migrant Labour Organising in Southeast and East Asia." In *New Perspectives on Gender and Migration—Rights, Entitlements and Livelihoods*, edited by Nicola Piper, 249–275. London: Routledge.

Pla Julián, Isabel, and Amat Sánchez. 2005. *Luces y Sombras de la Reconcialiación: condiciones de empleo y trabajo de las empleadas de hogar. Congreso de Economía Feminista 2005.* Bilbao: Facultad de Ciencias Económicas y Empresariales del País Vasco.

Pratt, Mary Louise. 1992. *Imperial Eyes. Travel Writing and Transculturation.* London and New York: Routledge.

Pratt, Mary Louise. 2002. "The Traffic in Meaning. Translation, Contagion, Infiltration." *Profession 2002, Journal of the Modern Language Association of America* (*MLA*)(12): 25–36.

Precarias a la Deriva. 2003. "Notas sobre el continuo sexo, cuidado, atención." http://www.sindomino.net/karakola/precarias/notas-cuidadp.htm (accessed May 11, 2005).

Precarias a la Deriva. 2004. *A la Deriva: por los circuitos de la precariedad femenina.* Madrid: Traficantes de Sueños.

Pribilsky, Jason. 2004. "Aprendemos a convivir: Conjugal Relations, Co-Parenting and Family Life among Ecuadorian Transnational Migrants in New York and the Ecuadorian Andes." *Global Network* 4 (3): 313–334.

Price, Joshua M. 2008. "Translating Social Science: Good versus Bad Utopianism." *Target: International Journal of Translation Studies* 20(2): 348–364.

Puar, Jasbir. 2007. *Terrorist Assemblages*. Durham, NC: Duke University Press.
Pühl, Katharina, and Susanne Schultz. 2001. "Gouvernamentalität und Geschlecht—Über das Paradox der Festschreibung und Flexibilisierung der Geschlechterverhältnisse." In *Geschlecht und Globalisierung*, edited by Sabine Hess and Ramona Lenz, 102–127. Königstein Taunus: Ulrike Helmer Verlag.
Querien, Anne. 2003. "Femmes, multitudes, propriétés." *Multitudes* 12:135–144.
Quijano, Anibal. 2000. "Coloniality of Power and Eurocentrism in Latin America." *International Sociology* 15 (2): 215–232.
———. 2008. "Coloniality of Power, Eurocentrism, and Social Classification." In *Coloniality at Large. Latin America and the Postcolonial Debate*, edited by Mabel Moraña, Enrique Dussel and Carlos A. Jáuregui, 181–224. Durham, NC: Duke University Press.
Read, Jason. 2003. *The Micro-Politics of Capital. Marx and the Pre-History of the Present*. Albany: State University of New York Press.
RESPECT and Kalayaan. 1998. *European Network of Migrant Domestic Workers, Solidar and Kalayaan. Taking Liberties*. Brussel: Solidar.
Revel, Judith. 2003. "Devenir-Femme de la politique." *Multitudes* 12:125–134.
Ricoeur, Paul. 2006. *On Translation*. London and New York: Routledge.
Riley, Denise. 2005. *Impersonal Passion. Language as Affect*. Durham, NC: Duke University Press.
Rollins, Judith. 1985. *Between Women: Domestics and their Employers*. Philadelphia: Temple University Press.
Román-Velázquez, Patricia. 1999. *The Making of Latin London: Salsa Music, Place and Identity*. Aldershot: Ashgate.
Romany, Celina. 2000. "Themes for a Conversation on Race and Gender in International Human Rights Law." In *Global Critical Race Feminism*, edited by Adrien Katherine Wing, 53–66. New York: New York University Press.
Romero, Mary. 1992. *Maid in the U.S.A.* London: Routledge.
Rose, Nikolas S. 1999. *Governing the Soul: The Shaping of the Private Self*. London and New York: Free Association.
Sandoval, Chela. 2000. *Methodology of the Oppressed*. Minneapolis: University of Minnesota Press.
Santí, Enrique Mario. 2002. "Introduction." In *Fernando Ortiz: Contrapunteo y Transculturación*, edited by Enrique Mario Santí, 17–89. Madrid: Editorial Colibrí.
Santos, Boaventura de Sousa. 2007. "Beyond Abyssal Thinking: From Global Lines to Ecologies of Knowledges." *Review XXX* 1:45–89.
Santos, Boaventura de Sousa, and César A. Rodríguez Garavito. 2007. *El derecho y la globalización desde abajo*. Barcelona: Anthropos Editorial.
Sassen, Saskia. 1999. *Globalization and Its Discontents*. New York: The New Press.
Satterthwaite, Margaret. 2004. "Women Migrants' Rights under International Human Rights." *Feminist Review* 77:167–171.
Satterthwaite, Margaret. 2005. "Crossing Borders, Claiming Rights: Using Human Rights Law to Empower Women Migrant Workers." *Yale Human Rights and Development Law Journal* 8:1–66. http://islandia.lae.yale.edu/yhrdlj/PDF/Vol%208/satterthwaite.pdf (accessed March 5, 2008).
Saussure, Ferdinand De. 2002. *Écrits de linguistique générale*. Paris: Gallimard.
Scharlau, Birgit. 2004. "Repensar la Colonia, las relaciones interculturales y la traducción." *Iberoamericana* 12:97–110.
Schulte, Jan Erik. 2001. *Zwangsarbeit und Vernichtung*. Paderborn: Schöningh.
Schultz, Susanne. 2001. "Domestic Slavery oder Green Card? Feministische Strategien zu bezahlter Arbeit." *iz3w* 257:11–16.
Schumacher, Sebastian, and Johannes Peyrl. 2007. *Fremdenrecht (f. Öster.)*. Vienna: Ogb Verlag.

Schupp, Jürgen. 2002. "Quantitative Verbreitung von Erwerbstätigkeit in privaten Haushalten Deutschlands." In *Weltmarkt Privathaushalt. Bezahlte Hausarbeit im globalen Wandel*, edited by Claudia Gather, Birgit Geissler and Maria S. Rerrich, 50–70. Münster: Westfälisches Dampfboot.

S/Convegno (Manuela Galetto, Chiara Lasala, Sveva Magaraggia, Chiara Martucci, Elisabetta Onari and Francesca Pozi). 2007. "A Snapshot of Precariousness: Voices, Perspectives, Dialogues." *Feminist Review* 87:104–112.

Scrinzi, Francesca. 2008. "Migrations and the Restructuring of the Welfare State in Italy: Change and Continuity in the Domestic Work Sector." In *Migration and Domestic Work. A European Perspective on a Global Theme*, edited by Helma Lutz, 29–42. Farnham: Ashgate.

Sedgwick, Eve Kosofsky. 2004. *Touching Feeling. Affect, Pedagogy, Performativity*. Durham, NC: Duke University Press.

Servicio Domestico Activo. 2008. *Briefing on Domestic Workers Rights in Spain*. Madrid.

Servicio Domestico Activo. 2009. "Trabajadoras de hogar y su lucha,"http://www.latinomadrid.com/notica.php?id=7806 (accessed January 2, 2009).

Servicio Público de Empleo Estatal. "Employment Statistics." http://tasadeparo.com/inem-y-servicio-publico-de-empleo-estatal.html (accessed February 2, 2009).

Sommerville, Will. 2007. *Immigration under New Labour*. Bristol: Policy Press.

Spinoza, Benedictus de. 1976. *Die Ethik*. Edited by Friedrich Bülow. Stuttgart: Alfred Kröner Verlag.

Spinoza, Benedictus de. 1994. "The Ethics." In *A Spinoza Reader. The Ethics and Other Works*, edited by Edwin Curley, 85–265. Princeton, NJ: Princeton University Press.

Spivak, Gayatri Chakravorty. 1993. *Outside in the Teaching Machine*. New York and London: Routledge.

———. 1985. "Scattered Speculations on the Question of Value." *Diacritics* 15 (4): 73–93.

———. 1987a. "Can the Subaltern Speak?" In *Marxism and the Interpretation of Culture*, edited by Lawrence Grossberg and Cary Nelson, 271–313. Champagne: University of Illinois Press.

———. 1987b. *In Other Worlds*. New York and London: Routledge.

———. 1993a. "Feminism and Deconstruction, Again: Negotiations." In *Outside in the Teaching Machine*, 121–140. New York and London: Routledge.

———. 1993b. "The Politics of Translation." In *Outside in the Teaching Machine*, 179–200. New York and London: Routledge.

———. 1996. "The Woman as Theatre: Beijing 1995." *Radical Philosophy* 75:2–4.

———. 1999. *A Critique of Postcolonial Reason. A History of the Vanishing Present*. Cambridge, MA: Harvard University Press.

———. 2000. "Translation as Culture." *Parallax* 6 (1): 13–24.

———. 2008. "Position without Identity—2004: An Interview with Gayatri Chakravorty Spivak by Yan Hairong." In *Other Asias*, 237–255. London: Blackwell.

Statistik Austria. 2005. *Statistisches Jahrbuch Österreich*. Vienna.

Statistisches Bundesamt. 2007. *Lateinamerikaner in Deutschland*.

Stewart, Kathleen. 2007. *Ordinary Affects*. Durham, NC: Duke University Press.

Suárez-Navaz, Liliana, Raquel Maciá Pareja and Ángela Moreno García. 2007. *Las luchas de los sin papeles y la extensión de la ciudadanía. Perspectivas críticas desde Europa y Estados Unidos*. Madrid: Traficantes de Sueños.

Sveinsson, Páll Kjartan. 2007. *Bolivians in London. Challenges and Achievements of a London Community*. London: The Runnymede Trust. http://www.runnymedetrust.org/uplaods/publications/pdfs/BoliviansInLondon-2007.pdf (accessed January 2, 2008).

Tate, Shirley Anne. 2004. *Housework and Caretaking in the UK*. Unpublished report.
———. 2009. *Black Beauty: Aesthetics, Stylization, Politics*. Farnham: Ashgate.
Terada, Rei. 2001. *Feeling in Theory*. Cambridge, MA: Harvard University Press.
Unión General de Trabajadores. 2008. *Press News: Avanza la Igualdad entre mujeres y hombres, pero la diferencia salarial nos disminuye*.
Vega Solís, Cristina. 2009. *Culturas del Cuidado en Transición*. Barcelona: Editorial UOC, Niberta.
Wallerstein, Immanuel. 2001. *Unthinking Social Science—The Limits of Nineteenth-Century Paradigms*. Philadelphia: Temple University Press.
Waterman, Peter. 2009. "Labor at the 2009 Belem World Social Forum: Between an Ambiguous Past and an Uncertain Future." http://www.netzwerkit.ed/ projekte/ waterman/belem209 and http://www.ukzn.ac.za/ccs/files/LaborWSFBelem2009. pdf (accessed August 2, 2009).
Waterman, Peter, and Jane Wills (eds.). 2001. *Place, Space and the New Labor Internationalisms*. Oxford: Blackwell.
Werlhof, Claudia von. 1978. "Frauenarbeit: Der blinde Fleck in der Kritik der politischen Ökonomie." *Beiträge zur feministischen Theorie und Praxis* 1:18–31.
———. 1983. "Der Proletarier ist tot. Es lebe die Hausfrau?" *Technologie und Politik* 20 (7): 111–136.
Williams, Fiona. 1995. "Race, Ethnicity, Gender and Class in Welfare States: A Framework for Comparative Analysis." *Social Politics* 2 (2): 127–139.
Williams, Fiona, and Anna Gavanas. 2008. "The Intersection of Childcare Regimes and Migration Regimes: A Three-Country Study." In *Migration and Domestic Work. A European Perspective on a Global Theme*, edited by Helma Lutz, 13–28. Farnham: Ashgate.
Williams, Raymond. 2006. "The Analysis of Culture." In *Cultural Theory and Popular Culture*, edited by John Storey, 32–40. Harlow: Pearson Education.
Wills, Jane, Kavita Datta, Yara Evans, Joanna Herbert, Jon May and Cathy McIlwaine. 2009. *Global Cities at Work. New Migrant Division of Labour*. London: Pluto.
Wrigley, Julia. 1995. *Other People's Children: An Intimate Account of the Dilemmas Facing Middle-Class Parents and the Women They Hire to Raise Their Children*. New York: Basic Books.
Yeoh, Brenda S.A. and Shirlena Huang. 1999. "Singapore Women and Foreign Domestic Workers." In *Gender, Migration and Domestic Service*, edited by Janet Henshall Momsen, 273–296. New York: Routledge.

DOCUMENTARIES

El Tren de La Memoria. 2005. Directed by Marta Arribas and Ana Pérez. Germany, distributed by Iguana.
La generación olvidada. 2005. Directed by Ainhoa Montoya Arteabaro. Germany.
La Memoria Interior. 2002. Directed by Maria Ruido. Spain, distributed by HAMACA.
Wetback—The Undocumented Documentary. 2005. Directed by Arturo Perez Torres. United States, distributed by Open City Works.

Index

migration from
  Argentina 54
  Colombia 54, 181n63
  Ecuador 54, 181n63
  LAC 54
migration policies 55–7
migration to
  Caribbean 54
  Latin America 54
  Morocco, border controls 49, 50
racism 18
SEDOAC organization 3, 153
State Agency for Women 80
voluntary return program 155
speech acts 112
Spinoza, Baruch, on "affectus" 5, 129, 130
Spivak, G.C. 15, 20, 21, 27, 29, 36, 110, 111, 141, 142, 143
  cultural codification 110
subject, predication of 141–2, 143, 145
  on materialist predication 141–2, 145
  on translation 22–3
  on subaltern 143
  on value form 110, 143
standpoint theory 33
Stewart, Kathleen 4
stress, domestic workers 136
subject, predication of 141–2, 143, 145
subaltern 20, 25, 38, 92, 97, 145, 155
  Spivak on 143
  subsumption
    formal 40–1, 43
    real 41, 43
  symbolic power *see under* power
  symbolic violence *see under* violence

T
Tate, Shirley Anne 171n3, 180n50, 185n43
terrorism, and migration policies 48
tourism, and migration 64
trade unions, and undocumented migrants 151–2, 153–4
transculturation
  affective value 146–7
  concept 9, 24
  contact zones 4, 9
  Cuba 9, 24
  Europe 173n42
  household 9, 158
translation
  "Becoming Woman" 26–7
  Benjamin on 21

and colonial difference 19–20
double 21
domination, tool of 23
goal 21
"hearing-to-respond" 22, 27
and identity 22–3, 24
plurilingual communication 23–4
and plurilingualism 21
in research 30
Ricoeur on 21
Spivak on 22–3
transcultural 23–5, 35, 36
transversal 160
transversal understanding 35–6

U
UK
  asylum control 58, 178n2
  Border Agency, formation 52
  Borders, Citizenship and Immigration Act (2009) 58
  British Nationality Act (1948) 57
  British Nationality Act (1981) 58
  Citizen of the UK and Colonies status 57
  citizenship criteria 58
  Commonwealth Immigrants Act (1962) 57–8
  Commonwealth Immigrants Act (1968) 58
  cultural integration 52
  domestic work, regulation 76–8
  domestic workers, recruitment 77–8
  economic recession, and women's employment 178n19
  Highly Skilled Migrant Programme 59
  Immigration
    Asylum and Nationality Act (2006) 58
    points-based system 51
  Immigration Act (1971) 58
  "Justice for Cleaners" campaign 60
  Kalayaan organization 76, 77, 153
  Latin America, trade 57
  Latinos 60
  migration, "points-based system" 59, 77
  migration from
    Argentina 173n49
    Brazil 173n49
    Chile 173n49
    Colombia 59, 173n49
    Dominican Republic 80

Guyana 173n49
LAC 54, 59–60
migration policies 57–61, 79
Nationality, Immigration and Asylum
    Act (2002) 58
Overseas Domestic Worker's Visa 46,
    76–7, 150
undocumented migrants 59, 78
"undocumented migrants"
    Austria 66, 84, 85
    citizens, equal treatment with 154–5
    disgust at 14
    domestic workers 14, 43, 47, 51,
        72–3, 108
    employment limitations 34
    Germany 1, 64, 80
    and globalization 142–3
    human rights, doubling strategies
        154–5
    Latin American women 124–5
    portable rights 155–6
    and trade unions 151–2, 153–4
    UK 59, 78
UNHCR 65
USA
    domestic work, and slavery 92
    migration from, Ecuador 54

V
value
    coding 30, 140–1, 143, 145
    dynamics of 91–2
    exchange 90, 94
    Marx on 89, 90, 91, 143–4
    "particular equivalent form" 91
    social, domestic work 8, 88–9, 90–1,
        92–3, 95, 110, 140–1, 144
    social hieroglyphic 92

surplus 94
    production of 95
    textuality of 143–5
    types of 91
    use, domestic work 90, 94, 157
    see also affective value
value form 89, 90, 91, 140, 143, 144,
    145, 165
    domestic work 92, 110, 141
Vega Solís, Cristina 128
Vettor, Tiziana 101
violence, symbolic 116, 121, 125, 127

W
Waling-Waling organization 76
Waterman, Peter 156
Weimar Republic (1918-32) 61
Werlhof, Claudia von 13, 95
Williams, Fiona 74
Williams, Raymond 4
women
    labor, as reproductive labor 13, 26
    in labor market 68
    migrant support organizations 66
    professional 2, 67, 69
    happiness 135, 146
    personal narratives 68, 69
Women in the Informal Economy,
        Globalizing and Organizing
        (WIEGO) 154
women migrants
    Austria 66–7
    Germany 63–4
"work-life balance" 73
world, hierarchical classification 31

Z
Zapatista Movement 25, 109